THE LIVING LIGHT DIALOGUE

Volume 13

THE LIVING LIGHT DIALOGUE

Volume 13

⚜

Through the mediumship of
Richard P. Goodwin

Living Light Books

The Living Light Dialogue Volume 13
Copyright © 2020 Serenity Association

Through the mediumship of Richard P. Goodwin.

All rights reserved. No portion of this book may be reproduced—electronically, mechanically, or via internet transmission—without advance, express written permission of the publisher except in the case of brief quotations embodied in critical articles and reviews. No derivative work—games, supplemental material, video—may be created without advance, express written permission of the publisher. For information address Living Light Books, P.O. Box 4187, San Rafael, CA 94913-4187.

Cover design copyright © 2020 by Serenity Association
Cover photograph by Serenity Association, 2020; copyright © 2020 by Serenity Association.

www.livinglight.org

Library of Congress Control Number 2007929762
ISBN: 978-1-947199-11-8

FIRST EDITION

This volume of teachings is dedicated to the spirit friends who brought to Earth the Living Light Philosophy. With eternal gratitude, we pray that we may demonstrate these principles and continue to bring to publication these teachings.

CONTENTS

Acknowledgment ix
Preface xi
Introduction xv
A/V Seminar 19 3
A/V Seminar 20 27
A/V Seminar 21 51
A/V Seminar 22 75
A/V Seminar 23 117
A/V Seminar 24 147
A/V Seminar 25 179
A/V Seminar 26 207
A/V Seminar 27 233
A/V Seminar 28 249
A/V Seminar 29 275
A/V Seminar 30 297
A/V Seminar 31 319
A/V Seminar 32.. 341
Seminar 33 361
A/V Seminar 34 387
A/V Seminar 35 407
Appendix. 437

ACKNOWLEDGMENT

Grateful acknowledgement is made to the many friends and associates for invaluable aid in compiling this book, for their helpful suggestions, for their loyal interest and encouragement.

Special acknowledgement is due to those who painstakingly and selflessly transcribed and proofread the text.

PREFACE

It was through the mediumship of the Serenity Association founder, Mr. Richard P. Goodwin, that a philosophy known as the Living Light was given in more than 700 classes over a twenty-five-year period.

To be specific, the philosophy was imparted through Mr. Goodwin by a magistrate who had lived on Earth some 8,000 years ago. The former magistrate is known to Living Light students as "the Wise One," and he narrated the journey of his soul on the other side of life, the experiences—especially the difficulties—he encountered in having to face himself, as well as the teachings he earned to help himself through the realms in which he traveled. It was his decision to share the teachings with souls on both sides of "the curtain."

Prior to the advent of the Wise One, Mr. Goodwin had prayed for a teacher from the realms of light. Mr. Goodwin, since age fourteen, had been the instrument through which spirit was able to communicate with those seeking help. But he saw that his mediumship brought only temporary solace, because the people he was trying to help soon became fascinated with the phenomena and ignored the help that spirit was imparting. He prayed for someone who would bring forth teachings that would benefit any soul seeking a path to a greater awareness of himself and of God.

His prayers were answered in 1964 when the Wise One came through for the first time. Mr. Goodwin, at first apprehensive about what this new teacher would impart, was taken into deep trance and not able to control what was being revealed through him. Upon hearing the recorded classes afterward, however, he became convinced of the goodness of the teacher and of the value of the simple, beautiful teachings. This, then, was the beginning of the Living Light Philosophy given to Earth through the mediumship of Richard P. Goodwin.

In carrying out the request of the Wise One and Mr. Goodwin, students of the Serenity Association transcribed from audiotape the classes that had been brought through. Because most are in the form of teacher-student interaction, the classes became known as The Living Light Dialogue; and the students were instructed to publish the classes as a multi-volume set of the Living Light Philosophy. Volume 1 was published in the autumn of 2007.

The present book, Volume 13, continues the A/V Seminars series of classes, and includes A/V Seminar 19 through A/V Seminar 35. Although these classes were given by Mr. Goodwin on the third Thursday of the month at the Serenity Association temple, they were not given every month, but intermittently, and cover the period of time from January 8, 1987, until February 16, 1989. Most of these classes were recorded on video tape, with the exception of Seminar 33, which was recorded on audio cassette tape. A/V Seminar 35 was the last spiritual awareness class given by Mr. Goodwin, who passed from this world to the higher life on February 24, 1989.

The foundation of the classes—the foundation of the Living Light Philosophy itself—is the Law of Personal Responsibility which states, in part, that we are responsible for all our experiences, and that our experiences are the return of the laws that we have established with our thoughts, acts, and deeds. Through greater awareness of our thoughts and by exercising our divine right of choice, we may choose to establish laws of greater harmony and goodness.

The Living Light Philosophy teaches that we have come to Earth to learn the lessons that are necessary to free us from the dictates and limits of our own thoughts and judgments, which are the mental patterns that we follow through our own lack of awareness and are so very potent, forceful, and limiting. These teachings guide us in making the necessary changes in our thinking in order to free ourselves from those patterns and to express our soul consciousness.

The choice of guiding the direction of our life, as stated by the Wise One when he speaks of being with a person, place, or thing, is, in essence, of being in this world and not a part of this world. He further explains that no matter what experiences we encounter, no matter what we do or do not do, we—our spirit—may view the experience in objectivity from a soul level of consciousness where peace reigns supreme.

The teachings of this volume help us to restore harmony or balance in our life by flooding the consciousness with spiritual affirmations and prayers, a few of which can be found in the appendix. When reason is restored, by balancing our sense functions with our soul faculties, we will consciously experience peace. Without annihilating our ego or our sense functions, we will find a pathway of expression for our soul. Where there was once disturbance, now there is acceptance. Where there was disease, now there is poise. And where there was hopelessness and despair, now there is reason, divine neutrality; and peace shows the way.

If you make the effort to apply these laws, such as, "If man is a law unto himself, what are you doing with the law that you are?" and demonstrate the wisdom of patience, the truth of this philosophy will be your living demonstration.

As the teacher states in CC 130, "My journey of many centuries and much experience has brought me here to Earth to share with you these simple teachings that have come as the effect of a long, long, long journey. Let not your journey be so long in the realms of illusion. For it is not necessary for you. For in your evolution, you have earned an awakening. But it is up to you to do something that is constructive and worthwhile."

INTRODUCTION

[This introduction was written by Mr. Goodwin and originally appeared in *The Living Light*, which were the first teachings of the Living Light Philosophy published in book form. The entire text of *The Living Light* was republished in *The Living Light Dialogue*, Volume 1.]

"Think, children. Think more often and think more deeply."

The teachings in this book were given as a progressive series of lessons to a group of four students who were sitting for spiritual unfoldment with me beginning in January of 1964. The communications were regular until October of that year when nearly a seven-year silence ensued and resumed in 1971 to the present. They were received in three ways by me as a channel. The main text was taped from a direct control of my voice in deep trance at special sittings of our group during which I had no experience of the voice or what was being transmitted. A few scattered verses were given independently when I was privileged to see and hear our teacher clairvoyantly. I have also been a channel for this communicant when speaking from the podium at church and in answering difficult questions at our public seminars.

Nearly all we know about our teacher is contained in the lectures. He reports that he had tried for sixteen years to break through an interference barrier that the channel had to deep trance. When our conditions were in resonance with his patient wisdom, he came through ready to teach his understanding. I have seen him as an old man dressed in white with long flowing white hair. He has blue eyes, slightly smiling and deeply compassionate. I have always called him the Old Man. The students liked to call him the Wise One. He is surely one of those often called a Teacher of Light. I do not know his country, although he indicated at one time that he was from 6000 B.C. and a form of a judge in his time.

The text is often difficult but it is complete, having been transcribed word for word from the original tapes recording the trance voice. It is presented with a minimum of punctuation to be freer for the individual interpretation of each reader. The lessons given before the long silence are phrased with many allegories often paradoxical. There are repetitions and renewals of theme, but it is explained that if an understanding is not perceived, compassion dictates that it be said again. Some of the topics have but a simple mention with little development but all are revealed, we are told, according to merit.

The Old Man is a fine teacher. He has in a hundred ways intertwined his allegory, progressive explanations, unfolding exercises and timely references to reach a multitude of levels of individual understanding. A notable change is his more direct style of presentation beginning in 1971.

There is an endearing intimacy of person that can be felt through his lectures, a meaningful and loving encounter with a wise friend. Like an old man, he makes a mistake and conscientiously corrects himself a few paragraphs later. He listens often and carefully to our earnest discussions of his words. He consults with a group of experts on evolution and cites their learning in his lesson. His use of the direct address "children" or "my children" is not patronizing but infinitely loving and supportive.

A word must be said about the teachings. The Old Man makes clear that his lessons are not dogma, a creed or a narrow way, but simply his own understanding offered to us as a form of instruction to aid us in our own individual progression. When he speaks of Laws, he does not refer to man-made rules or moral traditions but to the cosmic and atomic way-things-are, the natural world of what-is, the universal laws of life, part of the original creative design and through which creation is fulfilled. These laws are beyond the possibility of being changed, suspended, transcended, or destroyed but they are ever a tool of mankind, not his master. First, through our awareness of the universal laws and then slowly through our developed understanding, the powers of creation are accessible to us. Not power over men's minds or circumstances, but power over whatever is selfish and imperfect in ourselves is the way up the eternal ladder of progression. When the Old Man cautions us concerning the Law of Responsibility or gives us a thinking exercise to explore the Law of Identity in a dynamic manner, he prepares us to take another step. And all move in accordance with the Law of What Can Be Borne.

Our teacher shows us how the two worlds are drawn together. In his realm, he describes, there is a great diversity of thought, many schools of understanding; but the Light is always known by the Light. Because of the interdependence of the two realms, listening to our discussions helped to clarify his teaching to others on his side of the curtain. His love and gratitude he humbly equates with ours.

The lessons to be perceived are not new, they are very old, but they are new to certain levels of our being. I would personally advise the reader, after reading this volume of discourses in full, to make a daily habit (or when there is a feeling or need) to sit quietly with the book. Open it at random and be guided to the Light by the passage that is there for the day. This technique is still used by the original students who were given the lessons and by many students after them who have studied in unfolding classes with me through these teachings.

Go beyond the words into feeling, into the immediate meanings for you. Touch into the inspiration that flows into the form of this book. It is from the Divine.

RICHARD P. GOODWIN
San Geronimo, California
June, 1972

A/V SEMINARS

A/V Seminar 19

Good evening, students. *[As the teacher greets the students, the clocks begin to chime and announce the hour. He pauses to allow the chimes to subside.]*

It is better to pause than be competitive in a world in which one is tempted to believe that they are. And so this evening, as we close the final chapter in our present residence in your world of our school and continue on with our preparations at our new northern coastal residence, I find it appropriate to speak to you this evening on the Law of Duality, time, the illusion, and the many symbols throughout your world that have been used to represent that illusion known as time, from your so-called sundials, designed to cast a shadow to tell you the time of day by the shadow that it casts, to the hourglass which must be turned upside down to tell you that time has passed, to the present clocks that the minds have designed. Please note that minutes always have the larger hand; that hours of illusion pass slowly. And so man is blinded by the largest form for he is intimidated by that which his mind considers is bigger and therefore better. So we are tempted, of course, by our minds to control that which we judge in our minds is bigger or better. Wise are those who accept the crumbs of the mind for they shall indeed guarantee the loaves of the heart.

And so this evening, in your world of creation, I am pleased to announce that in your world we have concluded what you understand as contracts and agreements for our new residence and what you understand as buyers will be arriving the beginning of this week. However, you, as my students, have indeed been well prepared. And so I'm going to spend a short time here with you this evening for some of you, my students, have not seen our new location. And therefore, I do feel that it would be of interest to those of you, especially, who have not seen it.

Surely of interest to those who care and would like to view it again later this evening.

And so, my good friends, this is the time for you to ask your questions. And prior to that, some of you may have noted over the years that you've known my channel that he's rather fond of what used to be a radio program in your world called, "The Shadow Knows." And so shadows know many things, and wisdom reveals them all. And so when you find yourself in need, remember, you've established the Law of Destiny and, of course, guarantee being controlled, for whoever believes in need is destined by the Law of Denial of what they are to experience dependence on something or someone they cannot, by the Law of Life, control.

So now is the opportunity for you to ask questions on this philosophy. And remember that this transition of location, though quick in your world—our classes will reopen at our new location. Time in your world, that great illusion, shall pass. And the support, spiritually, mentally, and materially, is required for the continuity in your world of these classes.

And so it's time in your world for your questions. *[After a short pause the teacher continues.]* No questions? I'm sure my channel will be very happy. He's been with real estate people all day. Yes, please.

Could you please speak on the significance of that time of the day known as dawn? In the story of Ulysses, again and again, the rosy-petaled fingers of dawn were mentioned.

Yes, indeed. Of course. What is, what is dawn the passing of?
The shadows. Night. The lesser light.
Yes. Is it not a time for rejoicing of the soul?
Yes.
Most of you students are aware: that which is of import in your life spiritually, let it be done prior to the noon hour for that is the change. Did that help with your question?
Yes, sir.

Yes. Yes.

Why is dawn the time of day for rejoicing, sir?

Because it is freedom from the bondage of belief. It is freedom from the darkness of mental substance. You see, all things are revealed when the obstruction is removed from the Light that is. Hmm? So man finds himself bound by what he has created, for man believes his thoughts, and in that belief, he solidifies them.

I instructed my channel a few weeks ago to speak to some of my students about what many of you, I'm sure, can relate to. You all understand the water center and how you drown yourself in the water centers of emotion. And so I instructed him, weeks ago, to inform you in no uncertain terms to dry out; just dry out. Don't dry up. No, you won't remain on earth. Dry out. Hmm?

And so what does it mean? Now there's two ways of drying out: there's the—creation is a dual law. It has only a primary and a secondary function to serve it. There are only two functions that serve creation. Two main functions. They have many, many children they have created. So there is the primary function and then there is the secondary function. When you find yourself controlled by the secondary function, then you must dry out. If you insist on identifying with your mind, you either have the water center or the earth center. And as you would say, of course, in your world, you can always buy it, if you're fateful [faithful] in creation to the primary function. Does that help you?

Yes...

Go ahead with the next question that you have.

Well, I don't quite understand.

Understand what?

What you just said in relation to dawn being the time of year to rejoice. I—

It is the rejoicing of the soul for it is the removal of the obstruction to the Light that you are. You see, that which is limited is only limited by shadow, only by belief. A person, they look and they see limit. But that which you are views, for there is no obstruction to what you are. There is only obstruction to what you believe, for man stands in his own light by his attachment to what he creates. Hmm? You see, it's like going out and you want to accomplish something. And what you want to accomplish is to experience and to receive what you think that you desire. If you permit your mind to judge the specifics of what you desire, then you are bound by what you have created. Now should you use wisdom, you will experience the principle, which is formless, free, and limitless of what you desire. And you will go through many steps. By going through those steps, you will have no emotional reaction for you know they are steps to what you desire. Do you understand that?

Yes, sir.

You see. And so what does it matter if you want a shelter in which to be sheltered from the storms of creation and that you want to be warm? If a stove warms you, what is it? Is it principle, is it reasonable to dictate that it must be electric, it must be gas, it must be wood? You see, you lose the principle by the dictate of the mind. Remember that the mind is personality. That's mental substance. Souls are faculties, their expressions are faculties. Minds, their expressions are functions.

And so your soul, that which you are, when it views warmth and comfort, it does not limit it; the principle, it experiences. Do you understand?

Yes, sir.

But it is the mind that binds us, for [to the mind] heat is heat only one way. You see? It has all these limits upon it. So you'll find in the mind of personality that it is not heat that you want; it is heat a certain way. In other words, you are now considering not just heat and warmth, you are now considering convenience and many other factors of the human mind. For a person [who] says,

"Well, now, if I have a woodstove to warm me, then I have to get the wood someplace. Then I have to bring the wood into the stove. Then I've got to light a match and I've got to get the fire started. Then it will only last so long." And so you are now considering many other factors. You are now bound by the dictates of your own mind. So that is bondage. Would you not agree?

I do, indeed. Yes, sir.

You see, you see, a crumb to the mind is a loaf to the heart. Hmm? Does that help you?

Yes, sir.

It's like a man that says, "I want a coat. Why do I want a coat? I want a coat to be warm. However, I want the coat to be made of this material. I want it cut a certain way. I want it a certain color, etc., etc." A man now does not want a coat; a man wants many other things. So he has lost the principle and sold out for the personality. Hmm?

Yes, sir.

Did that help you?

Yes, sir. Thank you.

Yes. You're welcome. Yes, please.

Thank you. Is all illness born in the water center?

All illness, what you call illness, is an effect of chemical changes within the body. Chemical changes are controlled by the human mind, not the conscious mind. However, whatever is in the inner or subconscious mind first was given birth in the conscious mind. Yes.

So the mind actually can hold the illness in the water center and that creates the illness?

No. The mind, making its judgments—do you understand that?

Yes.

—which is a thought solidified in the water center, for that's where judgments are born, in the water center. Now because there are many thoughts and because the human mind, through its errors of ignorance, believes it is the thought that it has created, [the mind] solidifies it in its own water center of emotion. You must understand that there are many, many judgments in the water center of consciousness that are certainly not harmonious; they are discordant. Now discord is the cause of disease. Does that help with your question?

Yes.

So when discord is removed, when the light of reason is cast upon the centers of consciousness, when a person makes the effort to rise to the center—Which two centers does the light of reason flow through?

The fourth and the fifth.

Yes, and that is the air and electric. Now, when you place your identification, your consciousness, in that center, reason transfigures you and your health is restored. It is restored only as long as you make the effort to express through that center, those two centers, fourth and fifth, of consciousness. Should you permit yourself the luxury of returning to the water center, those discordant judgments, activated by an over-identification with the limit, the belief that you are limit, you experience what you know as poor health, ill health, or disease. Yes.

Do you—does one consciously go to the fourth and the fifth cen—is that a conscious process?

That is conscious effort. Reason, the faculty of reason, the faculties flow through the conscious mind, not the subconscious. The subconscious is the domain of that which has been, that which you have already created. A person says, for example, that "I want money." Well, when they say that, identifying with themselves, they enter the water center of consciousness. There they have many judgments and the battle goes on. Then you experience in the conscious mind what you understand as justification. "I have this because of that. I don't have this because of something else." Yes. And you experience what is known, the king of the mind, known as fear. The more fear one has of their dictate, then the less they experience.

All we have to do is dictate to the Divine—[the] Divinity that is within us—all we have to do with our mind is to dictate to it and we will experience with our mind what we know as fear. Yes. Do you enjoy the water center?

No. Not at all.

Well, you are an individualized being. No problem at all; you have a lot of company. Hmm? And they have so little tolerance for one who is in it because they have so little tolerance for themselves when they go in it. Do you understand that?

Yes.

Well, there you are. You know how you went to the water center? You registered fear, only in the few minutes of this class.

All right.

Yes.

Thank you.

You're welcome. Yes, please.

How does one go to the air and electric if they're in the water center to get to, to—

Through the breathing exercises that you have already been given as students. Through a conscious, constant effort, you see? Yes. Declare the truth. Declare the truth. You are the truth; so declare yourself. Declare what you are. Declare your right to the goodness of life. Declare it in your consciousness. Yes.

Thank you very much.

We're not short of the power of the will. It's only direction that we, at times, are so tempted to use unwisely. Yes, please.

Could you go into more detail about a crumb to the mind is a loaf to the heart?

Oh, indeed, indeed! Our little minds tell us that we want many things, and we want them right now. And so in keeping with the law of our own merit, which is, of course, the effect of our own efforts in life, we receive a small, little portion, that is, in our mind of what we want. It's a loaf to our heart. And we usually can relate to that truth through what is known as hindsight. Aren't you grateful you didn't marry him last year? Pardon?

Yes.

Well, there you are. Wouldn't you call that a crumb to the mind, truly a loaf to your heart? Is there any other question?

No. Thank you.

You're welcome. Hindsight, they call it. Yes.

Is there an effect upon people who live by the ocean? The sea air I'm thinking of, salt air. What affect does that have?

Yes. To those who are not over-identified with their water center it can be and is extremely beneficial.

Now, you have opened a door through which we may have a little discussion on what the forms are composed of and what they require for their mobility; I think you'll relate best to that word. A form created by the human mind, known as a thought form, permitted to enter the water center of consciousness, is solidified. What does that mean? That means its substance, of which the mind—for example, you think of a rose and you have it in the mind and you judge you must have it, and you permit it to descend into your water center, there it becomes solidified as a judgment. And so all forms created require moisture [and] what you know, also, as oxygen. Because they are created in a water center, you understand, without moisture (water), they cannot exist. You understand that? Salt and water. I think they call them the salt of the earth. But anyway, you will find that these forms actually utilize oxygen for their mobility. Does that help with your question?

Thank you.

Someone else—pardon? Yes.

I was wondering if the salt dried the air.

Dried the air?

Salt is drying.

Yes, of course, it is. Yes, indeed, it is. I think you've answered your question. Yes, indeed. But I think that the oceans of life itself are very moist, would you not agree?

That's true.

Yes. So I think that should help you in that understanding. Have you not found—perhaps it has not been fully revealed by your medical profession yet. At the present time many of your medical profession are awakening to the value of the sound or rhythmic flow of the natural oceans. Some of your medical profession are aware of that. And they're also aware of a healing experience. They, however, so far are limited to believing that it is a psychological benefit, when it is actually a physical and psychological benefit. Hmm? Yes.

And because man is composed of so much water and because man uses so much water—each thought requires moisture from his own being—and because the water center [in] which man has created so many judgments that are not in accord, then, of course, man benefits from those conditions spiritually. Does that help with your question?

Yes. Thank you.

Yes, you're more than welcome. Yes.

Thank you.

Good evening.

I would like a little bit more understanding on what you spoke of earlier about primary and secondary functions—

Yes.

—in creation.

Yes, there are, there are only two functions: a primary and secondary function which serve what we understand as the human ego, the throne of individual creation. All right? Now we understand that man, not God, is a creator. The Light sustains and mental substance creates. All right. The words that were given to my students so many years ago in your world is *m-e-s*.

Money is the primary service to the ego of creation, and sex is the secondary function to the ego of creation.

Now Lucifer, which is the fallen angel—the only thing that falls or fizzles like an Alka-Seltzer is a human ego. The soul doesn't fall or rise. The soul is. It's only the human ego that rises and falls. Does that help with your question?

Yes. Thank you.

And so, Lucifer, by his own choice of over-identification with limit, Lucifer fell from grace and is doing everything possible to bring what's left down with him. Do you understand that?

Yes.

Yes. But, of course, that's contrary to the very law: you cannot bring down or cause to descend that which, that which sustains one. So as the Divine Light sustains the Lucifer as well as the angels—for, after all, Lucifer was an angel. And in Lucifer's realm, known as creation, he is now king. However, he's not the king of kings, only the king of princes. Hmm? And princesses. Does that help with the question?

Yes. Thank you very much.

Yes. You're welcome. Yes.

Thank you. Good evening.

Good evening.

In the beginning of the class, I'm not sure I wrote this correctly, but I would like some more understanding. I have [written] down here it's better to pause than to be tempted to competition to what we believe we are.

Do we not believe that we are illusion?

Yes.

Is it not, is it not best to pause than to step over the cliff?

Yes.

Into the bondage of belief in that which is no substance.

Yes.

Yes. A shadow is still a shadow, an obstruction to what we are. We know them as has-beens. They can only rise when we begin to believe we are in need. No shadow can rise in the consciousness until we consciously choose to believe that we are in need. For when we believe that we are in need, we deny what we are only to experience what Lucifer experiences: what we are not.

Thank you.

Did that help with your question?

Yes, very much.

Yes. It's the destiny of denial, and it opens up one of the servants of the primary function. One of the—that particular servant is known as greed. Whoever chooses the path of denial shall walk through the wastelands of need ever crying, ever in greed. Ever.

Yes, yes. Good evening.

Good evening. Would you speak on—because I've heard you all mention it several weeks now—one facing the pride or facing his pride?

Yes, indeed. One should face what one creates; it's known as personal responsibility. You know a father has a wonderful opportunity. He looks at his child and he says, "Now I am an instrument of how my son is acting for I am the one who has guided the child, hopefully guided him." For you are an instrument of creating or permitting those particular traits of the child to, to develop within the child. Certainly. Face the pride, for the pride we have created. Yes.

You know I find it noteworthy that we have no problem serving our vanity in the mirrors of reflection. However, we seem to sometimes have great problems looking at our own pride in its own reflection, don't we? Hmm? Yes.

Thank you.

You're welcome. Yes.

Would—is it an—is it wise to look at what motivates one's needs?

Well, what motivates one's needs is what one has created with their mind and judged that they are and insist on believing that they are what they have created. You see, it's our attachment to the fruits of action. The fruits of action being what we have created. Whoever attaches themselves to their fruits of action, to their own efforts—you understand that—is destined to their own belief and bondage and also destined to the adversity to that which they have created. Hmm?

Age does not guarantee wisdom. Adversity brings balance, and balance is wisdom. Hmm? Yes.

OK. I was thinking in terms of desire. What one would desire. Would it be wise to look at what would—what is motivating one to desire?

Why, certainly. Honesty is the only path of Light. Honesty with oneself, what they are. You see, we cannot separate truth from creation, what we are from what we are not, until we are honest. And when we are honest and we take a look and we view and we will see, and then we can begin our separation, you see. Does that help with your question?

Yes. Thank you.

Yes. Yes, please.

How does adversity bring balance?

Why, indeed, for example, we become attached to that which we create, known as the fruits of our action. And when we are sufficiently attached and we pay the price of that attachment, we move to the counterbalance. We are in a world of duality. We believe we are our mind: separate, individual, perfect beings. Yes. That which we create we are not. And so when you spend the time of attachment to anything or anyone, especially when you deceive yourself that you can control it and awaken someday that you cannot, then you become adverse to it. Remember, the human mind ever tempts itself to destroy what it has judged it cannot control. Pardon? So if we are truly attached to our fruits of action and it does not—that which we are attached to does not work out the way that we have judged that it will work out, then we are tempted to destroy it for we do not want to live in the adversity that is guaranteed. Every attachment guarantees its adversity. Every adversity guarantees its own attachment. That is the beauty of life; the effect of it is freedom.

Yes. Say that you create whatever you create and you finally awaken that it is not serving you well; you become adverse to it. You don't want it around anymore. Correct? And when you become adverse to it, you become freed from that which you have created. Now that which you are adverse to, you also, by directing life-giving energy to it, you guarantee your own attachment to that which you were once adverse to. In your world it's known [as] the honeymoon is over. The honeymoon with anything. It's of such short duration. And as one grows older, through so many experiences, you see, the honeymoons get so [much] shorter, so much shorter. Did that help with your question? Yes.

What—you explained the attachment and the adversity. And you want to destroy it after you become adverse to it.

You want to destroy it after you awaken that you can't control it. So you build up your own adversity, don't you? And that's how we get free—isn't it?—in creation. That's the Law of Duality. Hmm?

Yes.

If there are not two, then there is not duality, is there? Hmm. Complexity is the multiplication, known in your world, of course, as breeding. Multiply more and more. Bigger is better. Yes. Quantity, not quality, is the call of the human mind. Yes, please. Good evening.

Good evening. Thank you. The destruction can be accomplished in many ways.

Indeed.

Apart from acceptance.

Acceptance free—as I said to my students years ago, forgiveness is the path: to give forth. For we have stolen that from the universe. Give it forth. Forgive it means to give forth. When one gives forth anything that disturbs them—you remember that

that which disturbs us in truth is controlling us. So when we forgive it (we give it forth), we are freed from it [and] no longer controlled by it. Yes.

In our days of ignorance, we have believed that we, being the creator, can control it. So we create something in our mind. We let it go out in the universe to do its job. And when we find that there are other entities and forms out there doing their job and the battle goes on. Then we have what we know as experiences. Right? Yes. So when you create something and it is dependent on anyone that you do not have the divine right to control, then you find you'll have a problem. Hmm? See, a man creates what he calls love, and someone comes in to fill what he has created. He has already created it in his mind. You do understand that, don't you?

So someone comes in out of the universe, an individualized, divine soul, covered with flesh and mental substance. And then, at first, because he is so blinded with desire, that fits the bill. Isn't that what they call it? Yes. And then, time marches on, and there are other things that he begins to consider. And in so doing the Law of Comparison is established. Well, now, comparison is the ribbon that ties the box of judgments, you see. And then problems begin, don't they? Pardon?

Yes.

Yes, indeed. And so it is, that's the way—you see, look at it mathematically. It's the law. That's why I said, for ladies and gentlemen, you can always buy it. So anyone with any intelligence, if they must have any attachment, then let them be attached to a primary function. If you must believe, then at least offer yourself that intelligence to choose a primary function. Hmm? For it is not primary by chance. It is primary by priority and value to the king of creation himself. That help with your question?

Thank you.

Yes, certainly. Yes, please.

Could you speak on the significance of the element known as hydrogen to the forms and how they use it?

Well, I think that we should first consider salt and water, shouldn't you? Don't you think? Perhaps, you know, we're not all advanced scientists, yet. If we are, we don't recall it. And I think that we should perhaps remain with moisture. We seem to have plenty of that. And as I instructed my channel, I want all students dried out. I only want dried out students, yes.

Yes, sir.

And I think you, as students, know what that means. If you want to drown yourself in the pool, you note that there's not one here [at the temple]. We have no intention of building one. Thank you. Yes. Yes, please.

What chemical is most detrimental to forms?

What chemical?

Yes.

Well, if you will consider poison a chemical. Pardon?

Yes.

The poison gas of selfishness. It is a chemical. Selfishness is a chemical. How is it a chemical? When one directs intelligent energy to limit—do you understand?—the limit of their own form, they poison their own body. Yes.

You see, the human mind, you understand, it is the human mind and the judgments of the water center that affect our breathing, which affects, in truth, our oxygen intake. And all these created forms use these chemicals of our own beings, you see? You see, there's a difference, of course, between the nature spirits, a vast difference between a nature spirit and a created form, a thought form of mental substance. A nature spirit has a specific work to do in keeping—no one creates nature spirits. Nature spirits are. They are responsible to their realm: earth, fire, water, and air. The four basic nature spirit armies. And when they are upset—and they control all form; they control the flesh, the bones, etc.—then you have problems in your world. That help you?

Yes.

All right. Yes. Yes.

Is the giving forth, which is forgiving, is that, would that be, then that is the natural ascendancy—would that be the natural ascendancy into the faculties?

Why, certainly, for if you give forth everything you create with your mind, then your soul is free. Of course! But that is not what we find, is it? We find that, through the poisoning of our being by constant self-thought, that we hold tenaciously to what we have created, as a mother holds to her babe, as a father holds to his son, believing that he has created it, when, in truth, he's only an instrument. They'll soon be creating all of them in the laboratory. Yes. Does that help with your question?

Yes. Thank you.

Of course. Yes, please.

When there's a disturbance in the atmosphere, is that a result, an effect of the nature spirits that's been, oh, taken by mental thought forms?

Yes, well, mental thought forms have interfered with the work that they have to do. And so they go to war. Yes, that is true. Yes.

And, and, and nature spirits, well, they are definitely not under the control of Lucifer or, or—

Well, absolutely not.

Or any—

No, Lucifer has no control. Nature spirits are not good or bad in that sense. Nature spirits are not fallen angels.

Right.

No, they are not. Yes.

And Lucifer, mental substance is only hollow. They're hollow, soulless forms.

Well, there is no soul in a mental form.

Hollow.

No, there is, there is no soul now in that respect. Now if you choose to remain out to lunch for a long time, then, of course, there are the wandering souls of the astral realms who will come in because they're out in the cold and they're looking for a place. And, of course, they will come in. In your world you understand that as possession, yes.

Thank you.

And if you stay out too long, well, you never know how many different ones are in and out in service to that particular realm. Yes. That help with your question?

Thank you. Yes, it did.

You're welcome. Yes.

You've taught us that, that work is a soul faculty.

Indeed, it is a soul faculty.

Is it ever possible that mental effort could be work in . . .

Mental effort? Well, yes, of course, now, when we limit work to the movement of the physical body exclusively—there are many physical bodies that move, but they don't work. They do all kinds of—there are many mental bodies that move and do nothing constructive whatsoever because they spend most of the time dreaming and playing with what has been. You see, anyone who plays with what has been, that is not the work of which I speak; work as a soul faculty. Work, as a soul faculty, is accomplishing. It's something constructive, you see. It's in keeping with the Law of Evolution, change. Has-beens, you see, do not and cannot survive. They do not evolve. A judgment does not change. We only create a new judgment. Judgments don't change. They're very loyal that way. And all has-beens, you understand, are judgments; they do not change. Yes. Does that help with your question?

Yes.

Yes. Yes, please.

Yes.

Not yet. *[The teacher seems to be addressing Reddy, the church's dog.]*

OK. Oh, we create forms with our mind that could be considered as detrimental, and we create forms of our mind that could be considered as not detrimental.

Any form created by the human mind that it sends into the realms of reason is transformed. Therefore, if the thought form created by the mind ascends—it has to go through its purification process, of course—as it ascends it becomes a form to bring good into our life. Why, of course. Because it ascends with faith, and it descends with fear. And so we—you know, if you create a form and then you're waiting and waiting and you experience fear that it hasn't happened, you can be rest assured that the thought form you have created has descended into the water center. Why, of course. And it's in its process of solidifying into a judgment. Does that help with your question?

Yes, that helps with one. Also—

All thoughts are heavenly if they reach the Light for no darkness can endure. Does that help with your question?

Yes, sir.

Yes.

I'll think about that.

Well, if you were [concerned], you would guarantee it just went down into your water center.

OK.

Yes. Interest is a soul faculty. And what do you think concern is?

Ah, ah . . .

Does concern have fear?

Yes.

Is it guided by fear?

Yes.

Is interest guided by faith?

Yes.

Well, when interest becomes concern, you can be rest assured the water center has it. It is now in Lucifer's hands.

Yes, sir.

Yes. Go ahead.

How or what creates how nature spirits come to be?

Nature spirits cannot be understood by mental substance, for mental substance cannot control them. And what man thinks he can understand, he ever tempts to control. No, nature spirits are not subject to mental substance. Hmm?

OK.

They are the servants of Light. Yes.

Thank you.

The tree is not subject to the dictates of the human ego. The tree, however, must suffer being exposed to the human mind. Hmm? Yes. Bend like the willow and you will never break. Yes, please.

Yes, could you please speak more on the purification of the ascending forms that you just mentioned?

Yes.

And how would we be aware of that? What would the experience be like?

Good. And not dependent on anything outside yourself. [Not dependent on] anyone. Anyone. Because, you see, a thought form in order to enter the realms of Light is transformed, and all self-interest and concern is removed. Hmm?

Thank you.

That help with the question?

Yes. Thank you.

Yes. You're welcome. Yes, please.

I'm speaking on the same thing. Is that the, the purification, does that have anything to do with what we were talking about earlier about attachment and . . .

Adversity?

And adversity? That that process being purifying your thoughts.

That's something that takes place in a mental realm. [The other student] here was speaking on the ascendancy of a thought form. You see, for example, say that you have a thought form that you want to have happiness and joy; and that happiness and joy, of course, is if you have a faithful, loyal, good, supporting husband. You have just denied what you are. That type of form does not ascend. Do you understand that?

Right.

For you have dictated to the Divine a denial of what you are. That you, what you truly are, is whole, complete, and perfect, formless and free. So to tempt to take Lucifer's realm and form it into need and give it to God and expect God, the divine, free Light, that Principle, to put itself down into—what do you call those bottles with a genie? Whatever those things are in your world—is just stupid and ridiculous thinking. Hmm?

Thank you.

You see, you see, you cannot take and, being a servant of the denial of truth, and carry a message from Lucifer to the Divine Light and expect the Divine Light to go down to serve Lucifer. The Divine Light sustains Lucifer and his limit. But Lucifer and his limit cannot control the Light that sustains it. He tempted to do that and fell from grace. And whoever tempts to do that shall fall, also, from grace. Hmm?

Remember that hope's eternal and truth is inevitable. There is no way for the human mind to be sustained by the Divine Light and to control the Divine Light, for the human mind is very fickle. There are times when it doesn't want the Light; then there's times that it does want the Light. So for the human mind to have control of that which sustains it, the human mind would not long endure and, therefore, would not be a servant for the Divine Light to express through. Does that help with your question?

Very much. Thank you.

Yes. Because there are times when you wish you could die, and there are times when you wish and want many things. And if your very life sustenance was in the control of the human mind, there would be no continuity of the human species. Did that help with your question? Because it is so fickle. Because it is so dependent on things. You understand that? When you limit the love of God, when you limit it in any form, you lose the love of God, but you do get the counterfeit. You get the temporal thrill, and you get the charge, and you get the sensation. You do not get the continuity of peace and harmony. No.

So when, of course, a being is ready, they shall enter that Light in its fullness. But not until they're ready. For the dictates cannot go into the Light. They're burned by the Light of eternal truth. Hmm? And that's known as transformed. Hmm? All personalities, all forms go through the transformation and are known as principle, for that's what they truly are. We're shed of the cloaks of deception that, at times, we believe that we are. And as long as we insist on believing with our minds that we can control what is not controllable, then we, of course, in our senses shall suffer. Does that help with your question? Yes.

Yes, please. Time is passing quickly.

To, to reap the counterfeit of an experience means a repeat of the experience, right?

Well, people—

Of the lesson.

Yes. People take many, many, many, many repetitions before they're willing to make a change. "O suffer senses not in vain for freedom of the soul is gain." Yes.

So if, if we give something, I mean—all right—we had something that we were trying to manifest or bring forth—

For what purpose?

For what purpose?

Well, one must always ask what their motive is. Only through honesty can man ever free himself.

OK.

Now if one says it's for someone else, then one must ask themselves, "Now just a moment, is that person in God's hands, God's care? What is the law involved here?" Hmm? Yes.

Yes.

And then if one's asking for himself, then one must be honest and say, "Now let me see, what am I denying? What have I denied? How could I experience this need until my ego rose in its supremacy and denied what I am?" Yes. That help with your question?

Yes.

I don't think there's any question left then, do you? in that particular respect.

Thank you.

Yes. When acceptance is the divine will of goodness itself. Hmm?

Yes, sir.

But let us not confuse acceptance, the divine will, with dictation, the devil himself. Get him behind me.

Yes, you have a question, please.

Yes. Thank you.

Yes. Yes, I know. *[The teacher addresses the technician recording the class, acknowledging that the tape is about to end.]*

Could you say a few more words, please, regarding constructive work? And—

Constructive work. Fine. Constructive work. What is constructive work? What fruit does a tree bear? Is it a fruit of benefit serving the purpose of its design? Is that not a good question? So we take a look at the tree, and we see that it bears the fruit of the purpose of its design. If no one plucks the fruit, if no one eats the fruit, is it constructive work of the tree? Pardon?

No.

So whatever you do in life, if it is of constructive work, then it is serving a purpose for which you have designed it, correct? So if you work to make a chair, and the chair does not serve the purpose of its design, then it could not be constructive work, could it? Pardon?

No.

When you have worked and you have constructed the chair to serve the purpose of its design—whatever serves the purpose of its design and the Law of Balance is constructive work.

Now I want to—time has passed for us and I will instruct my channel for those of you who are interested, I don't think [all of you] have seen our new residence. Well, I want you to know—and there's just a few moments left here in your world—for those who are scheduled and have been [at] weekly classes, I want you to be assured that I will be present in the atmosphere. I may or may not be speaking to you. Certainly not in this way with documents that my channel has to go through. They come in by the hundreds. And there's so much to be taken care of. I expect your continued support, and I do view your presence at our new residence as the moons pass so quickly in your world. And thank you. And good day—or good evening.

JANUARY 8, 1987

A/V Seminar 20

Good evening, class.

Our discussion is moving on: fear, what is it? Its cause and cure. Fear is an experience in our emotions or water center which is an effect of the judgments that we believe that we are when they are threatened. We fear what we deny. For example, one fears that they will not have enough money in their life for first they have denied that they have it. And so denial, indeed, becomes our destiny in keeping with our belief in that which has passed. And so as we look each moment to moving on to something better, we fear the steps necessary to accomplish it for we believe that we are that which has passed. And in so believing, we fear what is to be.

Anticipation is a servant of fear. Expectation is a servant of fear. Acceptance is a faculty of freedom. And so whatever we see that is not in harmony with what has been, we fear that it may enter our lives for we believe we are the shadow, the event, the form, the judgment that we have created.

Creation is king of the functions. It offers, inevitably, to everyone, fear. It is and has always been the purpose of these classes to bring about a balance in the consciousness between the functions, which are servants of limit or creation, to bring the functions into balance through an expression of the faculties. As acceptance is a faculty, which is the direct balance of denial, man enters the Law of Harmony and is freed from the expression of fear which he knows as need.

You can do, yourself, a daily exercise. Whenever you experience this fear, which you have created and know as need, direct your consciousness to the corresponding balanc[ing] faculty of acceptance. When your mind tells you that you have not, then tell your mind that you have. For the have-not[s] are the shadows that, through your direction [of energy] to, are, once again, being activated and absorbing the energy through your lack of conscious direction.

Whenever you go to make the slightest change in your life, if that change is not in keeping with what you have already experienced, then you shall experience fear before, during, and after. Usually a person experiences the fear after the change. Sometimes during the change. And rarely before the change. They think they experience fear when they are aware of the change, but they do not experience the real fear until they have made the actual step of change.

Go to the store; you make a purchase. You go through many experiences, the effects of fear, for you are threatening the judgments you have made in the past. And when you threaten a judgment that you believe that you are, it reacts, and that reaction is an emotional experience that you know as fear.

Remember, we always fear what we first judge we cannot control, and we judge that we can control what we are already familiar with. For in the familiarity with anything we create within our mind the judgment that we can control it.

And so you, as a class of students in the Light, have had over these past few months much experience with your fears. Fear of change. Fear of the possibility of change. For as I stated, it is the nature of the human mind to fear what it does not first judge it can control. And yet you have received and continue to receive the laws that govern fear, and the way to bring fear, king of creation, into balance by directing intelligent energy to the faculties, which free a person from limit and from obstruction.

Now it's time for your questions on this evening's class. Yes, please.

Could you please define expectation? *And why is it a servant of fear?*

Yes. Expectation and anticipation are functions. All functions serve [the] king of creation, which is fear. The difference between expectation and anticipation, to the human mind, is that expectation presumes the cost; anticipation does not. When you expect something, you presume what it will cost you. And when you anticipate experiencing something, you do not presume a cost. That help with your question?

Thank you.

Well, for example, if you expected something from your relatives, your mind would presume what it will cost you. Would you not agree?

Yes, sir!

However, if you anticipated something, you would not have that function of presumption of what it will cost you. Think of that. Yes.

Then in anticipation, you're not conscious of any cost.

That is correct. There is no conscious awareness of any cost when one anticipates anything. When one expects anything, there is a thought of what it will cost. That is correct. Yes, please.

Is there a corresponding soul faculty to anticipation and, and expectation?

Yes, indeed there is. You see, for example, because anticipation and expectation are servants of the king of fear, then one should use the faculty, the king of the faculties, known as acceptance. You see, you've already had the understanding that acceptance is the will (the action) of good, the movement of God. And so as fear is the king of creation, Lucifer and his throne, so acceptance is the throne of God and the will of good. So when a person is experiencing any of the servants of creation, then one should flood their consciousness with acceptance to bring about a balance.

Now, for example, that all has to do with the illusion of time. To a person who does not desire what they are told is coming their way, time could be, for them, very short, for it is something they don't care to receive. Do you understand that?

Yes, sir.

Now if you tell a person there's something coming their way that they've been waiting for or think they're waiting for a long time and they want it very much, then time is extremely long for them. Would you not say?

Yes, sir.

You see—and so everything is dependent upon our perspective. If you will recall I drew on the blackboard for you some time ago a person's perspective, in your private classes. And it is where you are in consciousness that reveals to you what time truly is: it is an illusion. It is the conscious awareness of passing events. And so a person when they are waiting for something that is something that they truly desire, then—and they're told soon—soon never seems to come to them, you see?

Yes, sir.

And so it's all relative to the individual's own personal desires. Does that help you?

Yes, indeed.

Yes. And so as I gave to you some time ago: accept the possibility of experiencing the goodness that you are. You see, don't declare, "I accept the goodness that I am," for you will threaten that which you believe that you are. And when you threaten that which you believe that you are, you experience, from that threatening of those forms you have created and believe that you are, you experience what is known as fear. And so the thing that we fear, of course, befalls us because that which we fear, we fear it because we believe we are the judgments that have been threatened. And so if you want to attract something unto you, then all you have to do is to sufficiently fear it, and it shall befall you in keeping with the magnetic Law of Attraction, you see.

You see, you have a judgment that you believe that you are. The judgment rises up in the consciousness, and it tells you that it's being threatened. You believe that you are the judgment; therefore, you experience the emotion that you know as fear only because you believe that that which you have created is what you are. Do you understand that?

Yes, sir.

Now a person doesn't suddenly say, "Well, I no longer believe that which I have created," because the water center of consciousness, the emotions do not respond to the light of reason. That is a different center of consciousness. Do you understand?

Yes, sir.

You see. Now you can cast the light of reason over someone else if you are not magnetically attached to them. If you are attached to another person, then you are attached to them at the cost and the sacrifice of objectivity, which means that your faculty of reason is blinded during the time of your attachment, because the attachment is a magnetic center of consciousness, the water center of consciousness. Do you understand that?

Yes, sir.

And so anyone who permits their life-energy to be used to create must be willing to pay the price of the blindness and the loss of the faculty of reason, for they believe that they are that which they have created or are creating. Does that help you?

Thank you, sir.

Yes. Yes.

Fear is the effect of need?

Fear, fear is the king of limit or creation. Need is the effect of denial. When you deny what you are, you experience what you are not. And when you experience what you are not, you believe that that is need. You have denied what you are in order to experience what you are not. For example, if you believe that for the fullness of your life, the happiness, the joy, etc., if you truly believe in order for you to experience the goodness of life you must have someone in your life, then you have denied that you are a whole, complete, and perfect being. And so therefore, you place yourself in a position of being a victim. Do you understand that?

Yes, I do.

You see, now that is an effect of denying the goodness that you are. In other words, your goodness is dependent on what someone else does or does not do. You have first denied the truth in order to experience the falsehood.

Correct.

Now fear is in the realm of the functions of falsehood, not in the faculties of truth, you see. So if you believe because you have entered earth in a vehicle, a female vehicle, that you're only half there (you're not complete), then you must pay the price of victimization and dependence on someone else for you to be complete, for you have denied the truth and must pay the price of the falsehood. Does that help you with your question?

Yes.

Yes.

And since fear is magnetic and that's, that opens the door to all the forms we have created which kind of creates that blackout which is like the lack of reason?

Well, there is no reason in the water center, magnetic centers of consciousness. Reason does not exist there.

Right.

That's only where the shadows live. That's where the judgments are created. Yes.

Yes.

And so whenever one chooses to enter that realm of consciousness, then they must be aware that they are doing so at the loss of objectivity and the faculty of reason. And as one grows in the Light, one finds the temptation less and less attractive. Pardon?

Yes.

Yes.

Thank you.

Yes. Yes, please. I'll be with you ladies in a moment. Yes.

[The student clears her throat.] *Excuse me. Am I correct in assuming, then, that sickness also is derived of fear?*

That is correct because, you see, it is a discord within the consciousness.

OK.

You see, disease is a direct effect of discord. Yes. And that reveals that within the consciousness there is a battle and a struggle that is taking place.

Yes.

Yes. And there is, of course, there is a threat to whatever one believes that they are. Yes, that is correct.

And when one is physically ill, how can we continue to accept the goodness that we are, considering that we don't feel well?

Yes. Well, first of all, you have to change; you have to move from the judgment that you don't feel well.

OK.

Now remember that it takes a direction of the power of your will to experience that you don't feel well. That takes a conscious effort.

Yes.

Yes. For example, one, one thinks of themselves, all right? Now the more that one thinks of themselves, the more the shadows rise up into their consciousness. It is extremely detrimental for a person to sit down and to think about themselves because they will find that for any positive thought that enters their consciousness, there's at least 20 negative ones. Do you understand that?

Yes, I do.

Yes. So, first of all, one must choose very carefully and wisely whether or not they're going to stop and think about themselves, for if they think about themselves too long, for sure they're going to start feeling badly. For it's a 20:1 situation: 20 of the negative past experiences to 1 of the positives, you see?

Yes.

Because we're entering down into the magnetic center of consciousness, into the water center of consciousness. All right. One cannot afford the luxury of thinking of oneself. One cannot afford the luxury of thinking about the job or the work they have in life, for if they do—they're all related, you understand?—one will enter into that realm of consciousness, and the judgments will take the energy and the vitality—the energy from the vital body. And the discord will continue on within their consciousness and their health will deteriorate.

Yes.

You see?

Yes.

Now a person, when they have fallen into that, being what some students like to say, "only human," you understand?

Yes.

Being only human, and not animal, I guess that's what they mean by that. *[Some students laugh.]* Being only human that a person enters that realm of consciousness, that's the time—yes, indeed—that's the time to declare the truth: you are whole, complete, and perfect. And flood the consciousness until you are able to redirect it into something of your interest. And you will see what a wonderful healing you will experience.

OK.

You see?

Just pick up and force yourself to—

Yes, it must be something that is of interest to the mind, something that is desirable to the mind, and something that will keep the mind active, you understand, its interest. And the next thing you know, you will not be aware of the poor condition.

OK.

Yes. And by not being aware of it, you do not direct energy to it. And therefore, the law begins to balance itself. Yes.

OK.

And it passes that much sooner. You see, people who identify with their illness only are instruments for the illness to continue. That is why the workers win, the workers who move into something besides the thought of self. It's extremely detrimental. You see, self-thought is the most detrimental and destructive experience that a human being could possibly have.

Yes.

Yes. Now, for example, if you have an animal, and the animal is feeling a little poorly or something, you want to be sure and tell them how good they feel, you see. What a nice day it is and everything. You know, it's like training a child. You train a child: if you want the child to eat carrots, you first eat a carrot yourself, and you tell them how great it is.

Yes.

You see. Well, animals are the same way. If you want your dog to eat carrots, then you must first eat the carrot and tell him how good it is and only let him have a little, small bit of it. Very small. *[Some students laugh.]* You see? Until they have created that judgment that the carrot is a wonderful thing, like an ice-cream cone. You see, it's all in the mind.

Yes.

And aren't we so blessed? We know we put it there. You know, it'd be a very sad day if we believe someone else put it there, you see. But we know that we put it there, and because we know that we put it there, that puts us in the position in our mind to put it back out. You see, whatever you put into something, you can also take back out. So don't ever forget that whatever the experience may be in your life, pause and tell yourself the truth, "Hmm, I don't like this experience. I did put it there. I accept that responsibility. I certainly did put it there. Now I choose to put it out." You see?

Yes.

And you put it out, you see. It is true, in putting out things, especially if it was a little spark of fire, if it was a little flame of fire, it takes a lot of water to put it out, you know. Hmm? Yes, indeed. Do you understand that? Yes, you see. I mean, after all, some people start a little spark there, you know, a little flame, and things change and they evolve and move on, you see, and the flame keeps on burning. Well, they haven't put enough water on it yet. Does that help you?

Yes, it does.

Yes, indeed. Yes, and now [you] have a question. And then I'll be with the ladies over here. Yes.

When we go to make a change and after the change is made and then the fear rises up . . .

Yes.

And we go to express acceptance, what are we accepting?

We are accepting our divine right of conscious choice. For example, a person makes a change, and they experience the fear after. If they don't nip that fear in the bud, what will happen? That fear, those judgments, which are creators—you see, they create. We have created them, and they become little creators. So they will create for us every experience to justify that we never should have made the change in the first place. It's kind of like getting a divorce, you know. You see, after the divorce is over, then the wife or the husband, you know, they look around and they say, "Well, here's these mouths to feed. Oh, I never should have got that divorce." Do you understand that?

Yes.

You see, so it's the same thing. It isn't a matter of divorce; it's a matter of change. You see, you make the change, and if you don't nip it in the bud, if you don't declare the truth, "This is a change that I have made by my own conscious right of choice. I have made this choice without dependence on anything outside of my own divine right inside of myself. Therefore, whatever is entering my mind is something that I've put there from who knows how long ago. I choose to root it right back out again and accept the goodness right where I am, for this is the choice that I have made. I will not permit my judgments, my shadows of the past to rise in my consciousness and justify that I have made a mistake for I will only guarantee everything necessary to prove how right my uneducated ego really is." Do you understand that?

See, an uneducated ego is an ego that doesn't accept personal responsibility. An uneducated ego is an ego that will not look up to the light of one's own reason. Do you understand that? You see, an uneducated ego looks down to the water center. An educated ego looks up to the air center. That's the difference between an educated and an uneducated ego. An uneducated ego, in every devious way possible, looking down to the water center of judgments, does every devious thing to blame outside that they are the victim of circumstances—not that they have created the circumstances, oh, no!—they are a victim of what someone else created. Do you understand? That's what the water center offers, you see. Hmm?

And this is a very important class. I have—because I've already instructed my channel, prior to coming down here to class, that you students would be permitted, after class, to view our new location, which is, let me say, definite for there are no guarantees and warranties in spiritual substance. There's determination, [which] is a faculty. Definite. A faculty. And things of that nature. But guarantees and warranties, we don't have in these realms of consciousness. But I can say "Serenity Del Norte" will be shown to you after class.

Now someone else has a question here, do they? Yes, please.

You were saying that we have fear before a change and during a change—

Yes, and after.

But the real fear comes after the change.

Well, the real fear, it depends on one's awakening. An awakened person is aware of the fear prior to the event physically happening. They are aware during its happening, and they are aware after its happening. Well, it depends, you see. It depends upon one's own desire in reference to the fear. If one has had a great desire to be married, there's a little fear before the marriage. They're not too much aware of it prior to the marriage because there's so much desire, which is total blindness. Then during the marriage, after a time, a little fear starts rising up. And then after it's over, there's plenty of fear. All kinds of fear. Fear that the next one might be like the last one. You see, if a person doesn't change, of course the next one's like the last one. The next one of anything is like the last one of yesterday because they really haven't changed. Do you understand? They've only allowed into their consciousness what is in harmony or in keeping with what's already there. What does that—that I would not consider evolution, would you?

No.

You see, it's like a person saying, "Well, let me see, my first husband had blue eyes. My second husband will have to have blue eyes. My third one will have to have blue eyes [and] my fourth one and my fifth one." Well, tell me where the change is? Pardon? They're still supporting the first one in consciousness.

Right.

Do you understand that?

Yes!

You see. And so when a person, unless they are honest with themselves and they don't take a good look, they will see that with all of the people, places, or things that they have already had, there's a similarity here, a very strong similarity in each and every one. But, you see, that shows how much the person is growing and awakening. Do you understand that?

So it's just a reflection of—that you haven't really changed at all.

Outward manifestations, as [that student] there said some time ago, outward manifestations are revelations of inner attitudes of mind. So if your outward revelations in life are similar to what they were twenty years ago, then that tells you how much change you've made. Do you understand?

See, if a woman goes and she gets married and she's been married sixteen times, and sixteen of those times she's also been divorced, there's been no change made at all. I mean, you see, there is no law of the Divine that says a woman must merit a bummer every single time she gets married. *[Many of the students laugh.]* You see, that's no law of justice, divine or otherwise. Pardon?

That was good. Thank you.

Yes. Well, I'm sure in your world of creation you are aware that they're beginning to enforce in some of your states, that is, the states that have always been known for a little bit more discipline, they are enforcing the criminal law of adultery. Or aren't you aware of that? Pardon?

No, I wasn't.

You're not aware of that. Yes, well, several of your states still have adultery as a criminal offense. And a person's put in jail and fined sufficiently. Oh, yes, indeed there are. Yes, please.

Could you speak on the spir—

Well, that's adultery of either party, you know. That's not restricted to the men. I want to get that clear. Yes. Hmm.

Could you speak on the spiritual significance of the direction north in relation to our move?

Well, if you had studied the class—and I do think that you were present. If not, you should have those tapes. Why—were you in class when you were instructed to place your head north?

Yes. Yes, I was.

Yes. Well, tell me something about the human form: what gives us the most problems, the foot or the head?

The head.

You have your answer. *[Many students laugh.]* You do have your answer.

Thank you.

Yes, please.

Yes, a little while ago you said that to put out a little spark of fire takes a lot of water.

Indeed, it does.

Could you please speak more on that in regard to the water center and—

Yes, yes. In reference to that, I was referring to that little flame of lust that is born in the fire center of consciousness. I wasn't speaking of the higher centers. I was speaking of creation. And because it has been created by a denial of what one is in the water center, it takes a great flood of the emotions to put it out.

Thank you.

Does that help with the question?

Yes. Thank you.

Yes, we're speaking about functions now in speaking on creation. So a little flame keeps on burning unless you use a lot of water to put it out when it's in reference to the functions of creation.

Thank you.

You're welcome. Yes. Yes, please.

You were also speaking about when we registered fear and we do our cleansing breath.

Yes?

And we've risen to the higher centers.

That's correct.

And immediately our mind tells us—because I've experienced this—that, that we haven't reached there.

Well, of course, your mind would tell you that if you believe that you are that limit. That means that your consciousness is still directed in the water center where the judgments are created and where they use their soldiers of justification. You see, just before the victory come the hissing hounds of hell. Well, the hissing hounds of hell are the soldiers of justification supporting the judgments which you believe that you are. Why, certainly. As you're moving on the path of Light, as you get closer and grow more in the Light, certainly, certainly the soldiers of justification come up and tell you what a terrible job you're really [doing]; you're not even getting close. Definitely! Absolutely! They do one of two things: they tell you you're not even close; therefore, you've wasted all your time and money. Or they tell you you've already arrived; and therefore, why are you wasting your time? You could be at the movies. So you may take your pick. It's one or the other they're going to tell you.

And that's all they can tell you, too. Because, you see, they will do that so you will return unto them. You see, they'll tell you, for example, when you're working to get ahead in anything—not just the Light in conscious[ness]—[when] you're working to get ahead, they'll tell you, "It's not worth it. No, it's not worth it. No, no. There's no goodness. There's no beauty. There's no this, and there's no [that]." You see, you know who's using you then. You see, because you have to remember that you make a conscious choice to do what you want to do. If you don't make a conscious choice, then wake up quickly, please, because you're being used by those things. You make a conscious choice. You put in your time, your effort, your energy, and then, could it be—ask yourself the question—could it be those things that are talking to you that tell you you've been wasting your time, could they possibly be supporters of what you desire to do in life? Pardon?

No, they couldn't.

No.

They're telling—

They have to be supporters of something else, don't they?

Yes.

Supporters of the way you were, before you made the effort, correct?

Right.

Because they want you back. Because the reason they want you back is because they're starving and hungry. And you haven't been feeding them with your conscious attention, directing your energy to them. Certainly. They are created by self, and they're very selfish. You try to understand that those in these different realms and planes of consciousness, you see, of creation, one realm fights against the other realm; it does it within one's own mind. There is the battle going on. [It] goes on within those realms, you see. Now they all serve the king of fear, the king of creation, in those mental realms. Yet they fight each other all the time, like enemies. They fight each other. Because they are created from selfishness. They're created from limit. Do you understand that?

Yes.

Yes. Does that help you with your question? Yes.

So they never really stop fighting, but the balance of, of being in acceptance is, will—

They never really stop. They rise up very strongly when you are about to make a step into anything that you choose to make a step into. Then they give you all the negatives, and you experience the fear for you have threatened that which you have been a victim of. That's what it really is. You are threatening that which you have been a victim of by believing you are that which you have created in times past. So when you no longer service them, you are threatening them. And when you threaten them, you must pay the price of their threat, which is an experience in your emotions that you call fear.

Thank you.

Hmm? Yes, please.

Yes. Am I correct to understand that they only rise up because of belief?

Well, you are only aware of them by believing that you are them. That is correct. That's how they bind you. If you didn't believe that you were what you had created, then you would not have any awareness of their efforts of being threatened. Do you understand that? In other words, you would be disassociated with them. That which you are disassociated with in consciousness you are not aware of. And therefore, not being aware of them, you are not directing energy to them. And not directing energy to them, they do not have the energy to create negative experiences in your life. Go ahead.

Yes. I was—is—I was, I was trying to get clear on, on the indentation as opposed to belief.

When you create something, you believe that you do it. Is that correct?

When I create something, I believe that I do it.

You mop that floor. Do you believe that you are mopping the floor?

No, I believe that I, I'm, I'm, I'm supporting—

You just moved your foot—Oh, now. *[The teacher laughs.]*

I'm, I'm supporting the vehicle that's mopping the floor.

Yes. You are directing a vehicle. Now if you will remember that in all your other activities, you will never have a problem. *[Some students laugh.]* I can assure you of that! Just disassociate and say, "Now vehicle, here, you've got this ride to perform. Get it done and get it over with. I'm sitting back in the chair and watching you." You'll have no problem. I hope that's helped with your question.

Thank you.

You're more than welcome. You know, you know, when we feel it's a personal message it always is more effective, you know, for us. Yes.

Uhm . . . I, I don't know my question.

It's all right. It'll return to you.

When we feel fear . . .

Yes.

Is it those forms, a vibration from those forms?

That is correct. You see, it is a vibration created by the forms in the water center. And that is how they get your awareness. Do you understand? What they are telling you, they're telling you from that water center of consciousness that you are threatening them. Do you understand? That the thoughts that you have in your mind, that you're entertaining in your mind, is a threat to them. That's what they're telling you, and you experience fear. You experience what you know as fear. Yes.

And it, and it's them that's afraid?

They're the ones that are afraid.

And are they—what are they afraid of?

They're afraid they won't have enough to eat to survive. You see, you are threatening their survival in their belief. Now remember, they are composed of what their creator has composed them [of]. You have composed them. You've garnered them together out of the substance. So they have, you understand, what you have to offer them from a mental world for they are mental forms. So they have survival as a basic in—as a base instinct, you understand? And they have intelligence, the intelligence that you have granted to them in the process of creating them. And so they tell you in the language of the water center, in the language of emotions, they tell you, you are threatening them. Do you understand? You see, it's like the subconscious—when, now there is a time—and some students can do it and some it is not in their best interests—where you must talk to that inner mind there, called the subconscious. You must speak to it as you speak to a child, for they are children in their thinking. Do you understand? They're afraid there won't be enough food for their survival. Yes.

So then, is it—are we, also, are we accepting them?

Oh, yes, we accept them by believing that we are limit. See, whenever we permit our minds to believe that we are the form or the suit that we are wearing, then we believe that we are that which we create. We do believe it. And that is where the problem really exists. Yes.

And if we fight them . . .

They'll get worse. You see, you see, so many times—and I've taught you students for years, do not suppress desire. Remember, you have created those things of desire. Do not suppress them. For when you suppress them, you have really threatened them. And when they rise up, it's like a flood. Do you understand? For they are forms created in the water center; so they will flood your universe with emotion. And wherever there's emotion, the light of reason cannot and does not shine.

Now the human being is a being that has a faculty of reason. Reason reveals personal responsibility for all one's acts and activities, that includes whatever they create. All right? So when a person suppresses something, they guarantee the day when it shall flood their consciousness. And in their great weakness of emotion, they shall fall farther than they had before, for they had risen higher—do you understand?

Yes, sir.

But they rose the wrong way; they rose from suppression, which is denial. Try to understand that suppression is denial. It's a function. It is not a faculty. Being a function, it does not have the light of reason. It does not have faith. It does not have freedom. It has fear; it has bondage. And so a person who rises by denial, by the denial of the function, rather than the education of it, that person shall fall lower for they have risen higher during the time of the denial for they have fed no energy to the forms. You understand?

They're stronger.

They're only stronger. If you want the forms that you're trying to be freed from, if you want to, if you want to make them stronger, suppress, which is denial, suppress them, and you will strengthen them in ways that your mind cannot possibly imagine. You only guarantee the day of the flood. Yes.

Thank you.

Does that help you?

Yes. Thank you.

Yes.

We've been taught to get through a thing we must face it and face it again.

Yes, that is correct.

To confront it. What is it in this confronting this—our own judgment actually—

Yes.

What is it that gets us through it?

What gets us through it is, first of all, when a person brings it up in front of them, they are accepting this is what they have created. Do you understand that?

OK. Yes.

You confront any situation. When you confront it, you see, you are communicating with it. Do you understand? You are communicating with the judgment that you have created. Now that judgment, if you communicate with it, has to accept that you are the father. It has to accept you as master when you bring it forth to you, bring it into the light of reason. You see, in a moment when you are in the faculty of reason, you call up the judgment, you understand? It won't want to come up from the basement. But it will have to respond to you for you are the master; you are the creator of it. So it will have to obey you. You understand? First, you ask it to come up the stairs. You understand?

Yes, sir.

You don't waste a lot of time. You don't beg it. Then you order it up. It has to come up into your conscious awareness. That is the law. The master is greater than that which it has created. The creator is greater. And so it has to obey you. It knows it has to obey you, for you have created it. It lives in your house. And so you order it up, and then you tell it exactly its orders. And you also must instruct it what will happen if it tries any devices or shenanigans and doesn't follow the orders. And you get an agreement through communication with it. Do you understand?

Yes, sir.

And if it doesn't want to agree with its master, then you tell them what its master is going to do: that you will annihilate it. Because, you see, it fears. Because it fears, it will do what you order it to do. Yes.

Yes, someone else had a question? Yes.

So the communication is the beginning of the separation, that is the beginning—

Oh, definitely.

That is the—

That is where you begin to gain objectivity. That is where you begin to separate truth from creation. You cannot separate truth from creation without communicating with what you have created, you see.

OK.

It is the lack of communication that binds people to the so-called wheel of fate. It's their own lack of communication. Yes.

Thank you.

Because it's their own fear. You see? And if they would only face what fear really is: the effect of threatening that which they believe that they are, those has-beens. Yes.

So suppression can actually stop you from evolving or growing in a certain area that—

Why, certainly, it does. Because, you see, it is not a reasonable, intelligent—it—you see, an uneducated ego suppresses. An educated ego communicates. Now that's the difference, basically, between an educated ego and an uneducated ego. An uneducated ego suppresses; an educated ego communicates or expresses, you see. It communicates.

Now what keeps the ego from communicating? Well, I think you will all agree: they call it pride. It's the price of pride. Yes, please.

If that judgment doesn't cooperate and follow the orders, how do you annihilate it?

You threaten to annihilate it. It knows no better; it fears.

You—

You threaten to annihilate it.

Yes.

You'll have no problem the moment you threaten to annihilate it.

So you never have to really annihilate it?

No, because—don't you understand?—you cannot annihilate it. It does not know that because it's created in a water center and darkness of desire. It does not know that. You are its creator. You tell it, "You'll either do this or I'll annihilate you." And it will fear that annihilation. Now while you've got it up there, working with it, if you go and you say, "Well, now there's no way possible I can annihilate it," it'll take advantage of that, of that awareness. It does not have that awareness until you give it that awareness. Now if you create the form with that awareness, well, then you've got a problem. *[The teacher and many students laugh.]*

Yes, yes, I know. Thank you. *[The teacher acknowledges the technician recording the class that the tape is almost out.]* Are there any other questions? We only have a few moments left. The hours pass so quickly, you know. Yes.

Is it possible to consciously—you mentioned that it takes a lot of water to put out a little flame that has been—

The flame of desire takes a lot of water to put out. Yes, indeed, it does.

Can one consciously set about doing that?

Oh, absolutely! Definitely. You consciously—you see, if you make the effort to awaken, you consciously decide to be angry.

You consciously decide to be in love. You consciously decide not to be in love. You consciously decide whatever you consciously decide. You see, you have available to you—you are a creator. God sustains; you create. So you have all these things as you create. You can create intelligently, and then you say, "Oh, let's see, anger? You come up here." And then it will come up. And then you'll say, "Well, I don't feel angry yet. Bring me up an assistant." And it will go and it will look for all the things that made you angry in the past. And you won't have to worry about being angry. And they'll serve you very well, as long as you remember that they are not you. You understand?

Yes.

Yes, that's when the worker uses the tools, and the tools no longer use the worker.

Thank you. And I look forward to seeing you again. Thank you.

MARCH 12, 1987

A/V Seminar 21

Good evening, students.

Preparations for our new classes being well underway, this evening we will have a preview of those new classes, entitled, "Our Journey Through Space." Present, past, and future; power, force, and fear; Sun, Moon, and Earth.

The so-called miracle of life, known as survival, is only possible through the Law of Adaptation. And so in our journey through space, the questions, of course, first arise in the human mind: is there intelligent life beyond the planet on which you, as earthlings, presently reside? The answer is yes. Are they in material or physical form? The answer is yes and no. For intelligent beings do exist, have existed, and continue to exist on other planets in your solar system in material form and out of material form.

For those of you who are not yet aware, as I stated when I first spoke to you, our new classes, the preparations for them are well underway. To your world it is known as astral videography. That means filming the celestial realms, what you call physical, and the beginning of that has already been accomplished. Added to this evening's class will be a short film, which I will instruct my channel to show to those of you who have not viewed it. For your interest, of course, should be in the planet that most frequently you permit to control you. And what planet could that possibly be? Let me see the hands of my students. Yes, please.

Earth.

No. To the ones who were not present at what—yes, please.

Moon.

Correct. And why is the Moon chosen by the human mind to be permitted to use us so frequently? What does it control on the planet of earthlings?

The water center?

Indeed. Does [any]one have any contradiction to that demonstrable truth? *[After a short pause, the teacher continues.]*

Fine. And so our investigation in our new classes will, of course, begin with the planet in your solar system that you spend the most time in obedient worship of.

Now, as I stated, we have present, past, and future. We have Sun, Moon, and Earth. Those who fear are controlled by what planet? Let me see the hands of my students. Yes, please.

Moon.

Why by the Moon?

Because that's what, that's what controls the water center. And the water center is controlled by the emotions, which is . . .

Yes?

Higher.

How does the planet Moon control the water centers of your planet and those who identify with your planet are therefore the victims of it? How does that take place? Yes, please.

It's where we form our judgments and our . . .

Yes?

It's where they—if we believe that we are them, they—they're controlled—we—they control us.

Yes. Now how does the Moon—is it a source of light?

Yes, it is.

It is? Is it a source of direct light?

No, it's not.

Is it a source of reflected light?

Yes, it is.

Fine. So we understand, and it is demonstrable to your planet, that whenever the Moon is fullest in the celestial realms, in the heavens of your Earth, then we find that the emotions of those over-identified with their own form are easily affected, and they are therefore victims of it. Do you understand that?

Now the Moon reflects the light. However, it is not the light. Does anyone not understand that? How does the Moon reflect the light?

By bouncing the rays of the Sun off its surface to, to the Earth.

Correct. By becoming an obstruction of the light, is that not correct? By becoming an obstruction to the light, it reflects the light. Do you understand that?

Yes.

Therefore, the mirror—the Moon may be likened to a mirror. It is a reflector; it is an illusion of light. It reflects light, but it is not the source of light. Therefore, that is not where truth can be found. Fine.

Now as man permits himself to believe that he is the thoughts that he has created, then man becomes the obstruction of the Light that he is. Does anyone have any questions on that demonstrable truth?

And so are there intelligent beings on the Moon? No, there are not intelligent beings *on* the Moon. The man on the Moon, so-called, left eons ago. There are intelligent beings inside the Moon, not on the Moon. Are those intelligent beings in what you understand as physical or material form? Yes, they are in physical or material form. Why do they live on the inside of their planet? They are no longer, and have not been for eons of time, able to exist on the surface of their planet. Adaptation is the law through which the so-called miracle of life is made possible.

Now it's time for your questions. Yes, please.

Are the intelligent beings in the Moon, are they helpful to us? Are they helpful, please?

One might answer that question in this respect, Is a victim of a person helpful to the person that they are a victim of?

I would say yes, it helps growth.

To whom?

To the victim because you go through the process of being one. You would—

Is it painful or pleasurable? Or is it both?

Painful.

Is it very painful?

At times.

At times. Then it is very pleasurable at times. Is that not correct?

Right.

Fine. Anyone else have anything to say about that? Yes, please.

Are, are these beings less or more evolved than us?

That which controls is more advanced than that which is controlled. That is the Law of Evolution. Yes.

Is that to say that they control us? Or vice versa? I didn't understand.

Well, if we, from lack of effort, permit the influences of the planet to control us, we must understand the microcosm and the macrocosm. The Moon you see in the heavens exists within your being. If you believe you are it, then you are controlled and bound by it. Now people believe that they are that in varying degrees. The question must be asked, Do you lose control by its influences on the planet on which you live? If you find yourself losing control, then, of course, you are the victim of it. We are the victim of that which we believe in to the degree that we believe in it. Does that help answer your question? Yes.

Yes. Thank you.

Yes, please.

During the time when the Moon is full and it has its greatest control of those people on Earth who believe they are their form . . .

Yes?

How is that perceived or experienced by the beings on the Moon inside, during that period of time?

By the intelligent beings that live in the core of the Moon, that is perceived by—in compassion and understanding of their stages of evolution—the same as you would look, perhaps, at an insect on your planet and would have that consideration for the insect and accept its present state of evolution. Yes. Or even perhaps better, as you would look in the cages of your zoos and observe the various actions of the animals therein. Yes, yes.

And I'd also like to ask, please, the bright light spots that we see on the Moon—

Yes.

Is that the light of the beings in the inner core?

Yes, well, those questions will be answered in our continuing classes on "Our Journey Through Space." However, I'm happy that you brought that up because you make your effort with your studies and then you must ask yourself the question, Why is there a Sea of Serenity on that particular planet? Why is there a Sea of Tranquility? And those questions you must ask yourself as you make effort with your studies. Yes.

Thank you.

Yes, please.

Is, is water a required element of intelligence?

No, it—well, on your planet? Yes. On your planet, Earth, it is, yes. On other planets, no, it is not.

And so, also, is it a required element of form on other planets?

No, it is not.

It's not.

On your planet it is. Yes. Yes, does a rock require water for its survival?

Well, no, I don't think so.

Is there intelligence in the rock?

I'm sure there is.

Indeed, there is. You see, for example, we spoke to you some time ago on mathematics is the key to the universe, and you look at form and you do not stop to think: What is this? *[The teacher touches a glass of water with his left hand. For all his classes, he had a glass of water available for him.]* This is mathematics. You see it as a glass; what you have decided from your own acceptances, this is glass. This contains H_2O, correct?

That's what you believe and that's what you think. Yet what I am touching and what you are seeing is only a code of mathematics. That's all that it is. That's all that form is. And so you see different forms; so you see different codes or combinations of numbers. That's what you're really seeing. Yes. Yes.

Is there a significant reason as to why water, I mean, that can be revealed, why water is required?

For man believes he is the force. And because man believes he is the force, he experiences fear. That is the law that governs H_2O: force and fear. Yes.

Thank you.

Now remember that in the study of this journey through space; you must remember, there is no water on [the] Moon. There used to be. Now that which believes it is a thing and evolves through the thing that it believes that it is and continues to survive, through the Law of Adaptation, has earned its position to control everything that still believes what it used to be. I do hope that's helped with your question.

Thank you very much.

Yes, please.

On the planet Earth is the number five of—

That is correct.

—of faith.

That is correct. That is the purpose of your journey on the planet Earth. That is correct.

Right. Now as . . .

Are you not faced, moment to moment, between the choice of power or force?

Yes.

Faith or fear?

Yes.

Yes.

Yes. And as we evolve, all the intelligent beings on our planet, on this particular planet, and we disassociate from our form, *that changes the water contents and the chemistry of the whole Earth planet, like it, you know, like it did with the Moon? Did the Moon—*

You won't have to wait for that day, for the Sun of your solar system is, as in your words, is inching its way closer and closer to the planet Earth. So evolution cannot be stopped. Yes.

Right.

Now, for example, as I have stated to you many times, dry out. Dry out so that you may perceive what life is, for it is far greater than what your minds can conceive that it is. Yes.

Thank you.

You're welcome. Yes, please.

Is there any correlation between the density of matter and evolution?

Oh, indeed, there is. Now some time ago we spoke, in fact, [the student] there, I spoke to, speaking on density: the intensity of density is measured, mathematically measured, by acceptance, you see. So when you're asking your question on density, you must consider intensity, for if you do not consider intensity, you cannot accurately measure density. Does that help with your question? You see, you're asking a question that is a mathematical formula. Do you understand that? Now in any solution to a mathematical problem, you must consider all parts. Is that not true?

Yes.

You see. Now, you know, oh, for some time and you've heard it, I'm sure, in your world time and time and again. Perhaps you were in school. How disturbed people have been over what you call fractured mathematics. You know, it fractures your emotions. You understand that, don't you? You did get some understanding of that in school, didn't you?

Yes.

And you are a little bit aware of fractured mathematics. Well, the only reason they are fractured is from the lack of acceptance, you see? You see, the intensity of the density of the problem has not been considered. Therefore, the solution has been waning [wanting] for some time in your world. You see? So whenever you ask a question on density, consider intensity; by so doing, you will not end up frustrated with fractured mathematics. Does that help you? *[After a short pause, the teacher continues.]* Or does that confuse you?

It confuses me.

If it confuses you, then you have over-identified with fractured math. Do you understand that?

I can accept that.

Well, you have an engineering type of mind, you know. You do understand that, don't you?

Yes.

All right. Let us, for example, let us ask the question, How does 2 plus 2 equal 5? Ask yourself the question. Your answer is what? *[The teacher continues after a short pause.]* I'm speaking mathematically.

If, if 2 plus 2 equals 5, then 2 plus 2 equals 5.

But your mind tells you that 2 plus 2 equals 4, doesn't it? Isn't that what your mind tells you?

Of course.

Fine. Now what do you consider what your mind tells you, acquired knowledge or insight?

Acquired knowledge.

Acquired knowledge. Now how was that knowledge acquired? It was acquired by what you accepted, wasn't it? Pardon?

Yes.

Fine. Now your ability to accept that 2 plus 2 equals 4 (and not 5) depended upon the degree of the intensity of your density to accept it, didn't it? You had to accept what someone else told you, didn't you?

Yes.

In order to experience what you experience today as acquired knowledge. Is that not correct?

Yes. [The student speaks very quietly.]

Pardon?

Yes.

Now in order to do that, it required from you an acceptance. It required from you faith that the person who told you that was reliable and dependable and knew what they were talking about. It required that judgment in your young mind. You understand that, don't you?

Yes.

However, you're now much older. Therefore, you accept that 2 plus 2 equals 4, for everyone else that you know accepts that 2 plus 2 equals 4, is that not correct? So each time that you accept that 2 plus 2 equals 4, you demonstrate your faith in something that you acquired when you were a child. Do you understand that?

Yes.

Fine. Therefore, emotionally you feel comfortable that you are not different. Do you understand that? In other words, you have support for what you believe. And having support for what you believe, you feel comfortable, is that not correct? That's what is known as mass thinking. Birds of a feather flock together.

Now man created that 2 plus 2 equals 4. He could have created 2 plus 2 equals 5. He didn't create 2 plus 2 equals 5. He created 2 plus 2 equals 4. Do you understand that?

Yes.

Therefore, we demonstrate as adult, intelligent human beings that our acquired knowledge is supreme. We demonstrate that because we fear being different. Do you understand that?

Yes.

Now for you to go to work one morning and tell your coworkers, "I have decided that 2 plus 2 equals 5. Because it takes faith on my part to believe that. It also has taken many years of faith on my part to believe that 2 plus 2 equals 4. I now decide, as an independent, intelligent being, that 2 plus 2 for me will now equal 5." You fear to do that. You fear to demonstrate that. What does that reveal to you as an individualized, intelligent being? It demonstrates to each person that they not only fear being different but the fear of being different is much greater than their individualized choice to be an individual, intelligent being. Does it not demonstrate that for all of you?

Yes.

Well, there you are! So you're here in these classes. They are not classes for mass thinkers. They are classes for individual thinkers. Do you understand that? For your individual right to decide if you want 2 plus 2 to equal 4, instead of to equal 5. Is that not your individual right? Is it not your individual right to, to choose that you will either decide what you're going to do or you will do what everyone else does for you fear the possibility of being different? Does that not reveal how over-identified one is with this so-called planet Moon? Can we question why we are victims when we fear so greatly to be different than anyone else?

Yet we take great pride when we look in the reflector, the mirror, and we see, "I am special. There's no one else in the universe quite like me." What kind of thinking could that possibly be? That in one area we take great pride in being different and in another area, we have paranoia, frustration, and fear that we should tell anyone that 2 plus 2 equals 5. Do you understand that? Pardon?

Yes. Thank you.

Yes. Then how can we possibly hope for truth when we have such great fear of being different, different than the ones we want something from? Is that not true?

Yes.

What do we want from our employer? Well, of course, we want him or the business we're in to think of us, that we are such and such, for we first look at them and we judge what they are. And having done so, having made, first, the judgments, then we fall in. "This is what they judge I am. Therefore, I shall play that part." Do you understand that? "And I fear not to play that part because if I do not play that part, I will be different. Therefore, being different, I will have no friends." Hmm? Is that not true? What can one say that that is truth? That's dependence! Certainly, it's dependence. Absolutely. It is absolute dependence in what we have created: our image.

We cannot create the Light that we are. The Light that we are already is. Everything else we've created. Yes. Yes, please.

Is the faculty of pride, humility?

Since when has faculty become pride? Since when has pride become a faculty?

I mean, I—

I think, first, we'll take some time to consider that. I don't recall ever having taught you that pride was a faculty.

Yes, sir.

Do you recall that in all the years you've been a student of mine? Do you recall that? Yes, I think you should take a moment to meditate on that. *[The teacher moves to another student.]* Yes, please.

Yes. Is there a relationship, a correlation between future, fear, and Earth?

You use such large words. What was the question? *[The teacher laughs joyously.]* You know, I've come down to earth here to speak to you as I would speak to any child, and one talks of pride and another one uses these great big, long words, you know, that sends some of my students into confusion and bewilderment. I think you better first study, meditate on correlation. And we'll go here, please.

Do the Moon, the intelligent beings—

"Do the Moon"? Well, now, we want to keep proper English. Does the Moon—yes. *[Many students laugh.]* I didn't say that we couldn't use proper English. It's just, you know—yes, does the Moon what?

Do the Moon's intelligent beings, do they travel about?

Well, they don't travel about outside their planet in physical form, certainly not. Because, you see, they can no longer adapt to the conditions of their planet on the outside. Now do they travel with their other forms? Certainly, certainly. Yes, indeed. And so do the Saturnians. Yes.

Since—

The Saturnians have different forms.

Since you said what we perceive, like—is the physical form, is the mathematical arrangement of it—did I—

Yes, that's all that it is: mathematics. All form is a, is a mathematical code. And so all you've got to do is study and become frustrated with fractured math. That's all you have to do.

I'd like to—

It's all geometrical. Haven't we discussed geometry, a bit of geometry, here in one of our classes some time ago? Had a blackboard over there. I think it was several months ago. Yes.

Can these beings in their other forms, other than the physical, travel to the Earth and rearrange their forms mathematically so to us—

Yes, certainly. Adv—

Appear physical?

Yes, certainly. Advanced forms, certainly.

So we think we're looking at, maybe, a like kind, where it's really, maybe, a Saturnian that's rearranged it mathematically?

Correct. Correct. For example, I'll come right down to your planet. You look in the mirror, and sometimes you believe you see a certain image that you're not happy with. You get ready for a date or something that you desire; you look into the mirror and you make whatever adjustments are necessary so that you're satisfied with the image that is reflected back to you. That is created by a mathematical pattern. That's mathematical. You see, you go through a process in your consciousness that is a mathematical code. And when you get to that code that you really believe is you, to present yourself, your image—the image changes in keeping with the attitude of mind. The thoughts create the attitude of mind; the attitude of mind creates the rate of vibration; the rate of vibration is the mathematical code that you look in the mirror and you think that you see. Yes.

Now how is that all done? Well, that is done by the very natural laws. Of course, it is. Form is a mathematical code. And when you look in the mirror and you're not happy with your form, you make certain changes. Those changes put your consciousness into another mathematical code that the image reflected back to you, you're now satisfied with. Yes.

And could I clarify, please, did you say earlier that that change in the mathematical form is based on our acceptance?

The intensity of density is measured by acceptance. And in that respect, you are correct.

OK. Thank you.

Yes, certainly. Yes. You see, a person, a person looks at a form. And they instantly judge they are attracted or they are adverse. Instantly. Just by looking at the form. Then, if that code is satisfied, they'll move to the next one, the next one, the next one, and the next one, you see. That happens—your eyes look and they see; they conceive. The eyes conceive. That which conceives deceives. So perception is the path of a wise man, you see. For conceiving, you see, the eyes see dual. So they conceive and deceive. That is the Law of Duality. For when you see with dual eyes—well, for example, perhaps you've been asking on the intelligence of the beings inside of the Moon. They see with one eye for they only have one eye. So are they evolved or are they not evolved? Yes, now [this student] has a question there.

Yes, sir. Is there a connection between future—
You may use *correlation*. But let's get down to your planet.
OK. The corr—
You didn't think I don't know what the word means, do you?
Oh, yes, I know you know.
Well, I think I know what it means. Go ahead.
Is there a correlation between future, fear, and Earth?
There is a correlation. Of course, there is. For example, present is power.
Right.

Past is force. And future is fear. So if you move out of the present in consciousness, you move into force, which guarantees fear. And then you worry what's going to happen tomorrow. "How much money will I have? Will I survive?" I teach you that adaptation is the law through which the so-called miracle of life is made possible. So, you see, you—here you are in the present. This instant. This moment. That's the present. That's power.
Right.

Now when you—if you don't make the effort to stay there in the present, in the power, in the Light inside yourself, the only alternative you have is force and fear.
Right.

Controlled not by the source of Light itself. [But] controlled by the image reflector. The Moon is a reflector of the true light; it is not a source of light.
Right.

So whenever you move out of the Light, the present moment, you enter the reflection. You are therefore controlled by the shadows of past events. Being controlled by what has been, you fear what is to be. So whenever you move in consciousness out of the present moment, you move out of the Light and out of the power. Then it's inevitable that you move into the force. So then the mind, which is force, tries to adjust, manipulate, and change what is to be, for it fears what is to be. For that which has been always fears what is to be, for that which has been is force.

So if you permit yourself to over-identify with image, then image only exists in the past. You look in the mirror. You see an image of yourself. It is reflecting back to you. But as you look in the mirror, you're in a past event. You think it is a present event. It cannot be a present event for what you see is being controlled by what has been in your life. This is why you change the codes and you fix your hair this way and you do that and you do something else. That reveals to you, you are not in the present or in the power when you believe in image. So [when] you look in the mirror, you believe that is you only if it is in keeping [with] something you can manipulate and control.

So what is controlling you when you think of what has been? The obstruction. You have become the obstruction to the Light that you are and believe, as you look in the mirror, the shadows that the obstruction—the obstruction you have created by believing that you are the image that you cast—the shadows of what has passed is now controlling you. So you do not see what you are when you look in a reflector. Does that help you with your question?

Yes, sir.

All right.

Thank you.

Yes, please.

What happens to the Light when it is reflected off an obstruction?

What happens to the Light?

Yes.

In what respect? What happens to the Light? The Light is the Light.

Yes, sir.

It, it is the Source. That is the Intelligent Being, the Light itself. That's what you truly are.

Yes, sir.

Now when—you mean, when you look at the reflection of the Light? What happens to the Light?

I had originally thought of the question in regards to the Light after it strikes from the source, after it strikes, say, the Moon.

All right.

Something—

Yes, something does happen to it. What happens to it?

It's—

What happens to reflected light? What is the difference between direct light and reflected light? Yes.

It's diminished.

Of—and how is it diminished?

In keeping with the mathematical code of the obstruction.

That is absolutely correct! Absolutely correct. Do you understand that? *[The teacher addresses a different student.]* Pardon?

Yes.

Well, if you don't, say so.

No, I believe I do.

Yes, you think about that because these are your future, what you consider your future, classes. This is the class that is; it's a preview of what is to be. Let's stay with what is. And because whatever reflects light reflects it after its own absorption of it. Do you understand that? You see, in order to reflect something, you must absorb a part of what you are receiving. Do you understand that?

Yes.

You see, well, I think in your world it's known as secondhand. Now if you have your choice of getting something firsthand or secondhand, which do you choose? Yes.

Firsthand.

You want it firsthand. Why do you want it firsthand? Yes.
Less, less contamination.
Yes. One wants the original, don't they?
Yes, sir.
You see? For having the original, one can do many things. You can always make a copy. So everyone wants the original! Who wants to settle for the copy?! Isn't that correct?
Yes, sir.
You know, it's like this day was a day for our broker's opening and everything. We won't go into that, but specifically this: the question must be asked, Do you want a Xerox broker or do you want a genuine broker? That's the question. Do you want a copy or do you want something that's original? Well, of course. You stand for quality; you stand for originality. You see?
Yes.
And if you want [a] copy, well, just go get a copy. They have them at the drug store, I'm sure. Yes. There's a vast difference. You see, you, you tempt yourself when it is wiser to do without one's desires, the fulfillment of one's desires, than to take a secondhand copy. For it is in one's own best interest to do without, you see?
Yes, sir.
For in doing without, one demonstrates the wisdom of patience. Do without it, and then when you finally get it, get the original. The original, you see? Now I'm speaking of things in your life that sometimes a person wants something real bad. No one, I know of no human ego that's ever been satisfied with a copy of anything. They want the original. Yes. Yes, please.
It seems to me . . .
[The teacher laughs and says something that is difficult to transcribe.]
If, if the . . .
Yes, I'm, I'm just talking to one of my students while it's seeming to you. Go ahead and make your statement.

If the reflector . . .

Yes?

. . . absorbs Light before it reflects . . .

It cannot qualify itself to send it off—if it doesn't receive it, it can't send it.

Right.

Right? So show me any object, anything in any universe, that sends off anything equal to its receiving, then I'll show you the Divine Light itself. And I'm not capable of doing that, and neither is anything else that's in form. Do you understand that? You see? You see, reflection is deception. Reflection is deception. Do you understand that?

Yes, I do.

The reason reflection is deception is because it is not the source of what you believe that it is, you see. Now there was a time in your world that earthlings believed that the Moon itself sent off light. They did not understand that the passing of your planet—do you understand that?—was creating an obstruction to the light of your solar system. Do you understand?

Yes.

So when you study the celestial—for anyone who studies only the terrestrial cannot expect to fully awaken within consciousness inside of themselves because, you see, you are a part of the celestial as well as a part of the terrestrial. So both must be studied in order to bring about a balance. And balance is necessary for awakening, you see.

So remember, it is your planet that you have entered to awaken to faith. A planet that offers to you so much fear. The fear is because Earth and all upon it revolves and obstructs the Light that is and believes something else. Well, now, ask yourself the question—you don't have to be an astronomer. Do you understand how the Earth revolves?

Around the Moon.

It does revolve. And so when it's in a certain position, you look up and see, "Oh, there's a full Moon. That's a half Moon. That's a quarter Moon." Who is doing that?

The, the Sun is in between—I mean the Earth is—

The Sun's not doing it.

No.

Who's doing the moving?

The Earth. It's in between—

That's right. The Earth is moving.

It's, it's in between the Sun and the Moon.

And it is obstructing the light.

It's casting a shadow. Right, it's obstructing the light.

Fine.

And it casts a shadow—

All right.

—over the Moon.

Now you, now you'll perhaps get some understanding of your journey, your journey through space and the planet on which you are. You start on that which you are familiar with and you, as a student body, are very familiar with Earth, you see? Yes, indeed! And so we start with Earth and how it is obstructing the Light. You see, you look at your body; you believe that you are your body; so you are earth-bound. You believe you're Earth. That's it. Terrestrial. You see? Did I not discuss at one of our classes the difference between horizontal viewing and vertical? There's all the difference in the world. Yes. You have a question?

Yes. Did the Moon—was the Moon originally a part of the Sun and break off?

Why, I gave that teaching many, many, many years ago in your world. Why, certainly! You have a little booklet, a little story, a little fable that was given to you some time ago. *[The teacher may be referring to the pamphlet entitled "The Descent of Man." Please see the appendix.]* You have the—what you understand as the Sun is the source of all of the things in your solar system. But your solar system isn't everything. *[The teacher laughs joyfully.]* It had its children. It has its nine children, yes. Yes, certainly. Yes. Everything begins from the source itself. Yes.

The other thing that I was trying to understand was when I look at the Moon, there's only certain colors that I perceive.

Are you sure you're perceiving them or conceiving them?

Well, when I see it with my eyes—

That's conception, yes, of course.

I was wondering if there are some colors that are absorbed before the light is reflected?

Well, now, you see, there, in reference to that question, let us go to our judgments. Do animals see in color?

I don't know. Scientists say they don't, but I don't know if I believe that or not.

And what are they measured by?

Ah . . .

For example, man says that he sees in color. Is that correct?

Yes. He does say that.

And so he studies other beings on your planet and says they don't see in color.

That's what they say.

No one has asked them. *[Many students laugh.]* And they're being measured by the human species. In other words, if they do not have what human eyes have, that man has judged makes him capable of seeing color, then they don't see color. That's quite intelligent, isn't it? Wouldn't you consider that very intelligent?

No.

See, man has made the yardstick; it's acquired knowledge. Ask [that student] there. Right?

Two plus 2 is 4.

Two and 2—2 plus 2 is 5. Yes. Acquired knowledge. So when you are speaking to me on those things, you're speaking to me of acquired knowledge. You say that you see the Moon and you only see a certain color. What color do you see? Yellow?

No.

What color do you see?

I see . . .

White?

Blue—white, blue, violet, brown, and black. Basically.

Basically. Well, now, why don't you speak to [that student] over here, or *[The teacher calls the names of several students.]* And I can assure you they see differently. Pardon? So, you see, where does color exist? Hmm?

As a judgment?

Is that yellow or have you made it yellow?

Well, we put a label on it and call it that.

You call it yellow?

Yes.

Now some people will look at that and say, "That's white." Because you have people in your world who have set the measuring standard who are color-blind. And then those who—you see, take a—try to understand that, you see. They say, "No, no, no. We have a large group of people; they're color-blind because they don't see the way I see. Therefore, *they* are color-blind." If the majority see one way and a minority see a different way, the minority has to be the oddball in your world and, therefore, is incorrect. So you have to ask yourself the question, "Being different from the pack, does that make me right or wrong?" It depends on your needs. It depends on your denial of what you are, whether it makes you right or wrong. Do you understand that?

You speak to someone and they say, "No, no, no, no. The Moon is only gray and shades thereof. Therefore, you have a problem: you're a bit color-blind." To someone else, they say, "No, no, no. The Moon has kind of a yellowish, a little tinge of blue there, and a tinge of something else." Someone else may see a tinge of pink, depends on how much they love it, you see. "And so therefore, you should check with an eye specialist." Well, that's ridiculous. That's ridiculous.

Yes, someone else have a question here? Let's move on. Yes, please. Time is passing quickly, isn't it? Yes.

Are the Moon people magnetic people and do they—

They, they—you're speaking of the past or the present?

Well, I don't know. It's just . . .

You want to speak of the present? They have been. They've qualified themselves as, as magnetic beings. Now they control it.

So now—

Now they are the magnet. The magnet under control. Yes.

And do they use force? Are they, are they—rather than power?

They are not—they're on a planet that represents force. Now if you're on a planet that represents a certain function, then it is understandable that the beings on the planets are qualified in the function. For, therefore, they are on the planet, correct?

Right.

Now if you're an evolved—you are an evolved being. You're involved, say, in one of the planets. And you've already paid, what you say, paid your dues of being controlled by water. Pardon?

Yes.

And you're beginning to dry out, your planet is drying out—adaptation is the law through which the so-called miracle of life is made possible—then you go inside or wherever you can go on your planet to survive, don't you?

Right.

Pardon?

Right.

And so that's what's happened eons ago. Now were there rivers and—Moon was very similar to what you call the planet Earth eons ago. Eons ago. You see. And so it is well versed, as intelligent beings, of how to control that which is still in an evolutionary stage of self-image control. You see, those who believe in image are controlled by force. Do you understand that?

Yes.

And so this planet and the beings upon it, of course, it is the planet where you're to learn faith for you're offered plenty of fear. It's most understandable.

Does that mean that they are not good people? Well, of course, they're evolved, intelligent beings. Do you understand? And they have and bear great personal responsibility. They have survived eons of time. Eons. They no longer see—I think I already stated to you—they no longer see with the duality of conception and deception for they only have one eye. They see singly. Yes, does that help with your question?

I...

You have another question? Go ahead.

I, I forgot it.

It'll return to you because that which is of value and priority to the mind is never lost. Yes, please.

Then the Moon's inhabitants do not control those people identified with form to their detriment, to the Moon people's detriment?

Why, certainly not! Absolutely not. Certainly not. Yes.

I remembered.

Of course.

What do they need from us? That they want—

They don't have need. They don't have need. Survival, the law—you see, adaptation is absolutely indispensable. The Law of Adaptation is indispensable to life, survival! Now in the Law of Personal Responsibility, they're responsible for their survival, yes. Do you understand that?

Yes.

When there's a planet, such as the planet Earth, that passes so close to them, consistently, that has beings upon it who are absolutely identified to use force to get whatever they desire from a denial of what they are, they have a responsibility to themselves, to their planet, and to evolution—you understand—to see that the force used by the minds of the earthlings is not used to destroy the solar system. Does that help with your question?

Yes.

Thank you. I'll say good night. I have left instructions for my channel to show you a few moments of the planet that earthlings have such great worship of. And, of course, that which we worship, of course, controls us. And remember, tranquility is that faculty that we experience when we are not disturbed. And let us not forget that that which disturbs us, in truth, has controlled us. I look forward to our next class. And look up. Choose wisely what you look at.

Thank you and good night.

MAY 14, 1987

A/V Seminar 22

Good evening, students.

This evening I'm asking for your full cooperation and participation in this class that you will refrain, make effort to refrain from the censorship of your mind in discussing the most serious subject that could be discussed with you, as students of the Living Light Philosophy. In keeping with our teachings and knowing that seeing and feeling are subject to censorship, that we see duality and we feel duality, that viewing is the only true and clear sight that we can possibly experience, I'm speaking to you at this very special class on the greatest crisis that your planet and the human race has ever known since the beginning of your recorded, so-called, time.

It is a subject that most minds choose to refrain from viewing and, in so doing, limit their growth in consciousness because seeing, as I have stated already, is censorship. Censored, of course, by what we believe or don't believe.

Now we're all interested in success. We all know that success of anything is ever in keeping with our degree of tolerance. And yet we seem to have great difficulty with the things that we want to be successful with. However, if we were, in truth, successful with all the things that we thought that we wished to be successful with, then, I assure you, as you pause in the light of reason, you are so grateful for the failures that, in looking in hindsight, you thought you wanted as a success. And so success is something that's available to everyone, dependent, of course, upon their tolerance. But our tolerance is ever censored by whatever judgments that we believe that we are.

Now speaking on this crisis that so many people are not aware of, and those who are aware of this great crisis to your civilization refuse to view it, for some time, I have shared with you, as students, the increasing spread of the plague on your planet. You have given it a name. You have given it a name that is indicative of the virus itself. You call it AIDS. What you don't understand is the characteristic of the virus. What you don't understand is how much it has spread across your planet. Each of you students, before you leave the Earth planet, will be aware and affected by this great plague that's over your land. You will either be affected personally or you will be affected by dear friends that you are aware of. So it will affect each and every one of you. It will affect your emotions. It will affect your feelings.

The time to prepare oneself for anything is not after the fact. The time to prepare oneself is before the fact. Otherwise, preparation is not preparation. How does one prepare themselves for such a great disaster of experience in their lives? They prepare themselves by understanding, which is an effect of communication, which is an effect of one's own effort.

I note that many of you and it is—I find it rather pleasing—I'm sure my channel wouldn't—[are] concerned at the possibility that my channel has befallen with this condition. I can assure you that he hasn't just because I'm here using his form to speak to you. So you can free yourself from that troublesome thought. And I would appreciate you not sharing it with my channel and give him something else to concern himself with. You know, from everything from blood transfusions to toothpaste and toilet paper's going to be blamed. I spoke to you some time ago about cancer, and they've just about included toothpaste and toilet paper [as causes of cancer], not quite, but they'll soon be there.

However, on the serious note, I'm going to open up the class this evening for your questions on this very serious matter. I do not consider myself a teacher or prophet of doom. Just because we're speaking to you on such a great crisis in your world, it is for your preparation, for if one is prepared, the possibility of sharing that preparation, when it is solicited, will reach many, many, many others. So we'll take a few moments for any questions that you have in reference to the subject that we are discussing this evening. Yes, please.

What percentage of the American population is currently infected?

Currently infected, over 66 percent are infected. Now what you want to understand about infection is this: some time ago one of the students present asked me how long that the virus could incubate in a person's form. And we gradually eased them into the awareness, 5 years—that is before your medical science was even aware that a person could carry it so long—to 10 years, to 15 years. And now because your scientists and your medical profession is beginning to awaken, we can now increase it to 20 years. Yes. Does that answer your question?

Yes, sir. Thank you.

Now I would like to say one thing. Because of the emotions, which are controlling, and the fear, this evening's class will not be available, though it will be recorded. Not until there is a greater awakening of the people on your planet, for it will not serve a good purpose to have it released to anyone at this time. Go ahead with your questions. Yes.

Is that percentage representative of the percentages of the countries throughout the world?

Oh, no. That is, if you would look at countries, for example, a low percent, a midrange percent, a high percent, that is a midrange percent. Yes. You see, just because the virus remains what you call, perhaps, in a dormant stage and can do so for over 20 years, and because of the great changes that have taken place within the last 50 years for the societies on your planet, [there] has been a great spread of the virus. Yes. Yes.

What triggers the activation of the virus when it has been dormant?

Well, let us try to understand some of the characteristics of the virus: one, the virus is tenacious; two, the virus takes different forms and you now have, I think your medical science is now revealing that there are four types of AIDS virus. There is one; it wears many cloaks. Pardon? What was the rest of your question?

I'm sorry, sir, I've lost it.

That's all right. We'll come back to it. Yes, please.

Is it possible to have it within your system and have it not manifest?

Oh, absolutely! Absolutely, definitely. We were discussing the characteristics of the virus, such as its phenomenal tenacity, its ability to wear different cloaks, as a virus, and its patience. It does have patience, yes. What other characteristics does it have? It has the tenacity of survival. It is [a] very self-orientated virus. Yes. Yes.

Could you use that same—like, if you, if one had it within one's system and to keep it from manifesting could you use, like, a counter . . .

Well, let me say this in reference to the virus, in reference to any virus, and that also applies to this particular virus, especially to this particular virus: the thoughts, the attitudes, which are the vibration of the mind, have a chemical effect upon the body. Now the more concerned one is of anything, in anything, the more concerned one is, the more energy one is directing to that which they are concerned about. So concern, of course, is not a benefit.

Now acceptance is the will of God. Now God or goodness is the Law of Perfect Harmony. So if a person is desirable of restoring their health, then it is necessary for them to maintain and to sustain thoughts and attitudes of mind which are harmonious, which are healthy, which are good. Now, for example, denial is a discord in the consciousness; therefore, it is, in truth, a disease. It is disease. Harmony—acceptance is harmony. What one accepts in consciousness, they free themselves of. What one denies in consciousness, they destine themselves to. So our denials become our destinies. Our acceptance becomes our freedom. Does that help with your question?

Yes, it does.

Yes. Now, you see, because attitude of mind does bring about a chemical change within the body, attitude of mind is absolutely necessary in any type of infection. Now, you see, the thing is that people have two types of thinking. They have the type of thinking that, "Well, it takes an attitude of mind, but it also takes a physical change in the body." But the physical change is an effect; it's not a cause. It is an effect.

Now if you have a person in the final stages of the disease of cancer, for example, and you tell them to have a change of attitude, to start thinking good thoughts, to start feeling good, to feel positive—for it's not a luxury, it's a necessity—then you are speaking to a person whose chemistry is already very discordant to a very high percentage, for they're in the last stage of the disease. So [if you are] working with a virus, through the change of attitude of mind, which brings about a change of the chemistry of the human physical body, then it behooves a person, of course, to work on that in very early stages. Yes. Does that help with your question? Yes.

Yes, it does. I have just one more, short one.

Yes.

So in the acceptance, does that mean to accept the condi—to be more positive about it being present in one's system?

Well, first of all, with such an infection on your planet, it behooves students of the Light to accept a more harmonious attitude of mind for they are, in truth, weakening their own chemistry, creating an imbalance in their chemistry from negative thoughts, from frustration, from anything that is discordant, you see.

Thank you.

Does that help with your question? In other words, you don't concentrate on a particular virus and say, "Well, I have it. I'm going to keep a good thought about this." No, no, no. You keep a good thought about everything, and then your whole body, your chemistry shall react to that rate of vibration.

OK.

Do you see? Yes, for harmony is health. It is one and the same thing. Yes, please.

Yes, all viruses stem from denial. And what is the difference between—

Well, all disease is an effect of discord, and discord is the effect of denial. Yes, in that sense that is correct. Yes.

And what is the difference of the two viruses being cancer versus the AIDS virus? Is it from a different level?

Well, yes, indeed, it is because the present virus, the virus of which we are discussing, it attacks the immune system, the protection of the physical house or the human body. It breaks it down. In other words, what it does, it absorbs it. You see.

Yes.

You know, if you want to put it in mundane terms, I would say that it's the greatest freeloader virus known to your world. It lives off of something else. In other words, it enters, the virus enters, and it literally absorbs the very membrane of the cell. In other words, it becomes it; and by so doing, it destroys it and it multiplies. That's basically what it does. Yes. Yes.

And that has to do with the, with our thinking and the mass thinking of so identified, to the degree we are so identified with those forms . . .

Well, the more that one identifies with oneself, the more discordant one is in consciousness. And discord, the effect of discord, of course, is disease. So in that respect, the more one thinks about themselves, the more unhappy they are. Do they not find more to complain about? Do they not find more to blame someone else for their discord? Pardon?

Yes. Yes.

See? So it's a denial of personal responsibility, you see. You can't blame the virus. The virus has its characteristic. It has its own personality. And it absorbs and becomes whatever it attacks. And by so doing, it multiplies off of those cells, you see. It becomes it. Yes.

Thank you.

Yes. Yes, please.

So that even though if we, if a person has been exposed to the virus, carries the virus . . .

Yes.

It might not express, necessarily, until the percentage of his attitude had dropped in self-thought on a regular basis?

Well, until the discord is sufficient to activate the virus. Do you understand that?

Yes, sir.

You see. You see, when a person in consciousness reaches a, a certain level of discordant experiences within the consciousness and denies responsibility for them, then one is more receptive to the activation of the virus. The virus is in 66 percent of the population of your country. You already asked that question. I think you asked that. Yes. Yes. Good evening.

Good evening.

Yes.

Do the tests that they, that the medical scientists currently have to detect the antibodies are, do they—can they detect antibodies at any point during this, this incubation period?

Not with their present efforts, they are not.

OK.

No, not with their present efforts. No. They will, in time, yes, but not at present. Yes. Yes, please.

Yes. Then when the virus attacks the membrane and becomes it . . .

Yes?

Does it change its appearance and so—
It multiplies.
It re-identifies?
Well, it multiplies. It has many little children.
Oh.
Why, yes. That's what it does. You see, that's what I said. It could be known in [other] words, it's the greatest freeloading virus that you're going to find. It's quite a freeloader. Because it denies personal responsibility. It's dependent on—you see, look at the characteristics of the virus, then you can understand states of consciousness that create discord in the human mind that make one receptive to its activation. It denies personal responsibility. It is dependent on something else for its livelihood and its multiplication of self-interest. Do you understand the virus now?
Yes.
You see, first of all, it denies responsibility. It freeloads on something that it attaches itself to. It so identifies with what it attaches itself to, it believes that it is the cell. It actually absorbs right to the membrane; you know, it comes in total harmony with the membrane of the cell. So it so believes that it is the cell, it becomes the cell, and it multiplies off of it, you see. Do you understand that? So that attitude of mind, that type of thinking, that denial of personal responsibility, that dependence on something outside is the characteristic of the virus. Pardon?
Thank you.
You're welcome. Yes, please.
What is, what is the future for the, for the human race if, if I understand correctly, in so far as we're all on the path towards the Light?
That is correct.
And very few are so close to the Light that, as a percent—
Yes?

That we're able to accept personal responsibility to the degree that the virus could be resisted by, by establishing a pattern of, of firm acceptance . . .

Yes?

That in the short term, will there be many people left? Or—

Well, there'll be a 40 percent decrease in the world population. You see, there's good in all things, you see.

Of course.

If the light of reason of the masses will not bring about the necessary changes, then the effects of the over-identification and self-orientation will bring it about. So there's good in all things. But let us not forget, in our understanding, that if we permit our minds to believe that we are the form that we are presently using—remember that that is a mental attitude. And when the physical body goes, the mental body is wide awake. Pardon?

Yes.

And so we must not forget that it exists within the consciousness. If we believe we're going to shed the virus by shedding the physical form—we have not shed the thoughts of it, have we?

No.

And we have not shed the, the suffering and the torture, depending, of course, upon how attached we were to the physical form at the time of being driven out of it. Do we understand that? Yes.

Then the disease is going to provide a vehicle for the, for the evolution of, of those that, that view it as, that are able to release through the disease.

Yes, indeed. Of course, it will release untold numbers into the other realms. The most important thing is to communicate and to help those when it is solicited. You see, the greatest sabotage that's being done by the mental world is the refusal to take a look at what is happening on your planet. It refuses to look at it. It refuses to view it. Yet it is everywhere. It is everywhere. Yes.

We have discussed it many times but not in a class or to the extent that we are discussing it this evening. Because you are students of the Living Light Philosophy you bear a personal responsibility to make effort to gain some understanding of the virus in an intelligent, reasonable way without emotion. Yes. Yes, [that student] has a question, please.

Yes, you just spoke that at present we don't have any testing to test if anywhere along the incubation . . .

That is correct.

. . . period. How long will it be before they do?

Well, at the present growth of the efforts being made by the medical profession of your world, it will be 15 to 22 years. Yes. Yes.

May I also ask, presently with their testing that they have for the antibody after what they call a six-month window . . .

Yes?

What is the percentage of accuracy of that test?

Well, the percentage of accuracy on the present testing is approximately, out of 10 percent, it is 2 percent. It's 2 percent. It's 2 percent out of 10, or 20 percent out of a 100.

Accurate.

Accurate. Correct.

Thank you.

You see, because it requires change in the thinking of the masses, change they're not even willing to look at, then they refuse to look at it at all, you see. From lack of understanding, it is from lack of understanding. The virus can only be transmitted by the fluids of the body. There is no other possible way to transmit the virus of AIDS. It's transmitted through kissing (mouth to mouth) and it is transmitted through intimate contact of an exchange of bodily fluids.

So it's the fear. The fear, although the virus has been growing rapidly for some time, the fear of the virus is worse than the virus itself because it will cause more problems for society. It is the fear of it, you see.

You cannot contact the virus by touching a person, unless you touch a person in the mouth where there's fluids and you have an open cut on your finger, then you have a possibility of contacting it. You have, of course, you have it from blood transfusions and wherever there is a contact of the fluids. That's the only way that it lives. Now the virus, if it's laid out on a table and you look at it, it disintegrates. It dies. It has to have fluids. It will last for a time, certainly, under certain laboratory conditions, but you're not going to catch the plague by touching it. I do hope that my students understand that. Yes. Yes, please.

Yes, how soon will it be and what kind of care facilities are seen in the near future for all the people?

Well, if you mean in the near future within the next two to five years, very, very little. As long as the thinking of the masses can restrict the virus to the minority parts of society, then you're not going to see the changes that are necessary by the government. No, you won't. Yes, please.

When one goes, dips down into the water center, are they more receptive to triggering the virus in their system?

Absolutely.

The water center, since that's a water, fluid orientated—

Absolutely. It's the same way with cancer or any of the diseases. That's where the discord is, because that's where all the judgments lie. That's where they're born. So, of course, the most detrimental thing you can do is to get into emotion in reference to any effort to bring about changes with the spread of the virus. Definitely. Absolutely. Yes.

Thank you.

Now I know that some students would like to know, well, if [it's] just a little small kiss, if they would contract the virus. Well, it doesn't matter how small or how big the kiss is, if there are fluid exchanges. Because that's how it's transmitted. That's one of the absolute, definite ways that it is transmitted. In fact, one of my channel's guides spoke to one of my students some time ago and said, "Well, just kiss them on the cheek. Or kiss them on the forehead." You know, it depends on how much you value your life, you see. Yes. Yes, please.

Yes. How many years, then, are we looking for the education of the masses, the children, the school system, all of that?

Well, at present—which part of the country are you speaking of? Are you speaking of this particular state here of California? Or are you speaking of the—

I would like to know—

Well—

All of it.

Well, all of it is—

I mean, California and the country.

Well, California is one of the most progressive. However— so you're living in California; let's speak on California. Now, first of all, there is some effort to bring about an education in the schools. Education in the schools should begin in the grammar school. Absolutely. Definitely. Because the children should learn about such a serious thing for their own survival very early in life.

Now, however, you must understand from lack of understanding and communication, there is great fear. And that fear is making great effort to bring about separations of certain minority groups in your country. We do not see that succeeding. However, it will take great effort from educated, intelligent people so it does not succeed.

Now as far as education in the public schools in California, that we do see passing. There will be changes and it will be watered down because there are those who would rather have their children pass from the plague and from the disease than have any education in the public-school system. Oh, of course, there are. There's, there's [a] certain type of religious type of people [who] would much prefer to have their own children pass from the plague than to have them have an education in reference to sex or anything of that nature. Yes.

Thank you.

You're welcome. And [that student] has a question, please.

Yes, sir. The disease, is it, is it going to take force to, to bring about a change? Is, is, I mean, is the disease in itself force?

The disease in and of itself is force. Its characteristic is force, yes. Yes.

And—

I would like to say one thing, though, for a moment there.

Yes, sir.

Let us not delude ourselves that this plague is something new. It's not new. We are awakening to it, but it is not new. So let us not believe that this plague is new. The spreading of it is the greatest crisis that your planet will experience. Go ahead with your question.

So by, by having the characteristic of force, there's, it's working, it's working with the fear, in a sense it's working hand in hand with the fear inside an individual.

Of course. Of course. A person fears being lonely, they fear this, they fear that, and they become victims of it. Why, certainly. Certainly.

So it's, it's a mental change that's going to be made.

The virus is a dependent virus, the most dependent known to your world. It depends on something else. It depends on something that it is not. It, through its own dependence and over-identification, it actually becomes a part of the cell. And in so doing it uses it and multiplies itself. Does anyone not understand that? Because that's how the virus works.

What—is, is all mental substance dependent?
Pardon?
Is all mental substance dependent?
I would like to see one that isn't. Does someone have a mental substance—does someone have a thought that's not dependent? An idea, I can accept as independent, but tell me a thought that's not dependent, please. Hmm? Yes, all thoughts are dependent. What are they, what are all thoughts dependent upon?
Probably, well, judgments.
All thoughts are dependent on judgment.
Right.
What created judgment?
What created—an over-identification.
Experience?
Experience.
Denial?
Denial.
Yes.
Comparison.
So they're all dependent, aren't they? Pardon?
Yes, yes.
Yes.
Thank you.
You're welcome. [Yes], please.
Yes, will we eventually have this virus under control before we colonize space and come into contact with other peoples?
Well, I don't like to say "well"—great effort is being made by other intelligences that you shall not contaminate the universe. That is—yes.
Thank you.
I can say that.
Thank you.
Yes, please.

Yes, why is this happening, like, why this and why now?

Why not? *[Many students laugh.]* See, the question is, Why not? You know, when you have the masses for the last, well, fifty years thinking of self, self, self; discord, discord, and, "Not me. It's not my fault. Someone else did this. Someone else did that." You see, and denying, denying personal responsibility, denying one's own personal freedom, then we must ask the question, Why not? Why shouldn't it come now?

Perhaps we should even think, Why didn't it get here sooner? [It's] been around quite a while, you know. You see, you've only been aware of it, perhaps, what, in these five or six years. Well, it's been around a long time. The virus itself is not something new. The spreading of it and your awareness of the spreading of it is what's new. That's what's new, is the waking up. That's what's new. Yes.

And what finally caused the spreading of it? What was—was it just the saturation point?

Tell me something, tell me something. When you think of self and believe that you are self and you completely over-identify with it, is it something easy to get out of?

No.

Does it spread?

Yes.

Do the people around you want to be around you?

No.

They want to, they want to be immune from you, don't they? Well, now you understand the virus.

OK.

Yes.

Thank you.

Someone else had a question. Yes, please.

How old is the virus, then? And where did it begin and how?

As old as the denial of man.

Is that, then, the beginning of man?

Well, I don't think we need to go into the Garden of Eden tonight, but as old as the denial of man.

Thank you.

Yes, please.

Has there been a spread and an outbreak like we're facing here now in the past in the history of the Earth planet?

Never to this extent. The planet has never experienced it to this great crisis. Yes. It has taken its toll over the centuries. Never ever to this extent. No. Yes, yes, [that student] has a question, please.

Does that mean that we're, we as, as a, a group of people are, in time, are more into denial as time marches on?

That is correct. We are more into denial and we're more into variety, aren't we, as a society?

Yes.

You see? There used to be a day when a man would say, "Well, [I have] 2 pair of shoes. Shoes are shoes. They'll cover my feet." Now it's 20 or 50 or 100, isn't it?

Yes.

So, you see, as we enter more denial, we also enter more demand. Is not society more demanding than ever before in the history of your—recorded history of your planet? Well, it's much more demanding, is that not correct?

Yes.

I mean "man" as humanity.

Yes.

You see.

Yes. OK.

You see, more demands reveal more denials.

OK.

The more denials a person has, the more demands they have, don't they?

Yes.

For example, if you take a look, say, just say if you're courting and you have, you deny this one, that one, that one, that one, that one, your demands increase, don't they? Yes, proportionately they do increase.

Yes.

Demands increase in keeping with denial. Yes. That help with your question?

Yes.

Yes, please.

Yes. So am I correct to say that man, each and every man, ever, ever since the first man walked on this Earth . . .

Yes?

He had the virus within him?

I did not say that.

Oh.

I said since the time of denial.

Since the time . . .

Since the time of denial revealed the time of dependence, didn't it?

OK. Yes.

When Adam was in heaven and paradise, you don't suppose they had the plague in paradise, do you? See, that didn't come until denial came. When you deny, you depend. The virus reveals the state of consciousness. When you deny, you depend. When you deny that you're happy, you depend on something, something outside, for you have denied it inside. Pardon?

Yes. So, so man, OK, man made a, man pulled—are you— I'm, I'm trying to say, man pulled, a, a—he had—it's not like the immaculate conception. But in a sense—

Yes?

It, it was, it was a positive and negative pole that touched in man's consciousness that brought, that, that conceived this virus within him, since at one time he didn't have it.

Let me say it this way.

Yes, sir.

That which separates denies. Hmm? So when man separated in his consciousness, he denied his wholeness. And when he denied his wholeness, then he pays the price. Wouldn't you agree? *[The teacher addresses a different student.]*

Yes, sir.

As long as you deny the wholeness that you are, you must accept the bondage of dependence on what you believe that you need. Hmm? You can't experience need without denial. The virus is a perfect example of need, is a perfect example of denial. Hmm? Does that help with your question?

Yes, sir.

You're welcome. [Yes], please.

Would it, it would be like a woman thinking she needed a man to take care of her, that thinking.

That is correct. She first has to deny that she's capable of taking care of herself, which first has to begin with a denial of personal responsibility. Pardon? Yes! We're speaking of the denials of conscious[ness]. That is correct. Yes.

Ah, ah, I . . . ah . . . [The student has difficulty expressing her question.]

We'll come back to you because you've been giving it much thought. Yes.

Some of the societies of the past that archeology cannot explain in their seeming sudden disappearances, could, or have any of those societies disappeared as a result of this virus?

Some of them. Not all of them. Some of them have. Yes, some of them have. I can say this to you, dependence is the heavy cross to bear. The virus shows what dependence offers. Yes.

Will it bring about, eventually, the change in consciousness of separating truth from creation?

Oh, indeed, it will. It will not only reduce the population of your planet but it is the way that the mental world has chosen to fight its war. Pardon? Yes. Yes.

What will be the years that the masses awaken to the condition of the plague? What will be the crisis years?

Well, the crisis years are yet to be. The crisis years are already being prepared, but it will be years before they manifest. The crisis years are the great fear. Now the fear has been rising over the past two years especially, over the past two years. Ever since your medical science has become aware and it has revealed to the masses that the virus is not restricted to certain minorities of your society. For example, the, the awakening of the masses is, if I recall from these records here, began in Haiti. It was the Haitians who had the virus. Then it was the Africans. Then it was the, the narcotic addicts. Then it was the gay communities. Then it was the prostitutes. You see, they're going to run out of minorities to blame it on. Because, you see, each time they can find a certain segment of your society, by thinking that they are the only ones who have it, then the masses don't have to change their thinking. Do you understand that, that type of philosophy they have? "So we don't have to do anything because it's that group over there that's got it. So all we have to do is, perhaps, spend a little money to, to send them off to some island someplace." Do you understand?

And so the fear is the terrible, terrible danger because the energy then goes to that realm instead of going to education. The best thing that can be done is education; number one [is] education. Because of the great crisis. And the way to work on it intelligently is through education. Now without communication and understanding, there is no education. Education is the number one thing that the energy should be going to. Secondly, is research. However, the great fear of bringing about more education of it, more communication and understanding, is that people will have to change their particular lifestyles, you see. Better to change one's lifestyle prior to the plague than to tempt to change one's lifestyle after the plague. Wouldn't you say? *[The teacher calls on a different student.]*

Yes, sir.

Why, certainly. Yes.

What future do you see for the sex-promotion tax?

Well, first of all, it is the recommendation of our Council as a fair and just way of raising—your cost, you're presently facing in the next 4 years, is [a] $37 billion tax. Now facing a $37 billion expenditure and looking with the light of reason over the situation, then we, of course, recommend that those who have profited from the disease, the profiteers, the ones who have promoted the license of the function, should indeed be the ones who are paying the $37 billion with an increased tax whenever they use that type of advertising. Of course, that's reasonable and practical. Whether or not that change will come about is dependent upon the leaders of your country; you're speaking of your country, the United States now, depending upon the leader of your country and depending upon your Congress, because it will be fought—what do you call it?—tooth and nail in the highest courts of your land under the blanket of freedom of speech. But what does freedom of speech have to do with the promotion of something that is creating a disastrous plague and an increase of it in the country? Would you not agree?

Yes.

So it is—every little bit of effort, of course, helps, and it is only fair that those who profit from something should be the ones that pay the tax for the effect of it. Wouldn't you agree? *[The teacher calls on a different student.]*

Yes, sir.

Why, certainly. They don't seem to have any problem in your world of taxing the alcohol or taxing the tobacco. And the alcohol and the tobacco can't come close to what the plague is doing to millions and millions and millions of people. Yes. Yes.

If it comes down to the point where we merit governmental leaders who are about to start something like internment camps to isolate these people, what can we as citizens—

That thinking is already in the minds of many politicians, yes. Yes.

What can we as citizens do to stand—

Well, you can, of course, you can, you can wisely vote. You can speak up when opportunity presents itself. The great danger—the cities that are at present in great danger, in considering their population and the spread of it, are New York, San Francisco, Detroit, Dallas, Texas, Houston, Texas, Oklahoma City, Cleveland, Ohio, and Miami, Florida. And don't forget Los Angeles. I did mention San Francisco, didn't I?

Yes.

Yes. Now look at these things in a little bit, perhaps, more light. You must also understand that in the bigger cities your health departments have a better reporting average than you do in many of your smaller cities. And also, there are many who have passed on, and who continue to pass on, where, for business reasons, their doctors will not report it because, after all, they have their clients to consider and their business. So if you look at it in that perspective, then you can see that the primary function is winning out over the secondary as far as reporting. Does anyone not understand that? Pardon? Yes. Yes.

Yes. If it's going to take quite a few years for the education process, what will happen—

You will have education passed in the legislature of your state before this year ends. Yes, I'm happy to say that.

Thank you.

I just received that report myself. You will have some legislation, watered [down], but some legislation passed. The reason you will have it is because one of your politicians just came down with the disease. He didn't just come down with it; it just started to take hold of him.

All right.

Yes. I think you're all aware of that politician. Yes. Yes.

Well, that would mean then—

However, the thinking is of a mandatory testing, which is the most detrimental thing that your society can do. The reason for that is that you will drive untold millions of people underground in the sense that it will spread more than ever before. And it is not in the best interest of civilization. Yes.

Already the care facilities are getting crowded. So where will the people go?

Home care.

Home care.

That is correct.

I see.

Yes.

In their own homes where people would come in to—

Well, if they have someone to come in.

Yes.

Because your insurance, you're going to have new clauses in all insurance: it will not cover the plague.

Right.

It will not. No. And big changes will come in your insurance. You see, whenever you're speaking about billions of dollars in a society, then changes that seem unrealistic to the mind, they do happen. Yes. Remember that the primary function is primary, and that's known as money, yes. The other is secondary. Yes.

So the facility, the one facility they have open now in San Francisco, under the name of Coming Home, those would be the facilities that you were speaking about?

No, there will, there will be more of the victims of the plague who will not have the funds. There will be no place to put them, even if they do have some funds, and they will pass, of course, in their own home, with or without care.

I see.

Yes. Yes, yes.

Thank you.

You're welcome.

There is currently a home care nursing program. Will that—

It will not be sufficient. It will not be sufficient, no. No, I don't want you to look at this with any kind of fear because fear is the most dangerous thing you could do. You want to look at it with some kind of reason. When opportunity presents itself and the information is solicited from you, you can share your understanding, your own understanding, you see. Yes.

Would it be—I know you just said that it wouldn't be efficient, but would that be a possible way to help the victims, through home care nursing?

The best care that can be given to a victim of the plague is home care. That's the best possible care that they could possibly receive. There is no stopping the, the virus once it has reached a certain percent of absorption in the human body. However, in the very early stages one can help retard its growth—do you understand that?—and its multiplication.

Well, it looks like we're going to be going over time here this evening. You have enough tape, do you? *[The teacher addresses the technician recording the class.]* Yes. We will keep this in reserve for you. *[The teacher reminds the students that their tapes of this class will not be immediately released to them.]* But it is in your own best interest that it not be copied until more awareness comes within the masses. You have to understand there are already officials in government, in the various state and city governments, and officials in your federal governments who are considering not just a mandatory testing—that is, that's guaranteed. If there's anything in your world can be guaranteed, I can assure you that mandatory testing is already on its way. Quarantine is in the consideration of many of your politicians. It's not the way to handle the plague. It is not. For example, if this city quarantines anyone with that and then there's the testing of whether you can get through the city or into the city. You see, it will just breed, through fear and misunderstanding, it will breed riots. That's what it will breed. The bonfear—bonfires are already lit. It will only breed riots and disaster. It will bring no good to bringing about the cure, which will come, but it is not in the foreseeable future. Yes. Yes.

A lot of people don't believe in a hereafter.

That is correct. So you don't talk to them in that respect, if you're trying to help people who have no acceptance of the continuity of life. Talk to them in terms that they can understand. You see?

Yes.

You see, you can talk to them and try to help them to divert their attention to something besides themselves. It'll be quite a step, but it will be helpful and it will be beneficial to them. Yes. Yes. Yes.

You mentioned the need to change lifestyle. And—

Yes, the lifestyle of one's consciousness. Yes, indeed.

In, in terms of, of addressing the or retarding the growth of the disease . . .

Yes?

In one's, in one's own body through the establishment of harmonious, positive attitudes and . . .

Yes.

In addition, are there, are there other considerations?

Well, yes. One cannot just think positive and go about with promiscuity and their past lifestyles no matter who we are, because, you see, we're battling ourselves. First of all, the awakening of acceptance to something greater in a more harmonious attitude of mind does not contain within it a dependence on something it cannot control. Do you understand that?

Yes.

You see. See, an acceptance that one is whole and complete, you see, an acceptance of good feelings, you see, does not contain within it a denial. It's a total acceptance. So not containing a denial, it does not contain a dependence. And not containing a dependence on anything outside, then it is free. Does that help in the thinking of the changing of [one's] lifestyle?

Yes. Thank you.

Because that's where it is, you see. You see, the characteristics of the virus reveal that to you very clearly, when you study the virus itself. You must understand it's not some bug, some foreign bug. It is an intelligent being. A virus is an intelligent being. It has a purpose, like all beings have a purpose. Its purpose is to survive and to multiply. And that's exactly what it does. So you mustn't look at it as something bad. It is an intelligent being. It has a purpose to serve, you see? And its purpose is survival and multiplication. Built within its characteristics is its dependence on something outside. Hmm? And by denying personal responsibility, it freeloads on those cells, you see. It freeloads on them by over-identifying with them [and] believes that it is them, right into the very membrane of the being, you see. Yes.

You mentioned at the beginning of this class that our name for the plague was indicative of the characteristics of it.

Of course.

And could you tie that in for us with the—

Well, what does, what does the word *aid* mean to you? What does *aid* mean to you?

Well, to me it means to give help, but . . .

That's what the virus does, doesn't it?

OK.

Well, doesn't the virus help itself? I mean, doesn't it go in and gobble up the little cell and multiply from the substance of the very cell itself? Study the virus and you will see. Absolutely. It helps itself. Help is help. It just decided it'll help itself. That's why I say it'll probably go down in your history as the greatest freeloader virus ever known to mankind. Yes. Yes.

Yes. How far off are we looking at a depression and a—

Depression?

Yes, sir.

An economic depression?

Yes, sir.

They won't have any time to think about an economic depression. They're going to be thinking about survival. Now I would not concern myself with an economic depression. Everyone's going to think about survival. Pardon?

I mean, survival to—I mean, I'm talking about to the point whereas, I mean, people are just going to literally be indoors.

No, no, because before you get into a complete revolution in your country, the cure will come. I speak to you on this matter so strongly, perhaps, it's strongly to you, because so many people won't even think about it at all. Would you not agree? *[The teacher calls upon a different student.]*

It's true.

They just won't even think about it. As long as they have someone to, to set it on, "It's over there. It has no effect upon me," they don't even think about it, you see. So I must speak to you strongly so that you can understand how serious it really is. Yes.

How long will that take to get that cure?

Don't hold your breath. It's not in the foreseeable future. I think I answered that. It is not in your foreseeable future.

Thank you.

You see, you see, if it was in your foreseeable future, then the change in evolution wouldn't come. You know, one would say, "Well, let's see, I've only got two years to wait. Why should I make any changes?" Hmm? "I can hold out for two years." Hmm? Yes. *[Some students laugh.]* It doesn't work that way. Yes.

Then, is air the enemy of the virus? Air.

Yes, air is the enemy of the virus. You're absolutely correct. Because it has to have water; it has to have fluid to transmit itself, you see. It is. Oh, yes, it is. Yes. Well, now you know more than I was even going to discuss. Now you know it's the water center queen, don't you? Yes. It's killed off by the king of the air center. That is correct. You're right. Yes, please.

So an actual movement from the water center into the air, for the light of—I'm thinking of moving from the air—the water, to like the fourth and fifth.

Well, when it moves into the air center, then it's not transmitted, you see.

Oh.

Oh, no, it can't multiply. It can't attach. Do you understand that? It dies off. Of course, in a laboratory it would last for so long a time under ideal laboratory conditions, and then it would—it dies off. It must have fluids to live on. It lives off fluid. You do understand it's a fluid virus?

Yes.

Yes, it's not an airborne virus. It's a waterborne virus, yes. Absolutely. Yes.

So in working with it, people working with it within their own system, they could actually help themselves by—is that possible?

Why, certainly. Why, certainly. Because when a person stays out of the water center and they enter the light of reason, then things are more harmonious, aren't they? *[The teacher calls upon a different student.]*

Yes, sir.

Well, much more harmonious. Yes. See, the virus is a waterborne virus. It is not an airborne virus. Now theoretically, I mean, you know, you could say that, well, if you had your mouth open and someone sneezed and that made contact direct like that, there's a very microscopic possibility. Do you understand that? Now if you had a big cut and it was bleeding on your finger and you were a dentist and you stuck your finger into someone's mouth, then, of course, there's a possibility, and a very good possibility—you understand?—of contacting the virus. Absolutely. Because you have fluid to fluid, you see. Do you understand that?

Yes.

Yes. I do hope so. You won't be all covered up or run around in a Faraday cage or something to protect yourself. *[Some of the students laugh.]* Yes. You're not going to contact it from somebody sneezing unless your mouth is open and that's a very rare possibility. And so you don't have to worry about all these masks and things. However, now if you are working in a hospital and you have your mouth open and somebody spits and part of that saliva gets into your mouth, then, of course, there's a very good possibility. So we must be reasonable, you understand.

Air is death to a water virus. All right? So it only lasts or survives so long [when it's] exposed to air, you see. This is why we have advised students who have asked, Isa has advised them, our good doctor has advised them, "Well, if you must kiss, there's no problem. Kiss them on the, on the cheek. Kiss them on the forehead." There's no exchange of saliva. Do you understand that? *[Isa Goodwin is Mr. Goodwin's mother. She would regularly instruct, guide, and correct the students through Mr. Goodwin's mediumship.]*

Yes.

Why, certainly. Now you have, for example, you have right in your United States now, you have the state of New York, of the City of New York, they already have started a program of advertising the only safe sex is no sex. Well, there's no such thing as safe sex to the virus; it doesn't exist. Safer sex exists. Safe sex does not. Well, who can guarantee—who knows, the balloon may bust? I mean, how do you know for sure? You don't, do you? Well, there you are. And how do you know, if you think you're giving a dry kiss that it may not be wet? Now seriously. Yes, go ahead, please.

Sometimes—

Seriously.

People have remissions.

Yes.

Are they just temporary or can they be permanent?

To God all things are possible, and they could become permanent, but it'd bring about a change in consciousness. Absolutely. Absolutely. After all, there are cases of people who do have the plague and who became aware of it very early, when it started to grow in their system. You see, it lies dormant for so many years, you know. Oh, so many years. Wait 'til you get to 25 years lying dormant. I've already discussed 20. Your medical profession is accepting 15, because they know so little about it, really.

So, you see, depending on the percentage of the activity that the virus is awakened, depending on how soon a person is aware and how determined in consciousness they are and bring about changes in their thinking, why certainly, it can help to retard it. It can actually keep it from growing any more. A battle goes on inside, you see? A battle of the chemistry and the virus. Absolutely. Definitely. Yes.

And, of course, you know, belief—because it is a virus which is directly related to bondage, to belief, to denial, to dependence, because it is a function virus, in that respect, because of that, belief—some people believe very strongly, very deeply; and through that belief, they create a change in their chemistry. We all understand that, I'm sure. Yes. Yes.

If the insurance codes are going to be changing and they won't cover the virus—

They will not cover the virus. No.

OK. OK, I understand that. How will people afflicted with the virus be able to survive economically?

Well, they won't. They won't survive, and it will be up to the taxpayers. It'll be up to the counties and to the states and to the towns and to the cities. This is why, reasonably, we see that the profiteers of promoting the conditions which spread the virus should be the ones paying a 10 percent tax on their promotion of the condition. Does anyone have any questions on that? If you, if you sell a box of cornflakes by draping the impression of some young lady on the box, then why shouldn't the profiteers who make the profit from selling those cornflakes pay for that? Because, you see, you must understand that through a constant repetition of anything you bring about change. Now when you have a philosophy, an advertising philosophy, that clearly states and brags that sex sells, and you sell everything from toilet paper to breakfast cereal, and the promotion of that in the consciousness of the masses is instrumental in spreading the fatal disease, then it's only right and fair that the profiteers making money from that should be paying. Don't you agree?

I absolutely do.

That is, you see, that is the recommendation that we have from our Council: that the billions of dollars necessary to care for the victims of the great plague that the profiteers who make money off of the promotion of it should be the ones paying for it.

OK.

Yes.

Thank you.

And if more of those recommendations get into the hands of the right politicians and to the right people, then effort will be made, even if it's on a city-by-city basis, you see, to see that the funds come from somewhere. Now if the funds do not come from an area of that, in that way, they will come from increased taxes. By increasing taxes, you start to divide the people. You divide the ones with it and the ones without it. Do you understand?

Yes.

Now through that division—because you are now, you now have as your battle cry the first function: money.

Yes.

"Why should I have to pay for people whose lifestyle is spreading this terrible plague across the land?" Do you understand?

Yes.

And so you're already moving with the situation where you can no longer say well, it's all of the drug addicts; it's all of the blacks in the country—you understand?—or it's all of the prostitutes. The truth of the matter is, when we look at the statistics, the professional prostitutes are the cleanest in the spread of the disease of anyone. Yes. I'm not speaking of streetwalkers. I'm speaking of the professionals, you see, because they have so much at stake. They have their business at stake, you see.

Yes.

Yes. And they make great effort, yes. Yes.

Right now, it's appearing to be more and more of a problem that all these new babies are being born with the plague. Is there any way at present to bring a child into this world without risking that they will have the plague?

There's no guarantee. There is no guarantee. No. No, untold thousands of babies are born every day with the plague. They don't usually last very long. Yes. Yes. Do you have a question?

Is, is there a, a region of the world, of the planet which is substantially less infected with the virus than, than the United States?

Certain parts of Asia. Yes. At the present time there are certain parts of Asia. South America, Central America, North America, Europe, it's quite contaminated. Yes. But then, it's also quite self-orientated, isn't it? Pardon? Yes. Yes.

Serenity's moving up to this rather quiet, little remote area in the northern part of the—

That is correct, yes.

Will it be more removed from the plague or will it be there?

Well, of course, the plague exists. The plague does exist in that particular area. Oh, yes, definitely. The thing is, sometimes by not having much, one's better off. They don't have very good medical facilities. They have very little. Their laboratories are a bit antiquated in many respects, and sometimes it's best. Yes, sometimes it's best. They are not free of the virus, no. No, they're not free of it. No. No. The atmosphere, conditions for promoting it, are better. You don't see as much promotion of the function in that area, do you?

No.

Do you see any billboards promoting it? Do you see those type of magazines in the drugstores and places, in the grocery stores? Do you go into the video stores and see those things all being promoted? No, you don't. You see. So there are other factors. The promotion of it is nothing like it is in the area of where our school presently is here. Yes. You cannot constantly promote something without the masses believing in its absolute necessity for their life. You see. So what it basically is, there's been a mass brainwashing.

Now when the mayor of one of your largest cities starts spending the tax dollars on safe sex is no sex [and] abstinence is only freedom from the plague, well, how many converts do you think he's going to get in New York City? Pardon? Who is he appealing to? He's appealing to the converted. Perhaps the fundamentalists or something, I don't know. But he's appealing to the converted, not the ones who *need* the message, you see. Do you understand? So in our view, things of that nature, though we know that abstinence is the only absolute safety, the only assurance of it—and then that's no absolute assurance of it either, because the people may already have it lying dormant. Do you understand?

Yes.

Yes, yes. Education, understanding, research. Those are the things and that's where the money should be spent. That's where the effort should go. And time should not be wasted in that respect. Yes.

You see, there are so many ways that you, as students of Light, can help this, this great plague across the land without ever mentioning religion—a lot of people don't want to discuss religion—without mentioning anything in reference to our philosophy, you see, by talking to a person when it is solicited, you see. And by first preparing oneself as students; to prepare yourself, you see.

Remember, the characteristics of the virus is dependence, denial. Its very characteristics reveal that in your laboratories, you see. So if you want to make a home for it, then the only type of attitude of mind you have to have is that which is similar to the virus, you see: total dependence and denial and the lack of accepting personal responsibility. The virus does not accept personal responsibility. It goes in [and] absorbs all that it can absorb. So it can multiply. Without the absorption of the cell, you understand, it does not multiply. Surely you understand that much about the virus. Yes.

In San Francisco in the gay community, there has not been a case in the past year. Is that contributed to the education of the—

To education and the banner of survival. You see, it's amazing what changes come about when survival is at stake. You see?

Yes.

It is through the effort of education and survival. Of course, there are no new cases because there's changes in consciousness. That's why there's no new cases. And there won't be any new cases until there's another change in consciousness, you see.

Yes.

You see, there's one thing about minorities: they unite to survive. Masses, they revolt and hope to survive. There is a difference, you see. Yes.

Thank you.

Because they're all special. You see, they're all special in the masses, you know. "That will never happen to me." The type of thinking [like], "That'll never happen to me; has nothing to do with me" is the type of thinking of a person who's waiting to be a victim. That's the type of thinking of a person waiting to be a victim. Yes.

If the, if the advertising were changed tomorrow, media advertising, etc.—

Yes?

Would the, would the effect in change, of the change in consciousness be so strong . . .

[It will] take twenty years.

Twenty years.

[It will] take at least twenty years, at least twenty years. You have a saying in your world: you can't teach an old dog new tricks. Take at least twenty years. At least. Now, see, the benefit of taxation upon those profiteers who are making so much money, have made millions and untold millions of dollars from promoting their products—I mean, after all, what does the secondary function have to do with eating a breakfast cereal? Really nothing, except to make more money. Is that correct?

Yes.

You see, you see, what has been done in this promotion is, it's an entrancement. Now your advertising interests have known for many, many years that if you can entrance a person, you can sell them anything while they're in a state of entrancement, you see, fascinated. So if you want to sell a person a bar of soap and you have in your advertising something that will entrance them, like looking at a pretty girl or something of that nature, you see—in other words, trigger within the mind something that they desire and sell them something else. Do you understand that, don't you? *[The teacher calls upon a different student.]*

Yes, sir.

You see, so that's what the profiteers have done for so many, many years. Why shouldn't they pay for what they have made so much money from? Do you understand? See, the thing is, is a tax upon those who use that function to sell their product when their product is not directly related to it. Do you understand that?

Yes.

All right. That way—you have what you call a free enterprise. You have the manufacturers who say, "Well, I'll no longer sell my soap by promoting that function." All right? "I'll sell my soap on its own merits that it cleans your clothes." You see. So you give them a choice. So you have those who make that decision, and you have those who are going to continue and say, "No, I'll make more money by paying the tax because I'll still promote it." You see? So you have that optional system; just tax them. Do you understand? And then you'll have the billions of dollars necessary to care for the victims of it. Pardon? Can you understand that?

Yes.

Do you think that interferes with free speech? If it does, then they're going to have to put new laws on governing pornography because you can't play pornography videos in the grammar schools, can you? There are certain laws that prohibit it, aren't there? Well, there you are, you see. It's a matter of degree, isn't it? Yes. Yes, please.

So, so in other words, when it gets to that point in the courts of law where they're trying to hide behind that free speech con game . . .

Well, didn't your pornography companies try that years ago in your—

Yes.

Well, how far did they get?

Not too far and—

Well, there you are. Yes, go ahead.

Then, then, in other words, would, would the judges of the land be then weighing that out as to, as to allowing that pornography to go into the schools, weighing that decision out versus the other?

It has to weigh against the first function. And the first function is not first by just, you know, some superstition. It's first by demonstration. When it comes to the first function, money wins out, doesn't it? Yes, it does. Of course. Of course. You'll have no problem. They'll have to pay. And, you see, because you're not talking about a million or two million or three million dollars. You're talking about many billions of dollars. You're talking about a world condition that will enter the zillions of dollars. Zillions of dollars. All right. Yes.

Will euthanasia become acceptable or legal in this country?

Unfortunately, it will be, what you would consider, nip and tuck. Because of so many afflicted and because of costs, should euthanasia pass, it will pass because of money costs to the government. We must take a look at it impartially, without emotion. That's the only thing that will cause it to pass. Yes.

You say "unfortunately," what is the Spirit's recommendation of . . .

Of euthanasia?

Yes.

Well, that's entirely up to the individual. If the individual has so freed their consciousness from the form, there's no problem because the form will not endure.

Thank you.

Yes, yes. I mean, I don't think we have ever in our classes ever recommended suicide, have we? Has anyone been aware that we teach suicide or escape? There's no escape. There's no escape. Now if a person has reached a point of consciousness that they are no longer so attached to their form, then they would not suffer from their form, would they? Pardon?

Right. Thank you.

Yes. Yes. Does that help with your question?

Yes. Thank you.

Yes. Yes.

If you have the opportunity to visit someone who is deteriorating from this disease and it's just dragging on and on—

Yes. It does drag on. Sometimes it's a year, year and a half, two. Yes.

Is it best to keep on seeing him to encourage him or does that hold him here?

Well, it depends upon the individual and what relationship you have as a friend. And it depends, of course, upon the receptivity of the individual: whether or not they have any acceptance of the continuity of life or whether they have the judgment of the ending of life when the physical flesh goes. That depends on what kind of thinking do they have.

I don't know.

Oh, if they were a friend, that's the first thing I would know.

Hmm.

You know, there's ways of finding out those things without coming out and asking a person, you see. Well, see, how are they? Are they involved in self-pity through over-identification, through denial? Are they—what attitude do they have?

Ah, at the—

Do they appreciate your visits? Do they seem to? Do they have many visitors or are they there and have no one, no visitors at all?

When I was last seeing him, it seemed that he was appreciating the visit and that he didn't have many visitors.

Usually, they don't, you know, because of the fear. Because of the lack of communication and the lack of understanding they have very, very few visitors, the victims. Yes.

However, it was my understanding that what was revealed at that time was that in his consciousness he was into self-pity and he was blaming himself at that time.

Most destructive force you can imagine. Keep it up and you just help spread it that much faster. Yes.

So I'm at the point where, where—
Well, when have you last visited the person?
It's been about a month and a half ago.
A month and a half!?
Yes.
Does it upset you to visit them as a friend?
No, no it doesn't.
Hmm.
It didn't the last time.
You visit them once in a month and a half?
Yes. I was visiting him regularly, then I thought that "Gee, maybe he really wants to move on." And maybe, maybe my coming there—
Did you ask him?
No, because he was at the point where he wasn't really communicating. He could hardly speak or anything.
Well, well, I can only say if it was a friend of mine, I would certainly visit him.
OK. Thank you, very much.
If they were a friend.
Hmm.
Unless I believed that they were the suit that they were wearing, and I couldn't bear to look at them.
Yes.
Yes.
Thank you.
[You're] welcome. Now are there any questions before we conclude this class this evening because we will not be discussing it at every seminar? And it is not in your best interest to permit fear to rise in your consciousness, because then instead of being instruments of something positive and something constructive and something good, and being inspired from within your own being to help yourself and in so doing to help others,

then you will just join the masses of fear, which will bring no good at all, you see.

You see, I know that it is difficult for you when you have many acquaintances and people out there you socialize with who don't even discuss the subject, don't want to discuss the subject and want nothing to do with it because it's never going to affect them. I like to relate this to the great holocaust you had in your world during World War II: to the millions who absolutely convinced themselves it would never happen to them. They have six million on the other side in many different realms of consciousness because they would not accept that a holocaust could happen to them, you see. It is that type of thinking, that self-confidence and self-assuredness that we must face head-on. It *is* happening. Untold millions, untold millions. I'm not allowed to give you the exact number of millions, but untold millions of people are already infected throughout the world. Hmm. Yes.

Yes. Will the, the—

With the active virus. Not lying dormant, but active. Yes.

Well, well, in the first twenty years will the bulk of the money be spent on research or health care?

Well, most of the money—you must understand that your medical doctors and your scientists have already judged and accepted number one: it's a fatal disease; and number two: there's nothing they can do about it. You have to accept that that's what they've accepted. All right?

OK.

Now, that leaves it in the hands of the researchers and profiteers, doesn't it? You not only have profiteers in promoting that function, you have the profiteers in coming up with all kinds of medicine-man gimmicks to make money. You understand? And so the gimmick doesn't work, but a person's belief in the gimmick might help them. Do you understand that? You see, like a rabbit's foot, you know, if you believe, "I got this rabbit's foot. I have real good luck. Well, when I got this little gimmick, things seemed better." So it's dealing with something else. There's a lot of—[it's a] big medicine show, you know, going on with all your pharmaceutical houses and with your stock market and everything. There's untold billions of dollars at stake there. Yes.

So it, one should, one should concentrate on health care, I mean, just health care period?

No, they're not concentrating on health care. They're concentrating on research. And hopefully they will concentrate on education. As far as health care is concerned, they've just given them up as hopeless cases. Pardon?

Yes.

Well, no, certainly not. When you're looking at it medically, they're doomed. They accept. That's it. They're just doomed. It's hopeless. There's no cure. It's just hopeless. Do you understand?

Yes, sir.

That's the promotion that goes on. Yes. Not the possibility that something could change, no, no, no, no. No, medical science has all these cases, untold cases throughout the world. It's hopeless, yes, in their thinking. Yes, please.

What is—I'm, I'm sorry but I forgot the name of the drug that the persons are going to Mexico to obtain, and is that drug in any way helpful to the people and is it—

Well, it's as helpful as their belief.

Yes.

You know, you can grind up an apricot seed anyplace. It's as helpful as their belief.

Yes.

Why, certainly. So if their belief is sufficient to bring about a change in consciousness to help slow down the spread in their system of the virus, then, of course, to that, in that degree, of course, it is helpful. There is no scientific value, material, scientific value. Only their belief that it is helping is, is [the] value.

Yes.

Thank you.

But they're paying plenty for that belief. I'm talking about money-wise. Yes.

Then the doom that the doctors are promoting are a plague in itself.

Why, of course, of course, because it gives more fuel to the fire of fear. Absolutely. Definitely. Not all doctors are thinking that way, but those in position to be heard by the mass media are certainly thinking that way and stating it very clearly. Yes.

And if you go to one of your doctors and say, "Well, I'd like to have a test. I want to know if I've got AIDS or something." And they'll look at you and say, "Oh, you don't need to worry about that foolishness." You see, because that's how they're thinking, so many of them. They don't want to be bothered. Don't you understand? You have a private doctor and if he reports that he has a patient that has AIDS and that gets out into the news media, don't you understand that his money, his business, and his profession, that's the end of it? Pardon? Because he's a business man.

Yes.

So the private doctor is not the one that's going to be reporting it. Do you understand that?

Yes, I do.

Not if he wants to keep his business. Yes. And so it's understandable that most of the ones that are reported are the minorities. They go to the public health services. The public health services keep records. So then when it comes to the information, "Well, all those people, they're all the blacks; they're all the IV users. Those are all prostitutes or those are all gays." Why, of course, because they go and use the public health services, which report those things, you see. The public health service is not in a profiteering business to make money for themselves, like a private doctor. You have to understand that. Yes.

Yes. Thank you.

So when the report goes out to the news media, "Well, here's the report and look at the percentages." The ones who use the public health facilities, who had their blood tested or something and got caught. Yes.

Well, hopefully, after this very special class this evening, that you will have a different perspective about the plague across the land. It is sufficiently serious that it was time to come to speak to you so that you, as students of the Light, could, when opportunity presents itself and when it is solicited, that you could help another; by helping yourself you can help another. And so perhaps you won't have these terrible fears that someone sneezed nearby because the virus cannot be transmitted, as I said, unless you've got your mouth open; there's probably one chance in ten trillion. Not that your mouth is open, but that it was at the same moment.

So let us see the good in all things because that's the greatest cure that you can do for this negative disease that's across the land. I thank you and good night.

JUNE 11, 1987

A/V Seminar 23

Good evening, class.

This evening we will discuss balance, the Law of Harmony. A balanced mind is an enlightened mind. An enlightened mind is a servant of the soul faculty of reason. Without faith, one cannot express humility. And without humility, one cannot express faith. Now faith and humility, the foundation of the triune faculty of faith, poise, and humility, is absolutely necessary for a balanced mind.

Ofttimes we have discussed educating the human ego. The human ego is a servant of the mind. The education of the human ego is brought about by the use of the triune soul faculty of faith, poise, and humility. That is the second triune soul faculty. The first triune soul faculty, of which you have been given some time ago, is duty, gratitude, and tolerance. And so we find that when the human ego, an expression of the mind, is the true servant of the soul faculty of reason, the ego is educated or brought into balance with its true purpose of creation. And being so, there is harmony, the effect of which is health in all our acts and activities.

We find in our expression in a mental world that ofttimes we lack faith, for we lack humility. We lack, at times, control of our mind from not applying the necessary tools through which it may be educated. We all have had many experiences when we find our self, from denial, we find our self in need. And so let us pause here for a moment and let us think about the need of the primary function of our mind, which is known in your world as money. That need registers in our mind from a lack of use of the balancing soul faculty of faith.

Now a person may say, "Well, I have faith that my need is being fulfilled." What we ofttimes forget [is] that the soul faculties are triune. One doesn't just say, "I have faith that my needs are being fulfilled," without an expression of humility, for humility is necessary in order to bring about a balance or an enlightenment of the human mind. A poised mind is a balanced mind. One doesn't think of poise and free themselves from the belief that they are in need. It requires faith and humility.

Now we'll take a few moments for your questions. If you'll be so kind as to raise your hands. Yes, please.

Would you give us a description of poise?

Poise is a perfect balance in the human mind. It is a soul faculty. When the mind is educated, a true servant of the faculty of reason, the mind is poised. For example, a person ofttimes believes that through a denial of the use of the second triune faculty the human mind will believe that their need is being fulfilled. But through a lack of applying the triune faculty—for example, of applying only one of the faculties of the triune faculty of faith, poise, and humility—their needs are not fulfilled, for there is not the full use of the triune faculty. There is only a partial or limited use. And in keeping with how much they use the soul faculty, the fullness thereof, are they freed from the belief of their particular need. Does that help with your question?

Yes.

You know, to say, "I have faith that tomorrow it will rain," [or] "I have faith that I am going to do such and such," unless you use the full triune faculty, then your faith, that you believe that you have, is limited. For humility and the experiences that it offers is not balanced with the use of faith. And therefore, poise or balance or enlightenment of the mind, it does not become the servant of the soul faculty of reason. Does that help you? Yes, go ahead with it.

Just one more question.

Yes.

Would, would the use of humility be if I, if you said, "I have faith that my needs will be fulfilled and the fulfillment of that comes from God?" Is that—

No.

—the use of humility?

No, absolutely not. Humility is a registration in the uneducated ego or uneducated mind of humiliation. Now humiliation is a registration in the uneducated ego that something outside of one's control is the problem or cause for their experience of humiliation. The soul faculty of humility registers in the uneducated ego as humiliation. Does that help with the question?

Well, the, the ques—how would humility register in the educated ego?

As humility, the soul faculty that it is. There's a vast difference between the registration of humiliation and humility. Humility contains within it, as a triune soul faculty, total consideration and the full acceptance of personal responsibility. Does that help you?

Yes. Thank you.

Yes. So, you see, a person [who may] say, "I have faith that my financial needs are being met by the divine law," doesn't go and [say], "Now how can I humiliate myself so that I may be freed from those needs?" The law fulfills itself. The mind does not dictate how the law shall work because the divine law is not subject to the dictates of the mental world.

Thank you.

Yes. Yes, please.

Thank you. So acceptance of what, however it starts to, it's brought forth, would be the key with humility?

That requires an expression of the soul faculty of humility. That is correct, yes. Yes.

That would mean not, not—like, if one was tempted to go into frustration or—

That is the denial of personal responsibility for the experiences that one is encountering, yes.

Thank you.

And a denial of personal responsibility closes the mind to the soul faculty of reason; that is an uneducated or unenlightened mind, yes.

Thank you.

You're welcome. Yes, please.

Continuing with what was being said, then when the mind is poised, does that mean you're expressing in a level of humility and faith?

That is correct. And we are, at the time of the mind being poised, we are a servant of the soul faculty of reason. That's when we are transfigured or transformed. That's when the things we have denied, in keeping with the Law of Personal Responsibility, are no longer registering in our conscious awareness.

Yes.

Yes.

So—

That is correct. Pardon?

So it's a peaceful state?

Yes, it is a peaceful state. That is correct. Yes.

Thank you.

This is why so often we, our minds, are able to look at others and to see the flaws and to see the reason why they are having difficult experiences. For not being personally involved, we do not have the personal denial of personal responsibility. So, you see, we do have a bit of objectivity when we look at someone that we do not feel attached to. You see?

Yes.

And we're able to see a bit more clearly. But only a bit. Because following that "bit more clearly" is the denial of the soul faculty of duty, gratitude, and tolerance, and especially tolerance. Pardon? Ofttimes.

Yes.

Yes.

OK. Thank you.

You're welcome. Yes, please.

In other words, when the mind is balanced or when we are in balance and in poise, there's no mental activity at all. Is that what that means?

That means that there is mental activity, but it is activity that is a servant of the soul faculty of reason. Now the soul faculty of reason transfigures or transforms a being because it is the fullness of total consideration and all of the soul faculties. Yes.

Thank you.

You're welcome. [Yes], please.

Yes. A balanced mind is the . . .

An educated ego.

Right.

Yes.

Yes. Is—the Law of Harmony is the effect of a balanced mind.

That is correct. That is correct.

And the Law of Harmony is—I'm—it's hard for me to describe. The Law of Harmony has a lot of laws within that law.

Well, may I say this—

Yes.

An uneducated ego may quickly say, "The Law of Harmony is definitely going my way." Now that's an uneducated ego, you understand.

Right.

Because an educated ego or an illumined mind does not register your way or my way. *Way* is what it is.

Right.

Yes, go ahead.

Thank you. So there's, so there is no differentiation between—which, which, you know, I know that—between the good and bad. The Law of Harmony is. It's, it's—

The Law of Harmony is. It sees no difference between ant and angel. Yes.

Yes. Thank you very much.

Yes. For there is no difference.

No.

Yes. Yes, please.

We lack control of our mind because we fail to make use of the tools necessary to establish that control.

That is correct.

Could you speak a little on the tools?

Yes, certainly. For example, and as I spoke earlier, you have these soul faculties that you are aware of. When you find yourself disturbed—whatever disturbs us, as we know, controls us. All right. Now we cannot have anything control us that we do not first deny responsibility for. The only things in our experiences that control us are those things which we deny responsibility for. For example, when we accept responsibility for our state of mind, our state of mind, through the acceptance of responsibility, no longer disturbs us. For no one chooses, "I wish to be disturbed." That is not a choice that the conscious mind makes: "I wish now to be disturbed." Or "I wish at any time to be disturbed." So it is a denial; first we must deny responsibility for the experience. We must first deny responsibility for the experience, before the experience can control us.

Now it is through the denial of the experiences that we have that we destine our self to be controlled by them, for we deny we have created them. By denying we have created them, we destine ourselves to serve them and be controlled and disturbed by them, for we place our self in a state of mind of hopelessness. In other words, "What can I do about it?" You see? "I'm not responsible for it. What can I do about it?" That's like saying, "Well, the country is going to pot. What can I do about it?" But the going to pot of anything is what is created by our own mind for it is our mind that is experiencing it, you see? So first we must deny responsibility for the experience in our mind before we can be disturbed and controlled by it. Does that help with your question?

Yes, sir. Thank you.

You're welcome. If there is anything to describe what your world likes to call the devil, then I would say the best description for that experience and experiences would be denial. The devil exists within the consciousness only through denial. Without denial, there is no existence of the devil.

What does the denial serve, though? We must ask our self, Why do we deny responsibility? Is it an experience of humility? Or is it one of pride? If it is one of pride, then that is opposite from the faculty of humility. It is pride, the uneducated ego, that registers the soul faculty as humiliation. And you know that pride is like a brass doorknob: it's constantly in need of polishing. It tarnishes at the slightest change of atmospheric conditions. Why does it do that? Because it represents the perfect uneducated ego. Of course, that's why it has to be polished constantly. No one chose glass to represent the uneducated ego, for we all know that we can see through glass. [The] difficulty is seeing through brass. What color does the seeming gold become of brass when it's tarnished? Yes.

Black and gray.

Wouldn't you say there's a little bit of green there?

Yes.

Yes, please.

Is there any . . .

I find an uneducated ego's like green apples. They certainly give you a stomachache in time. Yes, please. *[Many students laugh.]*

When a person loses the weight that the spirit says we're supposed to have [to be] in balance, is that balance related in any way to the balance that we're discussing tonight?

Well, now, first I would like to correct the denial of personal responsibility by saying that someone else says. I recall that our good doctor, at request and solicitation, shared with some of you, who were at that time ignorant of the balance of your forms, physically, and shared that with you. Whether or not one accepts it or denies it, of course, is their own personal choice. But if we want to come into balance, and we all want to come into balance, then, of course, we have to realize the more upset or discord there is in our mind, it reflects, of course, in our body. For example, we find that increase of weight has a great deal to do with the chemistry of the body. Our doctor has spoken on that repeatedly, many times. And to bring about a chemical balance requires a change in the consciousness because the change in the consciousness changes the chemicals of the physical body.

Now there are certain—every body, every mind, every form has so many of these chemicals. A little different in others, but similar. And some people, chemically, will put on more weight more quickly than other people who may consume the same amount and identical food because there's a body chemistry differential, you understand.

Yes.

There is a difference there. Now to bring about an increase in the necessary chemicals, there has to be a change in the consciousness so that those chemicals may be increased. They may be artificially supported because some already exist, only in lesser amounts than at other times. For example, you find that—well, you want to talk about weight—you find that you lose weight and then you find you go through different experiences and you gain weight, only to lose weight again, and back and forth. Well, that's where it is necessary to have an awakening within the mind that there are certain patterns, emotions, that are causing certain chemicals in the physical body to increase, certain hormones to increase and others to decrease, for the emotions have a direct effect upon the chemistry of the body. Does that help with your question?

Yes. Thank you.

You see. So sometimes, you see, a person will artificially take the chemicals that their body needs to get themselves started, but if the change is not made in the emotional patterns that are causing the chemical imbalance in the physical body, then they'll go right back to putting the weight on again because, you see, those chemicals are in short supply in that particular body. Pardon?

Yes. Thank you.

Yes. But that—don't—try to remember, students, that that's no denial of personal responsibility. That's an expression of personal responsibility because we're personally responsible for the house that we're using. And especially, even more responsible, when we are aware, personally aware, of how the chemicals of our body bring about—how our emotions and our emotional reactions bring about a change in the chemistry of our body. It's a chemical balance. Yes.

Thank you very much.

You're welcome. Yes, please.

Can knowledge, then, change the chemistry of the body as emotion?

Application of the awareness of the chemicals that are in short supply in the body, an application of the changing that is necessary that is related to those particular hormones, you understand, of course, definitely it would. But if you are short on certain chemicals in your body, you know, one doesn't say, "Well, I changed my mind," and the chemicals suddenly increase. It doesn't work that way. And so each situation is quite varied. Some will require an artificial input of those chemicals. But to permit the mind to become addicted to them and not manufacture their own, you understand, is extremely detrimental. It's one thing to use a crutch when you have hurt your ankle to walk and to use it for a limited time. And it's something else to use it for the rest of your life. Pardon? Yes.

Yes. Thank you.

Does that help with your question there? Yes, please.

Would that be like using a medication to [help with] illness, could that be likened?

Using a medication for an illness? Certainly, there comes a time when one weans themselves. It's like a person who cannot awaken in the morning unless they have an alarm clock. So what are they going to do on the time when the alarm clock's taken away? What will they do? That's the question one must ask themselves. Yes.

Thank you.

So one uses what is necessary always with the light of reason that it's for a limited time. And works to bring about the necessary changes in their attitude and their patterns of mind and their emotions so that the chemicals, the chemistry of the body is once again brought into balance. Yes.

Now that brings up an important point on healing. Many times students have asked about healing. You see, when a person registers that they are in need of healing or an improvement of their health and they've tried everything—they think they've tried everything—and they turn to something where they believe in God, and they try God. Or they try a healer or something. And they try some[thing]. They must not forget that the restoration of balance in their being is dependent upon their direct connection to the Divine Source of which they are an inseparable part.

Now when a person makes effort to pray or to come into contact with the source of their supply, of which they are an inseparable part, if they look clearly, they will see all of the forms that stand between their soul and the Source, the Divine itself, of which they are an inseparable part. The difficulty for many people with healing is that they believe they are those forms which are, in truth, an expression of the judgments that they believe that they are, that stand, like the hissing hounds of hell, before the gates of victory demanding, *demanding* their payment before the soul can make its contact. Do you understand that?

Yes.

So they must be removed. Now when they are removed, the person's health is restored, you see. And if establishing contact with the Divine Source, if the human being only allows that contact by first satisfying the judgments that wait there, the hounds before the gate of victory, and if that has been their pattern in life, then those hounds will scream very loud for their payment before they will allow a restoration. Yes, I think we've discussed some of those things before, however. Yes. And if one says, "Well, God didn't heal me when I've waited two weeks now and I'm still not healed and I'm still not better," well, they're just feeding those forms of judgments that they've created and those forms have decided you haven't paid enough yet, you see. That's all that is. Yes, that's all it is. That's all it ever was. That's all it ever will be. Yes.

Now you take a person, for example, who gets into a type of thinking, "Well, you know, there's never enough money." That seems to be so important to the uneducated mind. "There's never enough money." Well, when they go to declare their faith in God as the Divine Source, they establish a law to bring all experiences necessary into their life to bring about a balance or restoration of their financial—What would you call it? Picture?—of their financial picture or profile or whatever they call it. But anyway, and so when all of these experiences come into their life in keeping with the divine law that they have declared their faith in God as the source of their supply, they're not taking a look: in order to bring about balance once again, poise or balance in the mind and the fullness of life, they forgot all about humility over here, you see. So when humility brings its varied experiences, in keeping with the law—you see, we always get what we really want. Now if we want money and we demonstrate our faith of the true Source, we'll have money. But we must not deny what comes with money, what comes with faith: humility. So a person says, "Well, there was plenty of money there, but the humiliation that I put myself through to get all this money over here that I asked for was unrealistic. I'd never do it again." Wouldn't you say?

Yes, indeed.

Well, you see. So there is your—you see, I like to look at the application of this Living Light Philosophy. When you ask for something, relate that function that is asking—for, first of all, you're experiencing the need of it by denying the law that brings it about. So when you ask for money, or when you ask for sex, or when you ask for the glory of the ego, don't forget they are directly related to faith, poise, and humility. And faith, poise, and humility have their different registrations in the human mind. Hmm? Does that—yes.

That brings up a question for me.

Yes.

I don't understand why, for example, humility, the corresponding function to humility is procreation.

It is indeed.

Why is that? How does that—

Why is that? You have two functions that serve the human pride. Two.

Yes.

And I think everyone is familiar with them in a world of creation. It's money and it's sex.

Yes.

Now they serve the uneducated ego. They are servants of the uneducated ego. Now what is—you don't understand why procreation or sex, its balance as a faculty is humility? Was that the question?

Right.

Well, I think that you will find in all experiences in reference to that function that the uneducated ego registers that experience, at one time or another and often many times, as humiliation because it does not get its way. For example, you see, those functions establish the Law of Denial. First of all, they declare that they need money for they have denied, they have denied that they are the creators of money. They have first denied that. In other words, they first said, "Well, the money I don't have, someone or something else has it." So, you see, they establish—those functions, money, ego, and sex—ego being the great pride of it—only survive under the Law of Denial.

Yes.

They deny that they are a full person unless they have the secondary function. They deny their survival of their desires unless they have the primary function. Do you understand that?

Hmm...

How many people are living here in the world without money for bread on their table? Are there any hands? I don't see any. You see, it isn't money as something, a word that you—it is the security to the mind. And sex is the security to the emotions.

Yes.

You see, when a person believes that what will make them happy or satisfied is dependent on what someone else does or doesn't do, they have established the Law of Denial.

So it's our attachment to the function, to money or to sex, so—

It is our denial that we cannot be happy without them. That is, that is an expression of the uneducated mind, yes.

And that's when we are, we are not expressing in faith or humility.

We're not expressing in faith, poise, and humility. That is correct.

Yes.

That's when it registers. You see, when we accept personal responsibility, we open up the door to faith, poise, and humility.

Hmm...

You see?

Yes.

Now when we open up the door to faith, poise, and humility and, say, for example, that we're asking the Divine for an increase in supply in the primary function of money.

Yes.

All right? Now we're asking for that. As we do so, we must not deny that that func—that that faculty is a triune faculty. It will call forth, in order to balance it, it will call forth humility. You see?

Yes.

Faith, poise, and humility.

Yes.

So in order to bring that fulfillment about, that Law of Fulfillment, it will call that forth to balance itself.

Yes.

And then we experience the fullness thereof.

Yes. OK.

Did that help with your question?

That does. Thank you.

Yes. And, you see, if we remain in the faculties, you see, as the mental servant of the soul faculty of reason, then we will not register in our mind humiliation.

Yes.

You see?

Yes.

Humiliation is distasteful to the uneducated ego or the imbalanced mind.

Yes.

You see.

Yes.

You see, a person cannot be humiliated unless they first deny. You cannot experience humiliation until you establish the Law of Denial.

Thank you.

The Law of Denial is the Law of Separation. Pardon?

And the Law of Acceptance therefore is, is humility. It's not—
Well, yes, all soul faculties, of course, are under the, under the banner of acceptance, which is the will of God.
All right.
For God does not deny. The blade of grass receives its sustenance as well as the human being. Do you understand?
Yes.
Yes. Such as the lilies of the field. So God is a demonstration of the Divine Law of Total Acceptance and total consideration, you see.
Yes.
The only thing that denies is that which separates itself.
OK.
You see.
Yes.
You see, we cannot deny until we first judge separation. You know, we judge we are separate, different, unique. That's the only time we can deny.
OK.
Does that help?
It does. Thank you very much.
Yes, you're welcome. Certainly. Yes, please.
If we say—is this accepting responsibility, to say that I am the creator of money? Is that accepting responsibility?
Why, certainly. You are crea—you are the creator. Man is the creator. God is the sustainer. That is the law of the Living Light Philosophy as we've expressed for many years to our classes here. This class and many classes. That includes money. See? When we say that man is the creator, God is the sustainer, that is—man did create money. And you are man, as mankind, aren't you?
Right, right.
Well, there you are. See, you create it within your own consciousness. That's where it was created. I've always been one

to go directly to the source. So if I created a dollar, then I go right to the source: myself, for I am the one that creates or do not create it. But when you accept that demonstrable truth, do not forget, in the use of the soul faculty of faith, do not forget the balance is humility. And if your mind is educated at the time you are having your experiences, then you will not have any humiliation and your pride will not suffer. Does that help with your question?

Thank you very much.

Yes, certainly. Yes, please.

You were saying we always get exactly what we want.

No, I didn't say that. I feel rather like that, that soldier, that colonel there that you people have all been so interested [in]. *[The teacher may be referring to Lt. Col. Oliver North, who was in the news at that time.]* I did not say that! *[Many students laugh.]* I said, "We always get what we really want." Now there is a difference there. Do you see the difference between what you said I said and what I really said? Go ahead with your statement.

You always get—

There is a difference. Yes.

—what you really want.

That's what I said. Remember? *[The teacher addresses another student by name.]*

Yes, sir.

Yes.

All right.

We always get what we really want. That is true, yes.

What would cause a mind to, to think, to have an experience of having a desire, really wanting something, thinking it wanted something and then not getting it?

Well, not getting it when we, when we judge we should get it, is that what you're saying?

Right.

No problem. No problem at all. We have yet to graciously accept the payment that stands in front of it. *[The teacher laughs joyously.]*

To get what you really want?

Yes. Ofttimes a person says, "Now that's what I want." They're very determined about what they want, and they have faith that they're going to get it. And then all of the experiences start coming along, you say, "Oh, no. No, no. That's not my fault. I want nothing to do with that." Do you understand?

Yes.

It's too humiliating to the uneducated ego. Yes, that's what we've been discussing. Hmm?

Yes.

You see, the longer that we refuse, that we refuse to accept responsibility for the experiences in our lives, the more patience we had best have. For we always get what we really want, but sometimes we want something when we're 20 and it arrives when we're 70. That's how long we've refused to accept responsibility for it. Yes.

When you were speaking of healing, you said that the forms that are created stand between us and the Divine Source.

Our belief that we are those forms that we have created that stand between us [and the Divine Source], yes.

OK. And in that you said that—I wanted, I just wanted to know if this is what you said, is all. That you said that if we— were you saying that if we just go to the Divine Source when we are in need in the time, the greatest times, then those things rise up very strong at those times?

Why, certainly. Because, you see, you are going to receive something that you haven't paid them for. They're not about to not have their payment when they're used to getting their payment all the time. I mean, after all, each time the pride takes credit for some good in one's life and then that feeds those judgment forms that one has made. And then there comes a time, a great crisis in a person's life, and they do not bring to them, you understand, when they want it, what they want (the person), those forms they believe they are, don't bring it to them. Then they turn to something else. Well, you're going to an enemy of those forms, you see. You're going directly to the Source. You're going to that which sustains those forms. They're going to get paid first, as long as you believe that they're you. Yes.

So had one spent more time in going to the Source when not in the crisis, then it wouldn't be as difficult.

That is correct. That is correct. And one must not allow themselves the luxury of feeling badly because they didn't do so; otherwise, they just have more forms and more payments to make. You know, it's a new beginning. See, each moment is a new beginning because each moment one can change their mind, you see. And I find many people change their mind quite frequently. Well, of course, it depends. But it's nice if they know that it is their mind that is being changed. And not something that has convinced them that they are their mind, you see. Yes. Oh, yes. Yes.

How does humbleness fit into humility and humiliation?

And humiliation? Well, first of all, a humble person is one who is expressing the soul faculty of humility. Now a humble person does not react. They weigh out the experience that they're having. [A person] goes to the soul faculty of reason, their soul faculty of reason, and returns to their mind. And they make an intelligent choice. "This is the expression of this person. This understanding is taking place in my mind. I am responsible for my understanding of this person's actions." And they act in a light of reason. That takes humbleness, a servant of humility.

Now if a person at that moment, their ego is not educated at that time—because, you see, it doesn't mean that a person educates their ego and that's it; they never again express an uneducated ego. No, no, no, no. A person, at times, expresses an educated or balanced ego or balanced mind. Then, at times, they don't. So there's this fluctuation, don't you see, in the evolution of the being. And so if a person at the time of the experience has only 20 percent of their mind illumined in reference to educating their ego, then they can only get 20 percent sent up to the faculty of reason inside of themselves and can only get 20 percent back. Can't get back more than what one puts in, you know. And so if they got 5 percent educated, they get 5 percent worth, you see. Yes.

It takes 51 percent in the consciousness to make the change, of course. And so a person says, "I knew better than to do that. I did know better. I did have a flash. A flash across my mind." Well, the person's ego may have been 6 percent educated at the time of the experience. And so the flash registers as a flash, and 6 percent of reason flashed by, you see. So quickly, you see. I do hope that's helped with your question.

You know, I've heard some of my students say, "Well, I had a flash. I knew better." And I say, "Well, how long did the flash last? *[Many students laugh.]* Was it a 10-second flash? A 5-second? A 2-minute? Maybe a 6-minute?" "No, no, no, no. Just a flash. It just went swoosh!" But they knew better, but they did it anyway.

Well, you see, this is what this school is all about: to understand how that works. If you have a 5-second flash and you didn't do anything about it, but you knew better, then you can understand inside of yourself how educated your ego or balanced your mind [was] at the time of the experience, you see. Hmm? And how much glory the pride got out of it after, when it said, "Well, I knew better, but I did it anyway." Well, that certainly is not a servant of the soul faculty of humility, but it has a lot to do, I would say, with the thrill of an uneducated, imbalanced mind and an uneducated ego who thought it was just great that they had a flash and did their thing anyway, you see, even though they knew better. Yes. But it's an early step, of course. It's an early step, yes. Yes.

Is my understanding—

An early step.

—correct in this: the longer we fuse—we refuse to accept personal responsibility for that which we created . . .

Yes, and the—of course, you have the awareness and the experience. I've yet to find a person that's not aware of experience, especially their own. Yes?

I missed the rest of it. Is it the longer it takes for—was it the fulfillment of one's desires?

Why, certainly. But don't worry, you'll receive the tape. It is recording, isn't it, over there? *[The teacher addresses the technician recording this class.]*

Yes, sir.

Well, that's fine. Yes.

Thanks.

Yes. Yes, please.

So would responsibility be the triune faculties of humility and faith and poise—faith, poise, and humility?

But you cannot express faith, poise, and humility, you can't express faith without humility, or humility without faith. And they both bring you poise. Pardon?

So that's the responsibility involved in . . .

Why, certainly. Absolutely. Definitely. You see, a person wants something real bad, and it comes close to them and fizzles. Comes close again and it fizzles. Then you say, "Why doesn't it get together? What's happening here?" Well, what's happening is quite clear: the acceptance, the acceptance of personal responsibility [is missing]. And the sooner that's accepted, the sooner the bonfire gets lit and everyone's moving! Hopefully to something better. Yes. *[The teacher laughs.]*

What causes the fear?

Fear?

I'm sorry. [Perhaps the student apologizes to the teacher for speaking before raising her hand.]

Well, fear is an instrument, as we all know, of our judgments. Our judgments are the servants of our pride. Hmm? Certainly, certainly. If your judgments don't want to do something in facing personal responsibility, why, certainly, we've discussed that before, haven't we? They use fear. What is fear? Hmm? The mind's control over the eternal being. That's all it is.

Thank you.

Certainly. Absolutely. We fear we won't have enough money. We fear we won't have enough happiness. We fear we won't have this. Why? Because, you see, the whole thing is started by our judgments. And we start that with the ribbon of comparison. Study your tapes that you've received and your class notes. My, you have all of that. Hmm? Study and apply them to daily, *daily* experience. Hmm. *[After a short pause, the teacher continues speaking with the student who asked about fear.]*

Do you fear your hair might be gray when you sing?

When I what?

Do you fear that your hair might be gray when you sing the way you want to sing? *[The teacher repeats his question and speaks more loudly.]* Pardon?

I don't think so.

Good. Then you have no problem with the wisdom of patience. Don't misunder—misinterpret what I've said. I did not say that your hair will have to be gray or snow white before you sing and get what you want. But you [have] got to remember, when you want something badly, then be gracious in paying the price that stands before what you want. Hmm. Yes? *[The teacher and many students laugh.]*

[After a noticeable pause, the teacher continues.] When you hear your taped classes, one must wonder, perhaps, what you'll do during the long pauses. Yes.

When things, after a severe and lengthy struggle within you, start feeling good again, is that a sign of adapting or acceptance?

When there is a change in your experiences for the better?

When the—yes, in your thinking and just in how you feel. Nothing's happening differently. Why, I guess it's a change in experiences, of course.

Well, for example, a person sometimes, and many times, they find a situation that they're in intolerable.

Yes.

And if it's intolerable enough and they find they cannot remove their physical body from the situation and then changes start taking place in their mind and they realize that their mind can be wherever they choose it to be, and their physical body can be where they choose it to be. And that's one of the ways of changes, of course. It is an early stage of detachment from the physical form. You know, one might say, well, they're in an intolerable situation, and they just can't bear it anymore. And the next thing that happens to the mind, they dream they're on the beach at Waikiki or something that they like. And yes, I find that a very common practice in your world. In relationships and marriages, it seems to be quite common, yes.

Thank you.

You're welcome.

Yes, I know. Thank you. *[The teacher acknowledges the signal from the technician recording the class.]* Yes, please.

When I have an experience that allows or I allow my pride to well up and take responsibility for having had a, say, positive experience . . .

Yes?

Because I'm either not vigilant or I haven't—I don't have the proper state of mind so that the pride does well up. Is, after having experienced the pride, is there something I can do to, to counter the . . .

Effects of that law established?

The law I established?

Why, certainly. You can establish a counteracting law, equal in energy, which will neutralize it. Because the payment of pride is quite an expensive luxury, yes.

How, how would I do that?

Well, first of all, you've already started on the first step by recognizing that you did it. Most people don't even recognize they've done it, you see. And after the payment comes, then they're even more determined it was someone else's fault (the experience). Yes. First of all, you've made the first step by recognizing that the pride welled up, and you took full credit with the mind, you see. So [if] you want to neutralize that, that law, then you become consciously aware of exactly what you did—do you understand that?—and then you declare the truth: that you are an instrument sustained by a Divine Intelligence of impartial law, that anyone in the same situation and law as yourself would have received the same experiences by the same laws being demonstrated. Does that help with your question?

Yes. Thank you.

Yes. And so then, if you pour in equal energy—you know, it's just like the move of our little school here. And I explained to some of my students here just the other day. The time, which is the Law of Creation, for that is an illusion created by creation. It's an illusion. Time is dictated in creation by the domain of creation. As I said to some of my students, as much emotional energy as has gone out this last six months plus to not letting go of what they judge as their security must go into letting go and being ready to go, in emotions, in order to neutralize the law that has been set into motion. Do you understand that? So, you see, it's the same thing.

So here we are, here at this temple, in a process of bringing about balance, which is neutralization, you see, of the Law of Fear of many of the students of what they're going to do. Do you understand? And as soon as the law of ready to go emotionally and equal energy is put into [that as] the one of fear of what they're going to do or have to let go of—when that's balanced out, you see—then the Law of Harmony will flow unobstructed. And we'll all be in class in the north. Hmm? For the law is completely impartial.

You see, what we must understand: that there are several people making a change. Do you understand? There's not just one person or two persons or three. There are several people, you see. And so the growth process for each individual varies. You understand? So one cannot question, you know, "When will this happen?" "When will that happen?" because one can only ask oneself, "When will I balance out this negative law of not letting go or making the change?" And when that happens and it's balanced out, then you have the Law of Harmony and all obstructions are removed. When you are a part of a group of people and that which is happening affects the entire group, then you have a group consciousness of all of them to be considered. Not just one or two individuals. Yes.

It's like a company. You know, if a company decides it's going to move back East and they're going to close the present company where you were, then it affects every single employee in it, doesn't it? It not only affects them. It affects their families. It affects their relatives. It affects their so-called friends and associates. Do you understand that?

And so here, fifteen or so people, you're not talking about just fifteen people. You're talking about their relatives, their friends, their relationships, and all that they know. Do you understand? Of course. And if you look at it from that perspective, then you will understand how far we have really come in making this move in such a short six months or so. *[The teacher laughs joyously.]*

You know, it's like a person that says—a lady goes [and] she shows herself to her friends and tells them, "You know, I've lost five pounds of weight." And a lady says, "Oh, that's just wonderful. I'm so happy for you." And then take you out to a huge dinner with plenty of desserts. She's so happy for [you]. *[Many students laugh.]* You see, it's the same kind of thing, you know. Like a person says, "Oh, I'm so happy you're moving to the country." And at the time they're saying that, their mind is going, "Well, what have they done? How come that they get to go and move. And look at me, stuck here." And all that foolishness, you see. But they don't speak it, you see. They don't speak it. But it's the same, you know, as, as someone gets a new car and shows all of their friends [and they] say, "Oh, that's so wonderful. I'm so happy to see that," and everything. And then the next thing you know, it's got a great big scratch on it. And you wondered where it came from. *[The teacher laughs.]* Well, that's just the minds of ignorance, you know, that do those kind of things. But it happens. In your world it happens all the time. All the time, yes. Yes.

To the extent that the energy is balanced through the expression of faith and humility, poise is expressed.

That's when a person becomes poised. You see, a poised mind is an illumined mind, an educated mind, an awakened mind. And it is poise that's the servant of the soul faculty of reason, you see. That's where the transformation takes place. Yes. A balanced mind is a poised mind. Yes. Hmm? When your humility equals your faith and your faith equals your humility, you're in poise, yes, and you are transformed or transfigured, yes.

Thank you.

Of course, also at those moments, you must realize, you're not attached in consciousness. You just are. Yes.

Would that be the same as saying be neither up or down, just sort of be . . .

Yes, detached. Detached. Detached, of course, does not free oneself from responsibility for what they are responsible. Yes.

[After a long pause, the teacher continues.] Perhaps, *[The teacher calls upon a specific student.]* you would like to share with us your experiences on comparison during this silent time.

When you were discussing with the other student how the mind, the ribbon of comparison and . . .

What did you just write?

I, I wrote down, "I can't compare if I'm not separate."

That's why I thought we might like to discuss that, you know. It isn't too private, is it?

No.

I think [the student next to you] can look and see what I saw. Yes.

So if you're . . .

With the peripheral—peripheral vision, don't they call it? Yes, please go ahead.

So if you feel separate, if you separated yourself from the whole . . .

Yes?

And, I mean, if you haven't separated yourself from the whole, but if you accept that, you know, you're part of the Divine Intelligence and there is no separation, then there's nothing to compare with the mind.

Yes, but that's not what I see that you wrote.

Well, I wrote down "I'm not separate." I am a part of the whole.

Yes, that's what you wrote down.

Yes.

How do you feel?

Good.

That's very good. I'm glad that you feel good. That's why I asked you that question. Very good.

Thank you.

Yes. Don't you think you paid plenty for that?

Yes, I just wanted to make sure that I—

That's why you wrote it down. I'm very happy for you. Very happy for you. I'm happy for all of my students who make special notes of the things that cost them so much in their lives.

Yes.

Yes. So they don't have to waste and not experience need, you see. Hmm? *[After another very long pause, the teacher continues.]* Yes, the floor is still open for question. Perhaps we have too many classes, and there aren't enough questions of the students to sustain such frequency of classes. Perhaps we should reduce our frequency of classes. Yes.

Sometimes when I feel that I'm in a, a balanced mind, I am very easily upset into, by recognition of that balance by, by another person into a state of mind where, of embarrassment, almost.

Oh, because you're not paying attention to them?

Paying attention to?

Well, the one who observes that you're balanced.

No, after being recognized.

After being recognized, you feel embarrassed?

Yes.

Well, do you feel, first of all, do you feel that you've somehow offended them?

Not offended, no. I think more . . .

It's very important, you know, that the mind understand why it feels that way.

It's, I think, in part, because I, I don't think that I have a judgment, perhaps, against being balanced. That it is a, in spite of, in spite of my desire to be in a balanced state there's, there's always a judgment that says that it is, there's something not right about it. And I think that causes embarrassment.

I see. That's very important. I know, because you're not alone in that type of thinking. But then we must look at Nature herself to see whether or not it's in balance. Hmm? And to see what the mind has done with nature's balance. Wouldn't you say? Has it brought about harmony in the world in considering all creatures upon the planet?

I'm sorry. I don't understand.

Has man's effort to bring changes in nature's balance brought about harmony on your planet and in consideration of the harmony and balance of all creatures upon the planet?

No.

I think you have your answer. I certainly wouldn't feel badly that someone recognized the possibility that I had moments of a balanced mind. I would feel very good about it, myself. I like to feel that I have a balanced mind. Hmm? A balanced mind, as I have said, is an educated ego. It is a servant of the soul faculty of reason. And it takes effort to bring about a balanced mind because not many minds want to pay for what they desire. Pardon? Yes. So the only embarrassment therefore could be the judgment that you have that a balanced mind is not the thing to have. Hmm? Have you ever met anyone that you have judged has a balanced mind?

Yes.

Did you find them attractive to communicate with?

Yes. The, the feeling of peace surrounding a person in that state is, is very attractive.

I see. Then you must understand you have a problem with an educated conscience, and it's known as guilt. You don't feel that you have a right to have that experience considering other factors of your mind. Do you understand that?

Yes.

Well, isn't that ridiculous. It's such a destructive force (guilt) based upon [an] educated conscience, isn't it? You see, you see, for a person not to feel inside themselves—you see, "O man, think humble yet well of thyself"—for a person to think that they don't deserve this and they don't deserve that, for a person to think that they're not a good person, is a person who is in a process of self-destruction. Hmm? And I know very well you don't want anything like that. You see? You see, it comes from a type of thinking that one must have no temptations of the mind, one must not have any type of emotional expression, and, well, is, in truth, a glorified walking zombie. *[Many students laugh.]* Pardon? That's not the Living Light Philosophy for which I am responsible. *[The teacher laughs joyously.]*

Use it, don't abuse it. And enjoy the goodness of life for it's ever up to ourselves and our own mind. Thank you and good night.

JULY 9, 1987

A/V Seminar 24

Good evening, class.

Know what you want, for it is easy to attain. Frustration is an unpleasant experience in the mind, the effect of a judgment that what we depend upon we cannot control. And so once realizing and awakening to whatever it is we have chosen to depend upon and cannot control, then wisdom reveals that we change our dependence, the effect of which, of course, is a freedom from dependence.

For that which disturbs us, of course, controls us. But what is that control and that disturbance? It is the bondage of the error of ignorance of our own dependence. The best way, and the only way that works, is for one to face their temptations, for the temptations, once faced, reveal, of course, one's own dependence.

There is no limit to the things that the mind can and does choose to be dependent upon. Each time a person realizes and accepts that the true cause of their frustrations in life is an error in their own thinking, a dependence and a bondage, each time that is realized and accepted, one makes another step onward and upward on the path of freedom.

Now we have a few moments at this time for questions on this subject matter. Yes.

Sir, how can we convert our dependence from the temporary things that we normally do to God, the infinite, divine Source?

Whenever that effort is made by the mind, then what happens [is] a person becomes more frustrated, for they take a look, the mind does, at what it has, and it judges that an option of giving it up is accepting something that is not guaranteed. So, of course, that takes an act of faith, that takes a step in evolution. It is—the best process is the process that is taking place: the realization that disturbance and frustration is an effect of a judgment. So a person, once realizing what judgment the mind has made that has placed them in a situation of dependence upon anything or anyone that they cannot control, each time they realize that that is the true cause of their unpleasant, so to speak, experiences, they make an adjustment to another judgment. In time they realize in evolution that no matter what judgment that they make, it is the step of dependence and bondage.

Now to tell a person not to make a judgment is one thing; to experience the necessary things for the person to realize that judgments move us from one step of bondage on to the next [is movement along the path]. So a person makes effort to broaden their horizons. For example, a person may have had the experiences that they are very frustrated from an error in their thinking of a judgment of attachment to another person. In time, they can broaden that to their dependence upon the air they breathe. Now many people have judgments on the air they breathe. "It's, it's too cold. It's too hot. It's not this. It's not that." However, it is a broader perspective. So it's a matter of moving along the evolutionary path to a broadening of the judgments for no one suddenly stops and says, "I will judge no more," not as long as they believe they are the limit of the form in which they presently reside. Yes, go right ahead.

Well, how can we move to the next step then? In other words—

Well, facing—moving to the next step, yes. Well, for example, a person realizes that this person, they've been dependent upon, and so they move that person out of their life, correct?

Yes, sir.

And perhaps a few weeks or hours or months, or perhaps even years pass and they move to the next person. And so repetition of those experiences is the law through which change is made possible. Finally, they realize that it is not such a valuable situation to be in. In other words, by facing the temptation— you understand that—of the dependence, by facing it and resisting it—do you understand?

Yes.

One gradually broadens their perspective, you understand?

Yes.

And, in so doing, is finally freed from the condition. Now remember that also falls into the teaching that you've already received: do not be a reformer, for a reformer is one who expresses the suppression of their own judgments. Do you understand?

Yes, sir.

You see, they suppress that, you see, instead of expressing it and revealing it for what it truly is. Yes.

I see. So there's no way we can go from point A of a limited judgment to the end result of total faith in God—

Oh, no.

And not going through all of this, the other seeming—

No, no. Because, you see, even to attempt to do such a thing is simply to suppress it. And in so doing whatever we suppress, you see, we strengthen, and we weaken our resistance to it. So suppression is, indeed, a very, very dangerous path to follow. For example, it's like putting a person who has not awakened to the condition of their frustrations into a monastery and not having them face their own weaknesses and the various things they have to work on: to do so only weakens the person for it strengthens the things that their minds have depended upon. Yes.

So there's no, there's no shortcut.

There's, well, there's, there's no quick—what do you call it?—quick fix. No, there's no quick fix that is really a fix. No, no, it does not exist. Yes, it's a tempting thing to the mind, but it does not exist. Yes.

Thank you.

You're welcome. Yes.

How can we discern whether or not, in facing our own temptations, that we're facing them in the light of reason or just suppressing them?

Well, yes. *[The teacher laughs joyously.]* That's a very—you can tell from the experiences that you have. Especially after you have faced them. In your effort to resist, if you feel so proud that you have managed another moment and you permit your pride to take all the glory for the effort, then it's quite evident from the demonstration that you have suppressed it. Yes.

Thank you.

And it's waiting for you just around the corner. Pardon?

Yes, sir. Thank you.

Yes. Yes.

Let's say that one is dependent on the judgment that, that others or situations are the cause of his problems. He's not taking personal responsibility. And he goes from one judgment to the next. Step-by-step he blames this one, then that one. How does he ever get free from all that? Does he have to suffer through all those experiences?

Well, of course, when the experiences are sufficient for the individual, whoever they may be, when the unpleasant experiences have reached the saturation point, so to speak, for that particular person, then they begin to realize and to awaken: there has to be a better way. Now when the mind says to itself, "There has to be a better way," it steps upon the path to find a better way. Does that help with your question?

Yes.

Yes, certainly. Now I don't want my students to think that just because only men have been asking questions here that the women students have no dependencies. Yes. *[Some of the women students laugh.]* Perhaps they realize that they indeed are dependent and are rather weary of it. Yes.

Well, I was just going to ask about weary, the word weariness, which seems to go hand in hand with frustration, at least from a—

Yes, indeed, it is, because it is part of the process of the realization in one's own mind that they are dependent on what they have judged, finally judged, they cannot control. For example, take—now you have to understand how that process works.

A person finds themselves tempted, all right? Well, they are tempted to what? They are tempted to whatever they judge will bring to them something that they desire at the moment. Do you understand that? All right. So here they're faced with the temptation. If they do not fulfill that in their mind and in their experiences and they become frustrated—correct?—which the degree of frustration reveals how dependent in their mind they have become upon what they judge will bring them this goodness that they seek. Now the real unpleasant experience, of course, is when the mind realizes that it cannot control what it has permitted itself to be tempted to, do you understand? And that's when you really start the growth process of awakening. Yes.

So actually, the weariness is actually very positive.

Oh, indeed it is. Why, certainly. If a person gets weary of anything, in time they will let it go, you see? They will let it go for the mind will say to itself—you see, their survival is at stake. You see? That basic instinct of survival. The mind will say to itself, "I'm tired of this same old story." That's when you get the experience of weariness. Now if you have a sufficient amount of that, for your own mind, you will, in your mind you will say, "No, there has to be something better." You see, so weariness, in that respect, is a very positive sign, for you are moving closer to making another judgment to free you from the judgment that has caused the dependence, and the final effects are a weariness. Does that help?

Yes.

You see? So even though to the mind ofttimes a person says, "Well, this is a negative experience," the weariness, if you understand it, for what is taking place in the mind, you will see from a broader perspective that it's a very positive step. It is a step before making a change of a judgment that the mind has depended upon. Yes.

And you're actually going to go into another judgment that is going to be like a step up from—

You'll find it's broader than the last one. You know, the human mind is very inventive that way. Oh, yes, indeed it is. It will at least be a broader perspective. It will, yes. Yes, it will be a broader horizon of the next judgment. And the next one. And the next one. Yes. Yes, please. Thank you.

Making that, making that step up into a broader judgment...

Yes?

Is one automatically freed from a step backwards into—

No.

—the prior level so that we, in other words, in an environment where the other prior levels and judgments are still being expressed, can we be tripped back into that level?

The divorces in society reveal that it is an ever-waiting temptation. And ofttimes people go backwards. Yes, that is true. And it's fine when one goes one step backwards and two steps forwards, but sometimes they go two steps back and one step forward. So a person must be vigilant and remind themselves. You see, one thing about the human mind: it does not want to look at a past experience where it has judged it was the innocent victim. We all understand that, don't we? Pardon?

No.

No. Well, let me put it in another way then. A person—usually, most people do not want to look back at an experience where their mind judges that they were so foolish. They don't want to look at that. Would you understand it that way? Pardon?

Yes, I do. Thank you.

Yes. And so because of that, you see, the person is easily tempted and, in reference to your question, can ofttimes take one step forward and two steps backwards. Because, you see, an unpleasant experience does not mean that it is negative and is not beneficial, for in every negative, there's a positive. And in every positive, there is a negative, you see.

Yes.

And so a person, a student of the Light should not permit themselves not to look at a past experience and take the positive that is contained in the experience as a coat of armor for the future temptations which would place them right back where they were. For, you see, that would be two steps backwards. Do you understand that?

Yes, I do.

Yes. And so when looking at a past experience in an effort to change and evolve that way, one cannot afford the luxury of looking at the experience with the emotions.

Yes.

Only with the faculty of reason, in order to take from that experience the benefit that they have already paid for. Do you understand?

Yes.

You see, you see, you haven't paid the price of the experience. And having made the judgment to evolve and to keep oneself free from it, then one must look at it, you see, objectively in the light of reason, for that's their coat of armor in not being so weakened inside of themselves to go back to it. Pardon?

Thank you.

Yes. And, of course, all reformers are suppressers, you know. So one doesn't suppress something. May God free us from the reformers. That help with your question?

Yes. Thank you.

Yes. And [another student] is waiting.

Yes. Thank you.

Yes.

At the beginning it says know what you want for it is easy to obtain.

Oh, indeed. Of course. Yes, I think you can understand that. Yes, go ahead.

Yes. And then it talks about our judgments and the identification with them is what causes the obstructions to what we, at least, judge at that time is what we want.

For we permit the fulfillment of our judgment to be dependent on that which is not within the divine law for us to control. Pardon?

OK.

You see, you see, we direct our dependence for its fulfillment on something beyond our own individual divine right of control.

Right.

Did that help with your question? You see, whatever it—decide what you want for it is easy to attain. That's what I said, isn't it?

Yes, yes.

I didn't say, judge whatever you want for it's easy to control or get. No.

Right.

Decide what you want for it is easy to attain. What makes it so easy? *[After a short pause, the teacher continues.]* What makes it—

Acceptance?

It takes more than acceptance. Acceptance—

Personal responsibility.

There! There's your answer. That it is waiting for you inside of your universe. Now you have to be sure to keep your universe clean. You can't have all kinds of people in it that you're dependent upon.

Right.

For then it is not—you're not going to attain—what it is, is not going to be easy to attain whatever it is you want to attain. You see?

Yes.

Does that help with your question?

Yes, it does.

Yes, now [another student] has a question, please.

Yes, sir. What is it that, what is it that makes a judgment beyond our control? I mean, once—what is it that makes a judgment beyond our control? I mean, in other words, we're, we're set out to accomplish something based on a judgment.

Yes.

And, and, and we're not, to my understanding, we're not in control of the judgment or the situation that's going to manifest.

Is it dependent on something outside of you?

Is it dependent on something outside of me?

Yes. The fulfillment of your judgment. Is it dependent on what someone else must do? The fulfillment. Is the fulfillment of your judgment dependent upon what someone else must do?

OK. [The student speaks very quietly.]

Pardon?

I, I will write—I will write that down.

Yes, because if it is, then you are in bondage.

And that takes away—that takes it out of our control.

Why, certainly. Because it's now in her control or his control or someone else's control. And that's contrary to the divine Law of Personal Responsibility. You see? You see, now if you have a desire to attain something, then you must keep that working within your consciousness. Say, for example, you make a judgment and that judgment, if you take a look at it, is dependent upon what that person's going to do or several other people. Usually involves a few thousand people, the fulfillment of one judgment usually involves a few thousand people.

Now if you take a look at the judgment and say, "Well, in order for this to be fulfilled, look at all of these people that have got to do what I want them to do in order that I can fulfill this judgment that I believe that I am!" Not only that you've got this judgment now dependent on many people out there and what they will or won't do at any given moment, you also have all the other judgments that have been fighting in your mind for their fulfillment. So say that you judge you'd like a new car, for example. Pardon?

Yes.

All right. Now the moment that you judge you want a new car and you justify that you need it and you also justify everything else that's necessary in order for your mind to accept that you're going to work in that direction, you have all these other judgments that rise up in your own mind immediately [and] say, "Just a moment. I've been waiting a lot longer than you have to get what I want!" And they go to work and fight each other. And you have these distasteful emotional experiences. Do you understand?

Yes, sir.

You see? Now that's enough to contend with, but to even add more fuel to the fire, the judgment says, "Well, so-and-so will have to do that and that and that and that and that." It's a seeming miracle that anything gets accomplished, isn't it?

It is.

Yes. You're welcome.

Thank you.

Now, yes, [another student] has a question, please.

Yes. In praying for the removal of the obstructions between the goodness that you desire and the self, does, does that help— No. I'm asking the wrong way. I have been praying for that and found myself in a raging fury, almost, today. Could that have some of the judgments fighting me over that, or would that be something other than that?

Well, as you stated, in praying for the removal of an obstruction that stands in the way of something that you desire—

Yes.

You have to understand that in that act, you have accepted that you've placed those obstructions there.

Yes.

Now those obstructions, of course, only reveal the judgments that have been made by one's mind.

Yes.

And so, of course, they rise up. They are not going to be easily annihilated. And if one believes that they are that which they have created, then, of course, it would cause a great disturbance for anyone. Does that help with your question?

Yes. Thank you.

Yes, certainly. And so how does one free themselves from such a distasteful experience? By declaring the truth: "I am that I am. I am not that which I have created. I am only responsible for what I have created." Yes.

Thank you. I forgot that. Thank you.

Yes, certainly. Someone else here had a question. Yes, please.

Yes. I have a question about suppression.

Yes.

I'm trying to understand it. Because with the knowledge that we're given and the guidance and wisdom that we're given, to look at our dependencies with the light of reason, it seems like sometimes I'm suppressing my desires.

Yes?

Because I—maybe it's a judgment, you know. I think I'm using the light of reason, but possibly the judgment I'm making that if I do this, I will pay a certain price. And then it seems to sneak—the price really seems to sneak up on me, somewhere, because I've actually suppressed.

Yes, indeed. Well, the suppression reveals a lack of communication. Now a lack of communication is the effect of a lack of understanding. You see, exposure is what is necessary. Without exposure, there is no communication. And without communication, there is no understanding.

Yes.

And so to free oneself from the effects of suppression, one should make greater effort to communicate and to bring it out in the light of day.

Yes.

You see. However, that's difficult for the mind that wishes to cherish and to nurse its judgments, isn't it?

Yes.

However, it's much more destructive and detrimental to suppress it.

Yes.

Hmm?

So when you say communicate, do you mean communicate with them?

Oh, definitely. First, communicate with oneself in order to gain objectivity. "This is what I've created. It is not what I am."

Yes.

You know, you bring yourself into a state of consciousness where you're freed from the water center and from the emotions.

Yes.

You accept it is what you have created (the judgments). Do you understand?

Yes.

And the dependencies. You accept that.

Yes.

That separates you. Then from that effort of acceptance, it helps to free you from the water center of emotion. After having done that, through communication within one's own consciousness, then they communicate with the person that they have permitted their mind to judge that they are dependent upon. And one is freed from suppression.

Yes. OK.

It's not as difficult as it may seem.

Yes.

Yes.

Once you're unobstructed.

Pardon?

Once the obstruction is removed, then the expression just flows through.

It most certainly does. The only thing that is causing the suppression is the fear that someone one is dependent upon will judge that they are not the image they've tried to present. Does that help?

Yes.

You see? So really what is at stake is what is known as pride, isn't it?

Yes.

Pride cannot flow—Honesty cannot flow where there is pride.

Yes.

You see?

Yes.

The two cannot exist. No, not together. No. No, no, no. Yet honesty will free us. Hmm?

Yes.

Yes.

OK. Can I ask another?

Certainly.

OK. It seems that one—in one class it was said that it's better to be dependent on something you can control.

That's true.

As opposed to something you can't.

Absolutely!

And I took that to mean it's better to be dependent on an inanimate object rather than a person.

Well, sometimes inanimate objects, you know, they are subject to many bruises and warfares. It's better to depend on something in the mind that you, you can—it's more malleable. Do they call it malleable? I think in your world people love things malleable. You know, they can—you see, that means controllable.

Well, if you create something in your mind. Maybe you've created it and you've colored it pink and the next day you decide, "No, I like blue." So you paint it again and it is now blue. That's something you can control—right?—because it's inside your own consciousness.

Yes.

And you've kept it there.

Yes.

Now the moment you put it out there, then it's subject to all the battle scars that creation has to offer, correct?

Yes.

Yes. So it depends on where you keep it. Hmm?

OK.

If you judge, you see—what is the purpose for putting it out there? Well, putting it out there so someone else can see it, correct?

Yes.

And why does a person need the support of their judgment by putting it out there on display? Isn't that the question?

Hmm.

Pardon?

OK.

Because, you see, that means that one feels a bit insecure.

Yes.

Hmm?

Yes.

In other words, they think it's very, very good. Right?

Yes.

You know, you create something and you say, "Now this is really something special."

Yes.

"I must be a genius. It's so special!" Correct? After a time, though, that thought and that judgment that "this is really something special" requires someone else to tell them that. Is that true?

Yes.

And after the second person is told, then the next thing you know a third person has to agree. Isn't it correct? Then a fourth. Then four thousand, four million, and on down the list.

Yes.

And a person really becomes frustrated, don't they?

Oh, yes.

Ofttimes an artist is very frustrated and very negative and very discouraged. He listened too much to what others judged and became dependent on what they judge.

Hmm.

Pardon?

Yes.

You see? That's when inspiration turns to perspiration.

Yes.

Yes.

I see.

Does that help with your question? Hmm?

Yes. Thank you very much.

When one gives what they have to give in life, cares less what the world does with it, then one is freed from all of that.

Hmm.

You see? You see, the goodness is in the act of the doing within the consciousness. You see. Now anything beyond that point is subject to the duality of old creation. The goodness is in the moment of the inspiration within the consciousness. The moment it's released, it's in a dual law.

Yes.

Pardon?

Right.

Yes. Does that help you?

Yes.

You see? However, one can certainly benefit by saying, "This is what I have to give. I care less what the world does with it." You see?

Yes.

You cannot afford the luxury of the attachment of how someone else thinks about your efforts in life. Do you understand that?

Yes.

Because if you do, it will cast a dark shadow upon your inspiration in life.

Right.

For so many inspired souls long, long ago, [who] left your world were almost, mentally, completely destroyed by what others thought of their inspiration.

Yes.

Pardon?

Right.

Yes.

Thank you very much.

You're welcome. Yes, please.

When you have that experience of thinking that this is something special, really special, you have a good feeling about it, what happens that makes you have to go out to show it to someone else to get, for them to think that it's special too?

Oh, yes. Pride. Pride does not only ask, pride demands. Demands that you show it. Pride demands it. Yes.

Well, why does the feeling that it's special fade and make you want to do that, to go out—

Pride steps in.

Oh, I see. That's when—

When pride steps in, the good feelings start to go.

OK.

You see? That which flows from the eternal river of life is suddenly dammed up by the uneducated ego, and it loses its beauty and harmony. Yes. It's only the uneducated ego, an error of ignorance, that does that. It steals it for a time and has to pay the price of the theft. Yes.

So is there a way if you start losing that feeling and realize that pride is stepping in, how do you—

You don't have to worry about realizing if pride is stepping in; you'll have all of the experiences necessary and all of the negativity that the world has to offer. Yes.

Well, well, how do you—I mean, if you see that that's happening, you say, "OK, pride is stepping in," what can you do to cause it to stop so that you don't—

You have to stop. You have to stop yourself, your consciousness. You have to stop and pay the price. The secrets of the universe and the goodness of life are not given to blabbermouths. Hmm? Yes, please.

Yes, then how does one go through the—when someone, when you're inspired to do something and then fear rises knowing, the educated ego, knowing that pride is, like, waiting there, how does one get through that, that, even that initial obstruction to get through the fear or the pride taking it?

You don't have to worry about any fear or the pride. It's guaranteed. That's where guarantees are. Guarantees are in the world of creation. Warranties and guarantees are in the world of creation. Now it seems here we're getting into too much theory. Can't seem to relate to practical experiences. Now I'll have you relate to a few practical experiences here. Going off on these clouds of theory you know; let's get practical and right down to earth here. Now, for example, let's take my channel and his experiences. He has plenty of them and some of them you're familiar with or aware of, not all of them by far. Well, it was just here the other day. He spends ten years of his earth life trying to get grass to grow out here on this lawn out, out here. Ten years of his earth life here at this temple, all right?

Right.

Well, now one may say, "Well, what is ten years of trying to get grass [to] grow in sandstone?" Well, if you ask the human mind, it says, "Well, it costs us all this money for water. And it costs us money for fertilizer and it's cost all this money for grass seed. And it's cost all of this time and effort." And then he's suddenly informed, he's informed that five square feet of the lawn, that he's worked for ten years to get grass to grow, that one of students decided to rip it all up and throw it out. Well, what do you think about things like that? Let's get practical now. Let's get practical. Very practical. And so he has a responsibility. After all, he realizes it's not *his* lawn. It's not *his* garden. He's responsible, right?

Right.

And so he takes a look at a report, and the report says—from the board of directors, of which he's responsible, whatever they do. And he has this report from the directors that, for example, [a director] had instructed [the student] only to rake the grass there [and] the leaves. And according to the report, she [the student] said, "No, the grass should be pulled up," but she agreed not to pulling up the grass. And then [the director later] goes back, and there's five square feet of grass all pulled up. Well, now think about the—you want practical experiences.

Right.

Let's get off all this theory flying around in the universe up there, hmm?

Right.

Practical.

Right.

So what does that mean? Here are three directors. Here to— remember, he's been saying lately the buck stops here. Him and

Ronald Reagan. And they're both right: the buck does stop here, you see.

But you [have] got to look at it in another way. It has happened. Corrective measures must be taken. And to understand why a person would tear out five square feet of lawn that has taken ten years for the grass to grow. After having been informed, according to the report, by the board of directors of which he's responsible that they see that they do their job. Do you understand that, students?

Yes.

You see. Or let's take a better practical experience. But not better, but a different practical experience. It was only—what was it—last Friday you students had dinner here. The ones who come to Friday night dinner had dinner. Fine. There was a little, I don't know what you want to call it, it's kind of like a, a little—I wouldn't call it a saying. *[The teacher laughs.]* Well, it was a little paper that a waitress had shown to my channel in a restaurant. And, you know, humor is not only the salvation of the soul, it's a wonderful healing power. And so my channel's little guide, Crystal, informed him to get that paper. Well, the girl said it was the only one she had, but she'd make a copy for him. Well, she was kind enough to do that. And not only kind enough to make him a copy, she made him two copies. All right. And she gave them to him, and he thanked her. He then got permission—it was on upgrading a person's character, is what it was all about. Some of you, I think, have read it. It might still be here in this temple. And it was on an upgrading. We won't discuss the exact words in class, but perhaps you can see it after. It was on upgrading your life, you see, and your personality. And so he was instructed that it could be shown to the students there at the Friday night dinner. Do you understand?

Yes.

Fine. Now he had already been informed by the vice president that it wouldn't be in the best interest to show you that because they could take it and be sensitive, you see, and hurt their feelings. But, then again, the vice president and the board of directors don't make the final decisions, do they? No. And so anyway, he was instructed to have one of the students, I believe from the records it shows that [a student] was asked—Is that correct?

Correct. [The student who was named responds to the teacher's question.]

[So a student was asked] to read off this—it's a declaration is what it was; it's like a declaration—to read off this upgrading declaration, you see. And so [a student] read that off the upgrade. I'd call it an upgrade declaration. Definitely a declaration. And my channel observed all of the students as it was being read off. And one of my students in particular showed to my channel's mind—he [my channel] immediately saw, "Something is wrong." She doesn't look right. You know, the look like [she was] very, very hurt or upset or something. Well, a day passed, I think, or something. You had a report on that? *[The teacher addresses a director.]*

Yes. [The director responds.]

Was it the next day? Was the next day Saturday?

Tuesday or—[The same director responds.]

All right. Now to get to this, this scenario right down here to *terra firma*, the very next day was Saturday. [A student] brings some declaration that she has. And she, like an underground sharing of things, shows it to some of the students without permission. Well, we had untold hours of discussion here, my channel did and Isa, his mother, in that kitchen there. What was that, on Sunday or Saturday? Was it Saturday? *[Isa Goodwin is Mr. Goodwin's mother. She would regularly instruct, guide, and correct the students through Mr. Goodwin's mediumship.]*

Tuesday? [The same director responds.]

Or Tuesday! Tuesday! It was on a Tuesday. Well, I'm trying to get these reports straight here. All right. It was on a Tuesday and had all this evening's discussion. Now what was at stake? Now think. You worry about getting through an obstruction. My channel faces a hundred thousand of them a day in his service to keeping the school open for you.

All right. With much help from my channel and his associates, [the student who brought her declaration] revealed the truth with a lot of help: that she judged that her little declaration paper was better than the one that was read off here in this school. There's no problem. All the student had to do is to simply ask permission or to say clearly, "I have a declaration at home, and I think it is much better than the one that is being read here at the table. May I have permission to bring it?" Now, you see, that's honesty. That's honesty. You understand the difference? You see, that's honesty. Not suppression. It's honesty. All right. That is not what happened.

Because—let us look at principle. If one student in a school is permitted to show to some students in the school, while in school attendance, certain things, then other students take a look [and say], "Someone's getting to see or hear a secret here. How come I am left out?" Then you start all these experiences of rejection.

For example—my channel was guided to make it very clear. Now what if my student [A] there got a new pair of lace panties or something. And she was very proud of them, and she wanted some of the students here in the school to see them. But she didn't decide that all of them could see them. Well, what about the students who didn't get to see them? They would be in rejection. This school is a school of teaching in service to the Light. That's known as principle, not personality. What is the matter? Total consideration [was limited]. What if they're shown to [Student B], but they're not shown to [Student C]? And they're shown to [Student D], but they're not shown to [Student E]? Well, how does [Student F] feel? And go on down the list. *[The names of the students have been replaced with other signifiers.]*

So, you see, what it reveals is this: you must take a look of what the motive is, you see. "I am totally considering my selfish desire of the moment. I am not being honest and communicating my selfish desire of the moment. However, the fulfillment of my selfish desire will have a direct effect upon several people, many people." So, you see, others are not considered. The cause of wars in the world is that others are not considered. There is not communication for there is not understanding.

The selfish mind diligently works to destroy what it makes no effort to understand. No effort to understand. We destroy the little insects and the creatures of the planet. [We] make no effort to understand; [we] just blatantly destroy them. [We] judge they're an obstruction and they're in our way.

So when you think—you see, my channel, he could think about nothing [except] all these obstructions and be in terrible condition, you see, like anyone can. But you must take a look at the need of the individual. What is their need? It is an error of ignorance that they have chosen to fulfill their need, which is an effect of their own denial, in that way. Hmm?

Now let's go on. Now that we've, hopefully, come down to *terra firma* and we've got out of this cloud of theory, perhaps we can discuss something practical that's applicable right in the here and now. If one's allowed to show their panties or their new toy to this one and that one at the school and the others are not allowed to see it, then you have nothing but personality. Now all one has to do is say, "Now I want to show this to that one or to that one. May I have permission?" And you certainly will not get the permission from the Council that runs your church because "this one" is no greater in value in the Light than "that one." I do hope that brings about some perspective here in coming—what do you call it?—down to earth. All right. Go ahead with your questions now. I hope that answered your question.

Yes, it did. Thank you.

Yes, certainly.

Very much.

Yes, [a student] has a question, please.

I've noticed a pattern that in a given situation I become very emotional, upset, and frustrated. What is the process of tracking down or at least becoming more aware of the judgments that I'm over-identified with at that time?

Well, all one has to do is stop for a few moments and talk to the mind and say, "Permit honesty to flow inside of me." Be honest inside of yourself. Be honest, you see. And honesty is a full acceptance in the consciousness. You just be honest inside, and you will see what it is. You will see inside yourself. You don't need anyone to tell you. You see, my channel's been instructed to inform all students, for years, before you do something in a school of which you are a pupil, ask yourself the question, "What I am now tempted and about to do, what will my school be like if every pupil in my school is allowed to do what they choose to do? How will it affect my school?" Do you understand that?

Yes, sir. Thank you.

"If I have a desire to do something in my school and I just do it, what effect, if any, will this have when everyone else has their selfish desires?" Pardon? You see, you cannot operate a school of principle and permit it to be flooded and drowned with personality, you see?

Yes.

You can't have both. You see, now, for example, here like at the class this evening, if your school permits [Student A] to be out in the garage playing with the cat, then it must permit [Student B] to be out in the garage playing with the dog; it must permit [Student C], it must permit [Student D], it must permit everyone. Do you understand that? So when a person is tempted to do their selfish, personal thing, then that selfish, personal desire, taking place within a school, must be checked out with the authority of the school.

You know, it's like sitting at a dinner table and someone is used to the habit or the selfishness of picking their nose. I think that's what you call it. Well, shall you permit it at the table or shall you not permit it? For if you do permit it, then you must permit all others at the same table the same rights and the same exceptions. Do you understand?

Yes, now that's very, very important because ofttimes you forget you are not here for personality. You have come here for the principle and the law that, once applied, will free you from those selfish things that cause so much disturbance in your life.

As my channel was instructed there the other night, you see, now what if [Student F], so proud of her new pair of lace panties, decides she wants to show two or three students and the others don't get to see them? What kind of a school do you think you will have? It won't be very long—now my channel spent untold hours on that Tuesday evening. [Student G], you had a question, yes.

What—in order to assist us in identifying the cause of our feeling or the judgment and to possibly rise to another judgment, hopefully broader, would the breathing/cleansing exercise be of help?

Yes, it most certainly is. The cleansing breath and the power breath, but especially the cleansing breath, because, you see, as long as the breath is held, there is no activity in the mind, only that which you hold at that moment of inhaling the breath and holding the breath. The control of the breath is one of the indispensable steps in controlling the emotions. Now a person that doesn't practice that, ofttimes their emotions just explode! You see. Emotions that easily explode do reveal, through error, an over-identification and attachment with the self, you see. And so if a person wants to make effort to be freed from those things, then they should use their cleansing breath often.

Thank you.

Definitely. Now someone else here had a question.

Before you said the actual act of doing, the actual—I want to get back to, you—

Inspiration, yes.

Inspiration.

Yes.

That you, that the most important part is the, is the doing of it, but—

It's the actual act itself and the doing of it as you receive the inspiration. That's where the moment of all the goodness is, isn't it? Pardon?

Yes.

And the actual act, because that's part of the act, you understand, the receiving of it. It takes an effort of the will to put one into a state of consciousness to receive the inspiration, yes.

And so what you're saying is, what happens is you get the inspiration; you put it into action, but then the mind comes in and starts to care about what others think about it or what they're going to do with it, so on and so forth.

What it reveals [is] a person who's dependent on what others think. Pardon?

Yes.

You see? And remember that whatever we find our self dependent upon in life, we are diligently making effort to control. Right?

Yes.

And then we, as we find that what we are dependent upon is not doing what we want it to do, we become frustrated. Is that not correct? So, you see, that causes a great deal of problems to a person. Wouldn't you agree?

Ah, yes.

Indeed, it causes—it shows all of the dependencies, you see. You must understand that the human mind, just like here in school, it watches like a hawk to see what everyone else is getting away with. Do you understand that? You see? It takes a look and says, "Where's everybody? Who's missing? Well, what are they doing?" That's the way the human mind works in selfishness. And then if it sees someone doing something and it didn't have permission to do it, you have all kinds of problems, you see. That's the way the mind works, locked in the error and the ignorance of self. Hmm? Yes.

But you, you still can't let that stop you from—the important part is the, the action. Right? The inspiration being set forth—

It doesn't stop this student down here. He's decided that he's going to take a bath. *[The teacher refers to the church's dog, Reddy.]* Yes. Yes, go ahead.

So, ah . . . I don't know, I guess that was it.

What stopped you?

I kind of ran into a corner, and I didn't know where my thought was taking me.

We have to put a door in the corner. *[The student laughs.]* We'll come back to you when you get the door opened, all right? Yes, please. *[The teacher addresses another student.]*

What is the difference between putting an inspiration into action at the moment of the inspiration and pausing to give broader consideration to a desire or a thought that comes into the mind?

Usually—yes?

When is the first appropriate over the latter?

After you have made it your own in your own consciousness. That process takes at least seventy-two hours. Pardon?

Yes.

Because without that, you see, you don't get the coat of armor built up for the battle. Pardon?

Yes.

Because you have to understand it's all going to be shot down the moment that you reveal it. You do realize that, don't you?

Yes.

Yes, yes. And, you know, it's the same thing—it's like with teachings or anything. It's shot down by the minds in errors of ignorance. But if it wasn't shot down, it would not reveal that it had any value, you see? That that is feared by the human mind reveals its own value. Pardon?

Of course.

Would you not say?

Yes, very much.

Oh, certainly. Absolutely. Go ahead.

Then putting inspiration into action is, in effect, a, a building process over seventy-two hours in which it becomes our own.

Correct. That's when it takes seventy-two hours for that inspiration to be monitored in each and every realm of consciousness. And that's the time a person takes and makes that effort that it goes through all the different, what you would call to the mind, feelings and emotions and fears and hopes and desires. You must have a minimum of seventy-two hours to solidify it.

Thank you.

Yes. And once having solidified it, you've built up your coat of armor and let the chips, so they say, let the chips fall where they may. Pardon?

Thank you.

Yes, you're welcome. Yes, please.

I'd like to ask one more question—[The student clears her throat.] *Pardon me—regarding what I spoke of earlier: the frustrations of the day. Is that a good sign, actually that—*

Are you, are you weary of them?

Oh, I'm sick of them.

Well, that's an excellent sign! It means that you'll make the necessary changes in consciousness, and you won't have any more [of those frustrations].

Oh.

It's an excellent sign.

Good.

Certainly. Definitely. It's very positive.

Thank you.

Because when we're weary enough of anything—when you hit the bottom, there's no place left to go but up! Yes, did the door open? *[The teacher follows up with a previous question.]* Thank you. Go ahead.

Uhm . . .

Isn't it nice to realize that we alone create these things in our own consciousness? I'm glad you finally got the door open. Go ahead.

Thank you. So is it, would it be a good idea, so you, you sit down and you, you want to attain something. And you, so you have to be honest about why. Is that what you're saying? About why you want to attain it?

Well, certainly there has to be a reason. If there isn't any reason, it isn't worth attaining, wouldn't you say?

Yes.

Yes, so a person asks themselves, they're talking to themselves, "I want to attain this. Now why do I want to do that? For what purpose?" There's a reason for it. And so one asks themselves the question. They'll have several answers because several levels will get to speak. Indeed, indeed several levels will get to speak in anyone's mind. Then one learns, as they evolve, "Oh, no, the last time I had an inspiration, I listened to that level. I recognize that level very well. I'm not going to listen to that level again." You see? Yes. You can relate to that, can't you?

Yes, I can.

Indeed. Yes.

Is it important that the word attain *be used? I noticed you're using the word* attain *in reference to it's easy to attain something—*

That's correct. It is.

Rather than obtain.

Oh, no. Obtain has absolutely to do with all of the judgments, and there's a terrible battle goes on in that.

So that, they're treated the same.

No. Attain, attain is a soul faculty, and you're working with a soul faculty. Now a person attains many things. None of them do they obtain, for none of them do they possess. You see, the attainment of something is not the possession of it. The obtaining of something is the possession of it. The attaining of anything is not the possession of it. The attainment of something has the realization, the awakening that it is being loaned for a time. There are no dictates of when it shall be or when it shall not be. There are no dictates of the mind of how long it shall be with a person. That's an attainment. You see, a person says, "I'd like to have," for example, "I'd like to have a boat." All right? They would like to attain a boat, not obtain a boat. One day a boat comes into their life, only for one afternoon. They did attain the experience, correct? But they did not obtain it. Pardon? But then again, they don't have the monthly docking bill either, do they? Hmm? Well, there you are. *[The teacher laughs joyfully.]*

There are definitely, there are certain benefits to attainment [when] compared to the detriments of obtainment, you know. I think a person obtains a husband and they obtain a wife. Not attain them. They obtain them, you see. Yes, because, you see, that's where all the frustration is: that this, which they have obtained, they have purchased, they have possessed—correct?—then what are they doing? Who are they doing it with? Where are they going? And all the list of all of that foolishness. That's obtaining, of course. Now [another student] has a question here this evening.

When, when a desire rises and you want to attain something, I mean, in my mind what I do is I immediately judge how that's going to come about. And then I go—

When you decide to open the door for one to come up, yes.

Yes.

Yes, that's what happens, you know. Yes.

But you want to, or, like, when I think that I'm trying to change a law and then all of a sudden, my pride comes up and grabs hold of that and I lose it.

Yes.

In other words, the effort I'm trying to make positive [and] immediately my pride comes up—

Well, that's—

—takes authority for it.

That's when the mind steals the spirit.

Yes.

One's own spirit. It tries to steal it, and it always fizzles, for anyone. Yes.

There's a good feeling, prior to that stealing, in me. I mean, but it's, it's—but that's not the soul. I mean, because every time I have that feeling, I think that I'm moving ahead a little bit in a certain area or that I won.

Yes?

But I lose it. So I'm asking, Is there a way of, like, going beyond that?

Why, certainly, you know. Why, absolutely. It's just that the uneducated ego steals it.

Yes.

So what step must one make?

I—

Stop thinking about themselves is what's necessary. You see, a person who's constantly in self-concern and constantly thinking about themselves quickly steals the goodness that comes into their life by the divine laws of their own evolution. They very quickly steal it. So one should make the effort to stop worrying and thinking about themselves. Pardon?

So then should you just get busy as hell with something else?

In the mind? Yes. Absolutely. Definitely. But one who is in that state of evolution, at that stage also has a great deal, through over-identification, of self-pity and sensitivity, emotional sensitivity, and a constant need for one-upmanship, I think you call it in your world, a constant feeling of rejection and, and certainly not the goodness that they truly are.

Yes, it's true.

Hmm?

Yes.

See, one can work the physical body very hard, but if they're not making effort to work with the mental body—you know, when you have a feeling inside, you have that feeling whether or not your foot's moving or not moving, isn't that correct?

That's true.

You see?

Right.

So it's a mental process that's taking place. So one should work on those mental patterns. Hmm?

More aware.

Well, work on the mental patterns by stop thinking about oneself, you see, and start being—you see, it's the need of the mind to manipulate and to control. You see, think of how detrimental it would be for a person to say, "Whoops! I got away with that one. Uh-huh! I pulled a fast one here and a fast one there. And I got away with this and I got away with that." How destructive and detrimental that would be to a human being. It's extremely detrimental. Hmm?

Yes.

And I know that's not what you want, or anyone wants, really. No. Yes, we're really running over time this evening. Did anyone else have any questions? Yes, [another student] has a question there.

Exposure frees one of their, ah, mistakes, so to speak, their, their—not mistakes, but their—How do you understand better . . .

Exposure helps any mind to think more than once about what they're tempted to do with their selfishness. So the more exposure that a person experiences in life, as time goes on they're less tempted to try to do some of the selfish things that have such detrimental effects to others. And so a person—the more selfish a person is the more exposure that is required to help them to free themselves, yes. Were you thinking about five square feet of grass?

I certainly was.

Oh, I do hope that you'll consider that for a long time, yes. Because that's a wonderful lesson for you. You did get to do what your selfishness wanted to do, but, then again, one has to pay the price for everything, don't they? Hmm? Yes. Exposure frees the soul because it helps the mind to put a brake on, if only momentarily. Hmm?

Now we're going to take—now that we've run over time—just a few moments, a few moments to—there's been so much interest in, and it's ever increasing in your world from self-concern and all types of concern, about the, the condition and statistics of the world plague situation. I want to say at this time, and you may shut off that [video camera]. *[With that instruction from the teacher, the recording of this class ends.]*

AUGUST 13, 1987

A/V Seminar 25

Tonight, instead of your regular type classes or what most of you might consider formal classes, we're having an informal class on communication and the image transmitter.

Now I know we're all familiar with image because we spend so much time working diligently to gain approval from the best possible image that we can present. And so we do have much practice and familiarity and value for image and images. Now we have to ask our self the question, Why do we have so much value for image, images? And how well do we communicate the images or image that we have so much value for? Now to have value for anything, we must first arrive at a conclusion in our own mind of what it does for us. Once having arrived at that conclusion, we make great effort to present the particular image that we create and try, and work very hard, to communicate that to people that we care about. But we usually and often fail in communicating our most valued image.

Now, for example, we desire to have a new job or a new position or an increase in salary. And when we go through that thinking and the possibility that we may attain it, we go through an emotional process, a value assessment of our judgments in order to present to the person who possibly may be instrumental in making the decision whether to hire us or not, to present to the person our most valuable, to us, our most valued image. The difficulty is in maintaining and sustaining any particular image, for there are so many that we have already created that they can only be sustained, usually, for a very short period of time.

So we can see that the purpose of image creating and transmitting is, of course, a self-service design of our mind to attain what we believe we do not have. And we go, of course, out into the world, and we work to transmit a certain image to one person or to a group of people, and another image to another person or another group of people. However, these images have been created by our minds to serve [a] specific purpose, and they do not serve the purpose with all people, for in our effort to communicate and to transmit our most valued image, we must realize and understand that the recipient of our image and our imagery has their own images that they value. So we look, we see, we judge, and then we go to work to create. Therefore, for the mind, it is difficult to be honest with oneself for one moment we are honest and sincere to a valued image, only in the next moment to have another valued image to serve another specific purpose for our self.

Now the other evening I stated to our board of directors that a problem is merely a solution that we refuse to accept. Now let us think about a problem. Now we find that when we want to think about a problem and we judge that the problem is someone else's, we don't want to think about a problem at all. But let us think what we are really thinking and saying. A problem is a solution that we refuse to accept; therefore, we see that we are interested in solutions for our self, known as problems by our mind. However, we are not so easily interested or so willing in a solution for someone else.

Now why is a problem in truth a solution? Think about a problem for a moment. Make sure that it is your personal problem; otherwise, you will not be able to follow the mind as it goes through its various processes to a solution. So you have a problem. Everyone has a problem for everyone has a solution. The reason that we do not see our problems as they truly are (solutions) is because while we are thinking of the problem, we are unwilling at that time to make a change. Now a problem is a problem and not a solution as long as we permit our mind to tell us that the solution is in what someone else does.

A problem is a solution when we accept the possibility within our self of changing. The moment that we accept, in a problem, the possibility of making a change in our thinking, we instantly, clearly see the solution. Now many times you've heard a person

[say] they have a problem. They go to sleep with a problem and they wake up with the solution. But they go to sleep with themselves. When they go to sleep with themselves, with their own conscience and not someone else's, of course, they wake up to the light of reason. And their problem is indeed a solution. As long as we permit our mind to depend on something beyond its limits, then our problem shall remain a problem and we shall not find the solution that is contained within it.

As long as our health and our wealth and our happiness is dependent upon what someone else does or does not do, we're only half there. Therefore, we cannot see that a problem is a solution.

A negative attitude, we all know, is a self-destruct attitude. It is a mind that identifies only with the negative of any given situation. It is a mind not willing to make the slightest changes within itself, so that it may see and know beyond a shadow of all doubt that the problem they believe they have is a solution. The problem knocks at the door of our conscience and says, "Wake up! Wake up! You must, for your own good, for your own self-interest, make a change in your thinking, make a change in your attitude. If you do not, you will repeat the problems again and again and again and again. No matter where you go, no matter who you meet, no matter what you see, no matter what you do, the problem will ever be a problem and will not be a solution."

Now in this philosophy, of course, it is known as personal responsibility. Of course, it is known as the absence of depending and being the victim of someone else's fickle mind. We all have the tendency of a fickle mind because we all have the tendency of our mind of dependence on the goodness of life on what someone else will do. The goodness of life has never been, can never be dependent on what someone else will or will not do. It is true that is the temporary, temporary sleep of satisfaction, but in all sleep, there's a time that we awaken. To go to sleep with satisfaction and wake up with misery is not practical nor is it in one's best interest. To go to sleep in the light of goodness within oneself is to awaken with what you went to sleep with.

Now we can ask any questions that we have. Just raise your hands. Yes.

Yes. Then, simply, the problem is the denial of God and the lack of personal responsibility in any given experience.

The problem is the knock on the door of one's conscience, telling them, in every possible way, "Make a change within your thinking and your attitude of mind for if you do not, you will continue with the misery that you call a problem." Make the change in your thinking. It's the knock on your conscience. *[The teacher knocks upon the wooden table he is seated at.]* Sometimes it has to knock very, very hard, and it seems like someone's beating the door down. But you have to realize that it's knocking on the door of stubbornness: the unwillingness to change.

Now change is the inevitable law of image, form, and limit. It is a refining process. You cannot stop evolution. You cannot stop change, which is indispensable to evolution. All form, all images change. It is the Law of Evolution. If you deny it, you're only going against the tides of old creation. First of all, when you—you believe you are your mind; then you believe you are images and limits. So believing, problems are created by the mind. Those problems are knocking on the door to make changes in one's own thinking. Do you understand that?

Yes, I do. Thank you.

Hmm?

We are going against evolution by the stubbornness and the identification.

That is correct. That is correct. Any mind is, that refuses to move. You see, first of all, we believe we are the limit and the form. Therefore, we are bound by the laws that govern limit and form. And the laws that govern limit and form are the laws of evolution. And evolution is not possible without change. So any mind that holds tenaciously and stubbornly to anything the mind has created has problems because it will not let go when the problem is knocking at the door of their conscience to make a change in their thinking. Not a change in someone else's thinking, because then you cannot find what the problem is. The problem is a solution, you see.

The unwillingness to let go of that which is disturbing the mind by making a change within the consciousness—you see, we always want to change outside. We want something out there to change. We want the weather to change to suit our particular interests at any moment, but then there are millions upon the planet, billions, they want the weather their way. So everyone wants the weather a little bit different to suit their own personal interest at any given moment.

Now you take a look with your mind and you say, "I can't do anything about this lousy weather that I'm experiencing, except get on a plane and fly over to the islands where I judge the sun is shining." Of course, it may be raining that day. It's possible. You might be wise enough and practical enough to make a phone call to check. However, you see, that is identifying with the problem and not casting the light of reason upon the mind which would bring about the solution. You can change your attitude at any moment towards the weather or you can be dependent on what you can do outside. Then you become the victim of the airport, getting to the airport, the airplane, the fickleness of weather conditions, and etc.

Yes, then a problem's a very good thing. I mean, they're very—

A problem? Of course, it is—when it becomes extremely severe, then we do know how very stubborn we are and how tenaciously [we hold it], regardless of how self-destructive it becomes. The self-destruction is a change taking place within the mind, but it is a forced change, a change we have forced upon our self.

OK.

You see, you do not solve a problem by denying your responsibility for it. That is not where you find the solution. Now when the mind denies its responsibility for its experiences, it increases its dependence on people, places, and things that it cannot control. As it continues to do that, its problems increase no matter where the mind goes and no matter what the mind does because there is a denial of one's right to the control of their own mind. Does that help with your question?

Yes, very much. Thank you.

You're welcome. Yes.

Are you saying, then, that every problem is an image?

Every problem is a battle with the images that a person has created. Remember, the emotions and subconscious are all judgment images. And our own mind has created them, and our own mind tries, in its best way possible, to communicate [with] them for its own best interest, its own self-interest. Yes. Definitely. And so they go to war with each other, and we understand that as a problem. Yes.

When you said just now that the mind does its best to communicate, did you mean between the forms, or before you communicate—

No. It does its best to communicate with another mind, which reveals its dependence.

Oh!

That the solution to the problem they have created, someone else can solve it. Now as long as the mind thinks that way, the mind continues in its dependence and its own self-destruct victimization.

Thank you.

Now ofttimes the mind in its own deception says, "Well, things will be different if I do this or that." You see? Yet it has to take a look and see; is it now dependent on someone else? And, at first, one, the mind judges, "Well, yes, they're very trustworthy." And if you look at life, you'll see you move from this, to this, to this, to this. And it's always seemingly better. It's better when we let go in our own mind, then it's amazing, seemingly, how much better it really is. It's not a matter of the physical body, the mind moving the physical body to another dependence someplace else. A person may say, "Well, I just need space and I move out and I have new experiences." Certainly, you have new experiences. Certainly. They continue to reveal the dependence of something outside for the goodness of life. As long as we permit our mind to deny demonstrable truth of personal responsibility, the goodness of life will be the rainbow that we always chase and never catch. I'm sure that many of the ladies would agree, after several marriages or experiences, that it's always the rainbow that we chase and never seem to catch. Hmm?

Right.

But what is the positive and good lesson to be learned? That the solution is a change within the consciousness. Hmm? What if we held on to each day? How could we possibly experience hope? How could we even consider there'll be a better tomorrow if we won't let go of what we think we have? Yes.

As these images go to war and become, we see the problem, is it always, is frustration always accompanying a problem?

Frustration always reveals that a problem is taking place within the mind. A serious problem. Yes.

That is due to the images that are at war.

They're at war with each other.

With each other that are our own—

They're our children that we have created, yes, certainly. And they are dependent on what is outside. They're dependent on something outside. They are not dependent on personal responsibility. No, no, no, no, no, no, no. Children are not dependent on personal responsibility. They are *educated* to personal responsibility. The mind is *educated*. "If you want that, you work for it." The mind is educated, yes. And if someone doesn't do what you want, then stop wanting them to do it. So the solution is in the problem that you have created. *[A few students laugh.]* Yes.

Is a problem a belief? I mean, somewhere is there a belief then?

Oh, yes, the belief is the bondage attached—for example, one creates a judgment in their mind and there are untold thousands of judgments. They believe—they so identify with what they have created they believe that they are that which they have created, and that is known as their judgment. Now then, that judgment is a created image in their mind, and they feel it with their emotions. Now when they go to present their best image, they look through this whole supply that they have. And so they bring up this judgment and that judgment and that judgment and leave untold thousands not brought up, because they want what they judge is their best image and those particular ones they have created have served them, in their judgment, the best in the past. In other words, by using those particular images they've had past experiences that they got what they judge that they needed or wanted at any given time. Yes. Did that help there with your question?

You know, it's like a child. These things are learned very early by the mind. A child growing up, parents have a responsibility to train and to educate them, you see. Well, more properly is to educate them. Usually we train animals and educate humans. We like to think so. However, we like to differentiate between the two. Humans are better; so we educate them. Animals are lower in their intelligence; so we train them. All right.

So you have a child who learns very, very early, very early— the first few formative years—that if they do certain things, their guardian or their parents will give them what they want. So when they want something, they do certain things. Usually they whine, they cry, they make strange little faces, they appeal to one's pity, and they get what they want. Now they grow up and we call those spoiled children or spoiled brats. And, of course, they are the effect of spoiled parents or spoiled-brat parents, whose own self-interest is more valuable to them than what they have produced. Do you understand?

And so discipline is not something that a child values, as a child, when it's trying its various devices to get what it wants. And a child's mind, though ofttimes you see expressed in adult forms—for a child's mind still remains in an adult. And ofttimes adults will use the whimpering and the crying and the blaming that a child, a young child will use to have what it wants because it still believes, from its early experiences, by doing those type of things it gets what it wants. And what it wants is always dependent on what someone else does. Yes. That is childish thinking, not child-like, but childish. Yes. And a person who uses a childish mind as an adult, of course, reveals how well they were able to accomplish getting what they judged was dependent on someone else when they were very young. Yes.

Now years ago, myself, when I was in the other house there, on several occasions when there was the childish whimpering and whining and crying over different things from some of the past students who have left, I would turn the music on and turn the music up. So that they could, through indirection, get the message that I personally chose the harmony, the peace, and the goodness of the music that I enjoyed rather than the whimpering, whining, crying, and the denial of the God that I serve. And though, ofttimes many of my ex-students did not appreciate my selection, they wouldn't have appreciated anything that interfered with the whining and crying that they seemed to be so satisfied in expressing. Yes. Of course, some of my students present are aware that I am partial, perhaps, to country-western music, classical music, little bit of opera, little bit of jazz, and so I have a combination of all of it. And if there's too much whining and crying, I just turn the volume up. *[Many students laugh.]* It's known as survival, the miracle of life. Yes. I have yet to hear a human voice whimper and cry in harmony. It is indeed discordant to my ear. Sing in harmony? Yes. Whimper and cry in harmony? No.

Yes. *[The teacher calls upon a student.]*

When one finds oneself whimpering and crying and accepts responsibility for creating what's—

What they are experiencing?

—let's them do that, that they'd let themselves react that way.

Yes?

Is music a good thing to turn to, to change one's vibration from that space?

From the space of?

From the whimpering and the crying.

From the space of self-pity?

Yes.

Well, of course, it'll redirect the energy and the attention. And, of course, during that time if the attention is sufficiently redirected, they certainly will feel better during that time. Now if they make the effort, during that time, then they'll feel better when the music is shut off. But if they don't make the effort during that time, they'll just return to what they were doing in their consciousness before they turned their music on. Hmm? Now, of course, one has to consider that you can't always have music playing in your ears and especially the music that you may particularly like because not all employers will permit you to have the music playing and the music that you like because somebody else works in the workplace, too. And if they're allowed music, then they want to hear music that perhaps you don't like. So one does not want to become dependent upon something that they cannot use without having to cause a disturbance outside. Yes.

Then the music is really outside. So is the affirmations, should we say—

Well, the music is only—Are you all right now? *[The teacher addresses a student who had just coughed loudly and who had been coughing loudly for much of the class.]* The music is only outside because we judge that it's outside. That's what makes it outside. It's our judgment, which we, of course, we believe we are our judgment because we create [them]. See, our judgments are our children. We create them, and of course, a parent believes what they've created is perfect. You know, I mean, they may not go around telling the world, "I have created this. And, of course, what I create is perfect." But you have to go by the demonstration, yes. If it's not perfect, it's close to perfect if we have created it. If we really believe it's our original thought and it is something that *we* originated, then if we don't believe that it's absolutely perfect, then we certainly do believe it's close to perfect. Yes. Yes.

What, what would be a signal for me to know that when I feel self-confident about my projection, myself, my image, myself in projecting in a, in a work environment...

Yes?

In order to know that the, the image that's contained within that projection is, is not something that I'm creating because people expect me to be that way, but rather something that's coming from within me. It's really me. In other words, I, I feel that sometimes I respond to, to others subtle—

But images—

—expectations about what they want from me, rather than just—

Yes. Yes, of course.

—myself.

Because, you see, images are not what we are. Images are what we create, you see. So we are constantly creating images and servicing images we have already created. And we react to our environmental experiences, you see. If you go to work and half of the employees don't look at you or say hello, or if half of

your employees give you a very sad look—because, you see, we look at people because we look at our self. Do you understand?
Yes.

And so you immediately have a feeling. Is that not correct?
Correct.

You feel good or "What's wrong around here?" Usually, a person feels, "Well, what have I done?" That's usually what they feel. "How did I deserve this?" You see. Well, that shows and reveals the dependence of the mind on what others are doing. And so one is not, in truth, living for themselves; they are living for the servicing of other people's judgments and images. So they are reacting. They are not acting; they are reacting.

I understand that. And, and then sometimes, also, the, if, if I don't respond to other people's, of my perception of how other people are feeling about me, it, it could just be that I'm being totally insensitive to them, in other words.

Well, I'm very sensitive, I think. I think. Hopefully, that I am sensitive to people's feelings. However, for me to act according to the way they judge I should act, so that their feelings don't get slighted—no. No, I'm not interested in doing that because that just puts me into bondage and slavery, you see.

Yes.

So if you're in the work field, they've hired you based upon various images that you have presented, correct?

Yes.

Right. Now you already know the images you have presented, correct? You desire respect for your position. Do you understand that? And it is true. You have a right to respect for your position. How does one gain that respect? By respecting themselves. Hmm? Do you understand?

Yes, I do.

You see, when you have respect for yourself, all of the character assassination, all of the slander, and all of the slaughter will have no effect upon you, you see? It comes with the job. Each time you get a promotion in the work field, you are an instrument through which others create more judgments of jealousy and envy and greed. Do you understand that?

Yes.

Yes. And so the more that you rise in a material, mental world, the bigger target you become for assassination. It comes with the job. It comes with this job, too. Hmm? You see. Yes.

So you take a look and say, "Well, what I work for—just because someone has a temporary error of ignorance, I shall sacrifice all of that in order to satisfy someone else's images?" You understand? So when one is honest with themselves, has respect for themselves, does their work because it's right to work—you understand?—and it's right to do right and cares less what the world does with it. Pardon? For they will pay you and value you for what you produce in their judgments for their company for you to move ahead. Pardon?

So if a person does not make the effort to think well of themselves—do you understand?—in all areas of their life, then you can be rest assured they will enter the self-destruct level of consciousness. The pressures will become so great, they'll turn their back and walk away. Many have done it, and many still do it, you see. The opportunity a person has, once they have made their decision to do something, the opportunity that they have is when all the chips appear to be down, when all the rats have left because they judge the ship is sinking, that's the opportunity for any mind to see what their character really is. Not what others think it is, but what they know it is. The captain, if the ship is to go, the captain goes down with it, you know. That is, if he's a captain. Pardon?

Thank you.

He doesn't jump overboard with the rats. No. The captain stays with his ship. The rats are the first to go. Hmm? Did that help you?

Yes, it does.

You're more than welcome. Yes.

Is respecting oneself, does that—is that what you mean by living for oneself?

Well, I certainly do not mean that in the context that one should live only for their selfish mind and judgments, which the mind believes that it is the judgments or children it has created. No, and I don't think you meant to say that.

No.

But in respect to living in personal responsibility and not so dependent on images to impress others and be so frustrated and to have value for the goodness that one truly is, you understand?

Yes.

That's far different than all of these other problems and things. Yes.

Well, awhile back you said—

Yes.

—living for oneself. And I—

The true self.

The true self. I'm trying—

Yes.

—to make the connection between that and self-respect. So that would be true—

Well, you have respect for the goodness that you are. You do accept that you are good, don't you?

Yes.

Then that's all you have to do is to have respect for the goodness that you are. Pardon? For the goodness that—you see, the good that we see and the good that we identify [with] is the good that we experience. Pardon? Yes. Now if we are tempted to believe that our goodness in life is dependent on what others think about us, then when they don't think we're good then we have a serious problem. Pardon? You do understand that, don't you?

Yes. Yes.

You see. But, you see, to, to be dependent on someone else thinking whether you're good or not, you're depending on image, an image you created with the mind; that's a problem without a solution until one frees themselves from dependence. Hmm? You see?

You see, it's just like I was speaking there to [another student] in the work force. Wherever you are, no matter whether it's in a church or it's in a philosophy school or it's in the mundane work place out there, there are human minds. Do you understand that? You see. So those minds depend on what others think about them. You see, because they're dependent on the images that they present. Hmm? All right.

Now it's one thing to speak the truth inside of oneself. It is foolhardy to try to convince others. My work here in serving the Spirit and in service to this organization and to the angels is not to convince you of anything. My work is to reveal. You alone will convince your mind of whatever you choose to convince yourself of. My purpose in life is not to prove to anyone that life is eternal. I already know that in the depths of my being. Do you understand? You see? So the sadness is to be dependent with our mind on what someone else thinks about us. Hmm?

Now, being human, my goodness' sakes, I could be upset seven days a week of what people think about me. You have to understand, people I don't even know, that have never personally met me or spoken to me, have convinced themselves that I control minds and they're afraid of me. I *am* [a] mind controller. I work constantly at it: to control my own mind because I know without some control of my own mind, I know what my mind is capable of. I've already experienced it; it has a fine temper.

So, you see, to be accused of this and character assassinated at that—I've gone through the television assassination. I've gone through the newspapers and go on down the list. That's why I'm not interested in that foolishness. I'm not interested in convincing them that I'm honest. My life is my demonstration.

And everyone else's life should be their demonstration, you see.

Now some people, of course, in an error of ignorance, they're very jealous that I have a glass, perhaps, or a table or a this or have that or a clean house or something else. So? Is that going to change my life? Yes, if I am dependent upon them. Hmm? For by being dependent upon them, I am unhappy that I wasn't able to control their mind. Do you understand? I'm not interested in controlling their mind because I am not interested in depending on people, outside of this people—one person *[The teacher refers to his true self.]*—for my goodness in life. But anyone who's dependent on other people is very conscious and very sensitive to what they think or say about them. People think and say many things about me. But I don't live with them in my conscience. I live with myself. Hmm? Pardon? Yes.

What is their motive for character assassination?

The same motive that anyone has of character assassination. You see, a person takes a look outside, because they're dependent on someone else, you see. And so they look outside and they look at a person. Then they look at what the person has or does not have, according to their judgments. And so a person has very varied, selfish motives for accusing another person of mind control. It usually reveals it's what they want themselves and have yet to attain it. That's what it usually reveals. That help with your question?

Thank you.

Certainly. Yes.

Do we become dependent on people and what other people think because we are insecure?

Oh, we're very insecure because we are educated that way. We are educated—the average mind is educated to be dependent on what someone else will or will not do for them. We educate our children to be dependent on others, you see.

Because of our own insecurities.

Because of our own insecurities. Definitely.

And also, when, when I'm coming under attack from other people's judgments . . .

Yes?

And I feel my mind swaying and feeling like it wants to give in to those judgments—

Oh, it shows dependence on others for your security.

OK. What can I do at that very moment?

At that very moment? At that very moment, if at all possible, go someplace by yourself and start doing the breathing exercises. And in so doing those images—you've got to remember, you see, image reacts to image. They send out their images. Your images react in the atmosphere. Pardon?

Yes.

You see.

OK.

And so they don't have to—people don't have to say anything to transmit those images. You do understand that, don't you? They go right out in the atmosphere and you feel rather strange. Why, before this very class here this evening, I went to work to clear up some images. Isn't that correct? *[The teacher calls on the vice president.]* If you will recall there, images in the atmosphere. And, you see, it is through honest communication that you clear up disturbing images in the atmosphere.

Yes.

Now you cannot always honestly communicate out there, in the jungle of creation, with the people you're working with. But you can work on your own mind. You see, many people understand that as thought force. You know, a person becomes angry because they judge you are doing something that they don't want you to do or you have no right to do, and they're in a position where they will not say anything to you.

Yes.

But they say plenty in the atmosphere, and you can feel it.
Yes.
Pardon?
Absolutely.
You understand that, don't you? Yes, of course people sense that way. Animals feel those disturbances, too. You work on yourself, and you talk to yourself. You say, "I am not dependent on that person." And you start to go through a process in your mind. You take a look and you say, "I have lived this many years. What inside of me is tempting me to make this person my God?" You must ask yourself that question, for, you see, that which disturbs the mind controls the mind. So one must ask themselves the question, "All of these years I have lived and have worked for my life. This is disturbing my tranquility." Ask yourself the question, "What is tempting me inside of my mind that I would sacrifice my peace and my God, which is not dependent on people, for this person here? What will they do if I become their servant and their victim? Where will I be when their fickle minds decide they got a better deal?" Do you understand that?

Yes.

You think that way. You take your little break, and go to the restroom or pause for a few moments, and talk to your mind.

OK.

You will see a change. Definitely!

OK.

Absolutely! Because, you see, after you have that reasonable discussion with your own mind, that part of your mind, you'll feel better. It won't matter what they think or they don't think because you will no longer be dependent upon them. You will no longer be working so diligently transmitting images that are pleasing to their mind, you see.

Yes.

It won't matter to you anymore.

Yes.

See, when you don't want something out of them, then you're not dependent upon them. So you have this little discussion with yourself. Pardon?

Yes.

Yes. Sometimes my mind says, "It's a miracle I have any students at all," because they get so upset, some of them, at varying times, through errors of ignorance, to face personal responsibility, you see. Yes.

Yes. OK. Thank you very much.

You're welcome. Yes, please.

Is, is the difficulty in being honest the belief that—

Honest with oneself.

With oneself?

Why, certainly. We all know what we're doing.

Right.

We don't have to have everyone else tell us. And if they tell us incorrectly, well, that's just too bad, isn't it? We do know what we're doing inside of ourselves, don't we? What?

Yes.

There.

Thank you.

And honesty has nothing to hide. And truth requires no defense. Truth just is. Hmm?

Yes.

It just is. Yes. However, if we're depending on what others think, then we've got a problem and haven't yet arrived at that state in consciousness and evolution that we see the solution is right inside the problem in our own mind. Yes. Yes.

Thank you.

Yes. You're welcome. Yes.

So we're creating these—actually, we're creating these images to really control that which—

Why, certainly! Absolutely! We create them and transmit them for we are dependent on what others will do with them. Do you understand that? Hmm?

And then we become the victim of the very things—

We always become the victim of that which we desire to control, you see. If we come up against a stone wall and we finally make a judgment we can't control it, in other words, the images we present don't work on it, then what happens [is] we work to destroy it. You see? You see, the uneducated mind ever seeks to destroy that which it cannot control. Now the educated mind, it knows better. Of course. The educated mind sees problems as solutions because it accepts that it has created the problem in its own mind. The uneducated mind, the selfish mind sees only problem, you see. And so, of course, we become the victim of whatever we allow our self to be tempted to control, you see?

So when I am accused of mind control, I find it most interesting because it reveals to me (the accusation) that phenomenal effort has gone in to try to transmit that image to me, and it has not been successful. And it's self-destruct[ive] for the transmitter, you see? You see, it cannot affect me if I don't receive it. Now for me to receive it, I must be tempted by it. Do you understand that?

Yes.

Yes. I am not tempted by it because I know beyond a shadow of any doubt we become the victims of that which we seek to control out there because it is glory, the power-consciousness of glory, that tempts us to control that which is beyond our divine right to control. Yes. You just go right ahead.

So could—that process actually could happen—happens within oneself, too.

Oh, of course, it happens within oneself.

And the destroying process can start—

It will start to destroy what it, if it cannot have its way and you believe that you are that image that you have created.

Like one image is fighting another image.

That is correct. Absolutely. Definitely. It's known as discord. Its effect is disease. Pardon? Yes. You're welcome. Yes.

What is going on in our consciousness when we are easily disturbed by something unexpected in a work situation specifically?

Well, all of the images that the mind uses to present what you call its best side, all of those images are in a state of fear. Look what happens when there's a change that one is not prepared [in] their mind for. Take a look when there is a change and you haven't prepared yourself for the change and it is spontaneous. Hmm? Pause in those moments when you have those opportunities. See what happens to your mind and your emotions. Hmm?

Yes, sir.

Because, you see, your children were not prepared. Your mental children were not prepared. And they don't appreciate suddenly being called up to defend themselves. They weren't prepared, you see. They like to be prepared so they can put on their best face.

Well, look. When you believe you are image, when you believe you are form, then you wake up in the morning [and] you look into the reflector (the mirror) and you see an image. You say, "Oh, no!" And you take up all of these jars and different things and you know and etc. And you take another look, "Oops!" And then you go through another batch of paste or whatever, you see. Until finally you satisfy the particular judgment that is in control at that moment, who is now going to serve you, at that moment, through that image. All right?

Now you get on the bus, you get in the car, you park, and you get off the bus. The wind is blowing in the city or someplace else. You rush immediately, you rush right into the reflector for your child that you've created, that is going to bring what it judges it—[what] you judge it will bring you from past experiences, [and you] immediately put your face in front of the reflector (the mirror). And you go through this whole process, and you take whatever you have out of your pockets or your satchels or your suitcase and you go through the whole process *before* you now finally rush upstairs to present yourself. But you don't want to rush too fast, the judgment says, because if you do, you may have perspiration or look—etc. And there's this whole rigmarole, this ritual that people go through all of the time.

Now if you really believe in the children you've created when you were younger, before your hair turned gray, there's no possible way you can allow it to turn gray or white. Because you are still dependent on what those images that you created when you were younger brought to you. So then you go through the whole process to try to get the color just right, the way that it used to be when you were twenty or perhaps even thirty. Does that help you?

Yes, sir.

Hmm? Yes. True, it is an over-identification with the reflection of one's form, you see. You see, you look in the mirror, and the mind wants everyone to see you the way you see your own reflection. This is why so many people work so diligently to get their reflection, that they're looking at in the mirror, just so, because it's got to fit into the judgments they alone have created. And so then you walk out on to the street, and you really believe that other people see you the way you see yourself. They don't, however. *[Many students and the teacher laugh.]* It's such, such a waste of time and energy. They see you according to the judgments, the images they have created who are in control at that moment. If those images want something out of you, then they will be transmitted and see you in their own particular way. In the way that they believe that they can get what they want out of you for they are dependent upon you. Do you understand?

And, of course, it's a two-way street. It works back and forth both ways. Yes.

When I listen to my voice after it's been taped—

Yes.

It always shocks me that I sound a particular way. I—

Oh, don't feel bad. I'm terribly shocked myself. I have been ever since there were tape recorders because I judged that my voice is too high. *[The teacher laughs joyously.]* Yes?

Is it beneficial to, for me, perhaps in this case because it is a shock and I'm always—

Oh, it's a wonderful shock. The thing is, have you made the judgment that your voice is not now serving you well? Now if you've made that judgment, of course, you could go to school and try to make changes with it. It'll be a little difficult and take a lot of time and money. But you have to take an interest in "Well, now just a minute. This voice of mine has served me rather well. It brought me to where I am, along with the rest of me, at this point in time. So why do I want to change it just because I now judge that I sound shocked. I'm shocked at the way I sound." Well, you may be shocked, but [your friend] may be pleased, and you don't know. Right?

Right.

It depends if she wants something out of you; [if she does], I'm sure she would agree your voice is beautiful. *[The teacher laughs joyously again.]* So, you see, all of this effort, you see, is all this imagery; it not only is very expensive, very time-consuming, especially for people out there in the work field. To get up in the morning and to go through all of this tinting and dyeing and coloring and pasting and for what? For what? That's a good question. To be clean is one thing, but to go through all of that process—it is because we're dependent (our minds) on what someone else does. And we judge if we look this way and that way, then we're going to get what we want because they just cannot resist us. Pardon? I don't think changing your voice is going to make you irresistible, but you can speak to [your friend] there. Yes.

Is, is there any—

And I don't see anything wrong with your voice. It's your voice. That's why I see everything right with it. Now if it was [Student A's] voice or [your friend's], then maybe we'd have a problem. Yes, go ahead.

Is there—you just said that—well, I can't remember word for word, but is there any instance in which what we do to ourselves externally, or whatever, is just as a result of what we like, not because we're really trying to please anybody? You know, is there—

Oh, yes, there certainly is. And if one is not careful, they find there's a lot of disturbance because people, most people, don't like us when they find the way that we really are. Hmm?

OK.

Or haven't you had that experience yet?

. . . experience. [It is difficult to transcribe the student's response. Both the teacher and the student laugh.]

After they've passed through their images and they take another look and they say, "Oh, no, no, this is not the [person] that *I* know. I don't want nothing to do with that [person]." Surely everyone's had those experiences, right?

Yes.

Well, they suddenly woke up, you understand.

Yes.

Their images were no longer satisfied in impressing your images, do you understand? Because it's an image process going back and forth. One makes great effort to present the image that they judge is going to get them what they want. Certainly, there are times that one does not go through this process. "Let's see, there's no one around. I don't have to put on any images. Oh, I feel so great." And it's very refreshing.

Yes.

Pardon? You see? See, people usually can be more honest with animals than they can with their own species, you see. Unless they're trying to communicate with the animal and there's someone of their own species around, then they don't do it for the animal. They're doing it for the images which are, in turn, trying to impress someone else's images. Yes.

I guess what I'm trying to say—Is there any time when images are good or images are appropriate or—

Oh, certainly! Absolutely! They're definitely appropriate in the workforce. They're appropriate in many areas of life.

All right.

Oh, absolutely!

Because there's certain standards that you have to conform to.

You don't *have* to, but you do pay the price. I don't conform to a lot of standards, but I have other values and so I pay the price of non-conformity. Yes.

Yes. So is it just our attachment or identification?

It's our belief that we are the images that we create.

OK.

Yes. And so we work diligently to be conformists.

Yes.

To conform to whatever group of society that we choose to identify with. And we first choose to identify with any particular group in keeping with our own judgments, images, which are dependent on what they do and what we want out of what they do.

Yes.

I mean, we do understand that. You know, it's not all negative. Of course not. It's not all negative.

Yes.

That's why people, they will act and speak one way in one situation and become completely changed in another situation.

Yes. Right.

But that is so sad and distressing to a person in time. They get so weary of doing that. They don't feel good inside. Satisfied for a moment, but they do not feel good inside. They do not feel good. They must be constantly entertaining the mind. If not, they become aware of that not feeling good inside, you see. So the mind has to be constantly played upon.

Yes. So just be, express who you are at all times.

That's right. Who—and remember that how you feel inside, you see. So if, if you're in a situation where you don't have time to put your lipstick on, what does it matter, if you are being you? Pardon?

Yes.

The lipstick or all those things are for the images of impressing and dependent on what someone else will do or not do according to your judgments. So one justifies and says, "Well, all the women wear lipstick." So? They're conformists. Now what if all the women decide to wear black lipstick? Will they all wear black lipstick? I've already seen some black lipstick. But will they all do it? It takes a slow process. People do not change quickly. Do all women wear rouge now? Some do and some don't, you see. Some have broken away from that conformity. Correct?

Yes.

In a society [a] certain degree of conformity is necessary in order to maintain the society, correct?

Yes.

The United States of America is the greatest melting pot in the whole world, the greatest melting pot. It has the greatest opportunity because it has so much diversity and less conformity than all the other nations of the planet. And it has more opportunity to grow and to evolve.

Hmm.

Because change is indispensable to evolution.

Yes.

And you don't have change when you have total conformity.

Yes.

So you don't have evolution, whether politically or financially or in your health or any other way.

Yes.

As long as you have absolute conformity, you do not have evolution.

Hmm. So then, in some way it's good to, to not conform to everything, obviously.

If you want to evolve, it certainly is! It certainly is. You see, the masses do not lead for the masses do not change. Masses change by force. Wise people adjust through acceptance.

Yes.

It's the masses, you see, the masses do not lead society to greater goodness. They never have throughout all of history.

Yes.

Because they are basic conformists. They are the sheep that follow the leader.

OK.

And if the leader is evolving, you never know what changes are happening. It's like in a business. They say, "Well, you're taking a real chance because no one has presented the product in that particular way." Well, no one will ever know unless someone supposedly takes a chance. Otherwise, we wouldn't even have televisions today. We'd still be with the radios. We would not have the computer chips. It would not exist. Someone broke from the masses, from the mass thinking. And someone always will. Some will fall. Some will stumble and pick themselves up again. The changes are inevitable. They are inevitable.

Well, it's time to say good night. Thank you very much and we'll see you perhaps next month.

SEPTEMBER 10, 1987

A/V Seminar 26

Good evening, students.

This evening's class: Acceptance - something good is happening. Attaining your goal - Fulfilling your desires.

And so this evening you will make your own scoresheet for we do best with things with which we are most familiar. And one of the things that we are so familiar with is, of course, our desires and our score tally of their fulfillment. So let us write on our notes "Attaining our goals - Fulfilling our desires." And then let us write what we expect to receive when our desire is attained. And then let us write whether or not our desire is dependent upon person, place, or thing. Now list three of your most important desires at this time. My good student, Mr. Red, has listed his and moved to the chair. *[The teacher refers to the church's dog.]*

Now let us write the word *Concern* and opposite that word, the word *Acceptance*. Let us now write the word *Personal Responsibility*.

Now go to your first desire. Take a look at what you expect to receive from it. Mark down either yes or no, whether or not its fulfillment is dependent upon person, place, or thing. Either yes or no. Is it dependent upon a person? Then you write yes. If it is not, you write no. If it is dependent upon a place, you write yes. And if not, you write no. If it's dependent upon a thing, you write yes. And if not, you write no. Soon you will have your score of just one desire.

Now under *Acceptance*, you write yes (you have accepted the fulfillment of your desire) or you write no. If you write yes in the *Concern* column, you cannot write yes in the *Acceptance* column. For each time you permit concern, which is a negative expression of mental substance, to express in your mind, you question and doubt the acceptance of the fulfillment of your desire. If you have no in the *Concern* column, then you have yes in the *Acceptance* column. If you have yes in the *Acceptance* column, then you are demonstrating the wisdom of patience. If you have yes in the *Concern* column, then you are demonstrating the ignorance of impatience.

If you have yes in the *Person* column, then place minus 20. If you have yes in the *Place* column, then you write minus 10. If you have yes in the *Thing* column, then you write minus 10. If you have no in any of those columns, you have plus that amount. If you have yes in the *Personal Responsibility* column, then you have plus 40 points. If you have yes in the *Acceptance* column, then you have plus 10 points. If you have yes in the *Concern* column, then you have minus 10 points.

Because this is recorded on tape, I felt it would not be necessary to draw a chart for you, that you would have more impact from placing your own desires and making your own charts.

Now let us explain the laws involved. We have had much discussion on negative and on positive. We have had full discussion on how judgments are created. And we have had full discussion on the importance of faith, which is positive, and fear, which is negative. The other day I spoke to my channel in reference to whenever the mind is easily tempted, it reveals the degree of fear at the moment. A person who is easy to fear is quick to tempt. And, of course, a person who is quick to tempt is one who feels the pain of victimization.

The expression, of course, of fear is what is known as frustration. A person easily tempted is one who is fearful and one who is quite frustrated. Frustration is discordant, for it is disorder. It is lack of organization. It is lack of reason.

Now let us take a look at just our primary desire. Let us add up our score and let us see how far we are along the path of its attainment. The business of living is the lack of concern, for concern is a question, a doubt, and denial of acceptance of the fulfillment of one's own desires. Doing our part is accepting the good that is. It is not difficult to attain the fulfillment of one's desire once one applies the very simple laws that have, in so many different ways, been revealed.

Now it's time for anyone with a question—just raise your hand, please. Yes, please.

Temptation follows fear because in fear we place our attention on limit?

Temptation is the expression of fear. A fearful person is easily tempted. We fear the fulfillment of the desires that we concern our self about. So if you have a desire and you are fearful in your efforts to attain its fulfillment, the fear expresses itself by being easily tempted through the negative expression, the negative. It is a negative emanation of the human mind. It is measurable by instruments, scientific instruments. It is a negative emanation of the human mind. It attracts its like kind. Yes.

Thank you.

You're welcome. Well, for example, I'll give you—you know, it's important to have examples that you can relate to. It's this very day, for example, that my channel received a letter from the North and was offered opportunity, one might call it, to attain the ranch on which we have made a deposit, to make arrangements so that he would be able to purchase that and place it into escrow without having the full cash amount or prior to the sale of this property. I'm happy to report he had no problem nor hesitation in not bowing to that temptation once he brought it to the light of reason, you see. So, however, had my channel feared and denied that which he serves, then, of course, he would have bowed to the temptation from the fear of the mind and the negative emanation of its concern. Does that help with your question?

Yes, sir.

Yes.

Thank you.

In fact, I will inform him after class, so that you can see the letter yourself. You know, they say a picture's worth a thousand words and ofttimes a letter, so-called, official to the mind, is worth more than anyone's statements. Yes. Are there any other questions? Yes.

Can one understand—

Ah, just a moment. I would like to say one thing to the class. My channel, I'm happy to report, loves God and the Light more than he loves a house or a ranch or any *thing* else. Yes.

Can one understand that they are in concern and accept personal responsibility?

No, it is not possible to accept personal responsibility and have a negative emanation of the human mind, known as concern. It's not possible. You must deny personal responsibility for whatever one has created. You must first deny that personal responsibility in order to have concern, which is the questioning and the doubting of acceptance. It's contrary to demonstrable law. Yes, you cannot have concern and have acceptance. If you have concern, then you have denial. Do you understand? Yes, you cannot have both. Yes, they cannot exist in the same space at the same time in consciousness. Yes.

Thank you. Is it that the desire to attain our goals—because when it comes from the mind, the fear is there and so that the faith, in giving the desire up—Why do we fear so much of attaining our goals?

Because we rely upon what our mind has to offer. And if it does not happen in keeping with the time limit that has been created by the mind in the creating of its desire, then it enters concern and denies acceptance of what is.

I see.

You see?

Yes, I do.

Yes. You see. It denies. It's a house divided which denies itself. You see, as I stated, you cannot accept, you cannot have acceptance and personal responsibility—which is personal responsibility—you cannot have that and concern at the same time. Now you can vacillate between the two, between concern and acceptance, and acceptance and concern, but then you end up frustrated, you see.

Yes.

For you increase the fear.

Right.

You increase the reliance and the dependence upon the mind. And by increasing the reliance upon the mind, you increase its fear, for faith directed to the mind is fear.

Right.

You see?

Yes. Thank you very much.

Yes. Yes, please.

So then is being anxious also fearful, even though—

Anxiety is an expression of concern.

Yes.

A concerned person is an anxious person.

OK.

Yes, yes. Yes, please.

Are you saying that, that we are actually creating the time frame of—

In the creating of the desire, that is correct.

Of the desire.

That is correct.

In the beginning.

Ofttimes we are not aware of it. We become aware of it as months or years roll by. Then we are aware from our experiences that a hidden time frame was created by our mind at the time of creating the desire. See, whatever the mind creates, we must understand the mind creates—time is an illusion created by the mind. So whenever the mind creates something, it creates its own time limit. That's an indispensable ingredient to the creating of the forms in the mind. Does that help with your question?

Yes.

Now, you see, when a person demonstrates personal responsibility, acceptance, then, as stated many times, when our hindsight becomes our foresight, we then gain insight. And so the insight comes in the wisdom of patience, you see. See, a person creates a desire for anything, and in that creating they are not consciously aware that at the time of creating the desire form in the mental substance it contains a time limit. Do you understand that? Now they're not consciously aware of—usually, they're not consciously aware of the time limit. They become consciously aware of the time limit that was created at the time of creating the desire after time passes. For some, it's days. Some it's hours; some it's minutes; some it's weeks; some it's months; and some it is years. Yes. That help with your question? Now my student, Mr. Red, for him it was moments and he's over in his chair. Yes. Yes, please.

First there's the fear, and then the temptation, and then the concern.

Well, *[The teacher laughs joyously.]* that's—yes, yes, indeed, indeed. First is the desire.

The desire.

Pardon?

Yes.

Yes, first is the desire. Now what happens to the desire? It contains a form, a shape created by the mind, correct?

Correct.

It also contains a time frame. Pardon?

By the mind.

Yes, of course. In the creating of the desire, a time limit has also been created. Pardon?

OK.

Yes, now what was your question?

You answered it. Thank you. I was wondering if the, the temptation followed the fear and then the concern followed the temptation.

Well, of course, the more concern one has over the fulfillment of the desire they have created, the more easily they are tempted to fill the desire by whatever means the mind has to offer, yes.

But that, in doing it that way it seems to never go anywhere. It seems like there'll always be a dead end or nothing ever—

Well, one has many desires, and if you look in hindsight, one might call them dead ends. But in truth they are—the dead end was a fulfillment. That was the limit that the desire could take them. Pardon?

I see.

I know that more than one person who's been married and divorced would agree to that. There was a limit. They weren't aware of the limit at the time of creating the desire. The limit, however, was created in the desire. They just were not consciously aware of the limit, you see.

Yes.

Yes. Does that help with your question?

Yes. Thank you.

Yes. Yes, please.

Thank you. Could concern be telling us that our desire is ill-conceived? That it's not in our best interest to begin with?

No, the concern is the denial, the question, doubt, and denial of the acceptance of the fulfillment. You see, it is questioning and doubting based upon the time frame it has created, that the conscious mind usually is not aware of. The concern is the expression, a negative expression of the mind, which is impatience, that the desire created by the mind has not yet been fulfilled. Do you understand that?

Yes.

Yes. Does that help with your question?

So it, it really isn't questioning the, the basis of our desire.

No, it's questioning its fulfillment because the fulfillment has not taken place within the time limit that the mind has created for the fulfillment of the desire that it has created.

Thank you.

Now, as I say, sometimes the mind is consciously aware of the time limit it has placed on the desire it has created. Usually the conscious mind is not aware of the time limit that has been created at the moment of creating the desire. Usually, like a person, you know, they fall in love, and the desire's created, but they're not consciously aware of the time frame they've allowed for that desire. So they fall in love and then something, they say, happens out there. And they fall out of love. They are fulfilling the time frame they have created with the desire.

I see. OK.

Did that help your question? You see?

Yes, it did.

Yes, like a person says, "Well, I'm going to get married and have a family." Now there's a time frame they have created when they created that desire. Usually they're not aware of the time frame, you see. And when the time frame (its limit) is up, then you have divorces or justifications or excuses and everything falls apart, you see. Yes. Did that help with the—

Yes, it does. Thank you.

You're welcome. Yes, please.

When one confronts the time frame—

Well, you can't confront what you're not aware of.

Well, if you're aware of it and you face it.

Yes, yes.

If you choose patience or impatience, is impatience the same as force? And is patience—

Yes.

—the same as power?

Yes, because concern is force. It's a negative expression of the human mind. When there is a much better way, as the classes, over these many years that you've been in class, will reveal. There's a far better way, you see.

Success is, is—we're successful in all the things we do. We don't understand, it seems, sometimes, that we are successful. We're successful in being concerned. We're successful in acceptance. We are successful in whatever we choose to be successful in. Yes. Now ofttimes a person will say, "Well, now I worked real hard and, and I had nothing but failure." They don't understand what they have created. If they understood, they would feel better. They'd say, "Yes, this is a negative expression that I am successful in. Now, I call that failure," you see?

You see, we always get what we really want. We don't understand it when it arrives at our door. The reason that we don't understand it is because we have denied personal responsibility for the creating of it, you see. Pardon? Yes. As I explained to you earlier and as I will instruct, later, my channel to show you the letter, he understands that. He understands what temptation and fear is. He should understand, he's my channel. He *does* understand. So he is not easily tempted by trying to work something out mentally for he knows how much it will cost him, and he is not tempted to do it that way. You see, doing one's part is: create your desire; accept the fulfillment of it; keep yourself free from concern, for each time you enter concern you, you doubt, question, and deny acceptance of its fulfillment of your own creation, you see? So it's known by many prophets over the ages: you stand in your own light; you're a house divided, you see. Yes.

Thank you, sir.

You're welcome. Yes.

How does one tell whether they're just being tempted that this is the fulfillment of their desire or they—

Well—

... the fulfillment?

That is dependent on how much control the desire has over their conscious mind. Now if they are under a great deal of control by that which they have created, then they are blinded in the awakening that they are being tempted by their own fears of the fulfillment of that which they have created. Yes. Did that help with your question?

Yes.

Yes. You see, it's like with the temple. This temple, this physical structure, this property is sold. When the awakening comes to my students, they will have that realization. The more concern there is, the more denial that it is sold takes place within the consciousness of the student. Pardon? Yes. Yes.

If one has a pattern of slipping into concern whenever they think about it consciously, whenever they think about the fulfillment of their desires—

That they move into concern?

They move into concern.

They deny the fulfillment of their own desire.

What, at those moments, can we do to take, to free ourselves from that concern?

Accept personal responsibility, you see. You see, first of all, pause and say, "Now I have created with my mind this thought and this desire. I alone have created this. I alone am responsible for its fulfillment." If it is dependent on person, place, or thing, then you're minus 20 points on your score for person. For you have you as a person, that is minus 10, and you have the person that you've created in your mind, a minus 10. So that gives you a minus 20 on that scoring. Do you understand that?

Yes, sir.

You see, see, for example, if you say, "Well, this is my desire," and you create it. And you say to yourself, in the creating of the desire, on what that person there does, you have now created another image. You have your own image that you're responsible and you must pay for. Do you understand that? Then you have the image of the other person that you have created and their law is involved too. That's why it's a minus 20 if you have a yes in the fulfillment of your desire under *Person*. Pardon?

Thank you.

And you have a [minus] 10 if it's place and thing, for place, you see, you don't have another person's law involved. Do you understand?

Yes, sir.

So you have 10 percent of your own personal responsibility of creating place, and you have 10 percent of creating thing, you see. But when you step into another person's universe and you place them in your image of dependence, then you have—what do you say in your world? A double whammy, I think you call it. *[Many students laugh.]* Yes, I think that's what you call it, a double whammy. One must be greatly tempted, you know, to have their desires fulfilled with double whammies. That's minus 20 on your scoring. Yes. Yes, please.

To, to have, to consider one's just obligation is, is that something, would that be considered as a thing outside?

Just obligation is what one has created.

Right.

Do you have a person image in what you consider is your just obligation, a person image?

A person's image?

Well, do you have in your mind—in what you consider your just obligation, in the creating of that desire, known as just obligation, is there, under *Person*, do you have a person you're dependent upon?

No—

Or that you judge is dependent upon you?

No.

Well, then you don't have that problem there. Yes. One creates what they judge is their just obligation. What is a just obligation for one, another would consider "That has nothing to do with me. That has nothing to do with me at all." Do you understand? One creates that.

Right.

Yes.

Yes, yes, one, one does create that just obligation.

What is it that you're trying to understand?

Well . . .

How much weight of responsibility you may have incurred?

Well, well, OK, OK the weight of responsibility, yes. But that was, whatever it is, it was created by me and it's my just obligation.

I see. Yes, yes, of course.

OK.

And therefore, it's not dependent upon person.

Right.

Is it?

No, it's not.

Why, no. You have personal responsibility. Acceptance. Yes. See, we all know what is right, and we all know that it's right to do right.

Right.

Hmm.

Yes. Thank you.

Yes. Now remember, a problem is nothing but a solution that we refuse to accept. I think we've discussed that before.

Yes.

It's all a problem ever was and can ever be. It is a solution waiting to be accepted. Now, however, it requires change. Yes.

In that example that he was speaking of, would that responsibility, then, come under a category of a thing? [A different student follows up on the question asked by the previous student.]

Well, a responsibility, and if I understand [the previous student] correctly, he is speaking of a thing that he has created by his own mind. Yes, that would be classified under *Thing*.

OK.

Yes.

Thank you.

Because he did not declare that he was dependent upon another person for its fulfillment, so he would only have minus 10, you see, on his score in that respect. Yes. Because I think if he analyzes carefully the created desire, he will see that it was *Thing* and not *Person* that he created at that time of the just obligation. It was a thing created, a desire thing.

All right.

Yes, yes. Now the result of a desire thing can be very varied, you see. Indeed, very varied. Yes. That help with your question?

Yes. Thank you.

Yes. Yes.

So we create our own responsibilities, is that what you said?

Why—when we create a desire, when the divine expression is taken by the mind and formed into what we understand as our desires, we create that. When we create it, it's like a child we have created. We are responsible for it, you see. Pardon?

OK.

Yes, yes. We create. We create by creating the desire, of course, the responsibility of its fulfillment. Yes, indeed. Yes.

So are these the responsibilities we've incurred in life, that . . .

Go ahead with your question.

OK. So . . .

Tell me what you desire in life, and I will show you, to the mind, your weight of responsibility. Yes. You see? This is why the weight of responsibility must never exceed our love of God, the God within us, you see. Now to find the God within us, it is not possible without personal responsibility and total acceptance. Yes.

At the time of forming the desire, then, at times we forget the responsibility that goes with . . .

With the, with the fulfillment of the desire. Yes, indeed. You see, this is why we have this law revealed: Put God in it or forget it. What does that mean? That means just exactly what it says: total acceptance is the will of God. Now if the created desire is over 51 percent—51 percent or over, then the will of God is only 49 percent. So the ruling force is the 51 percent of the mind's creating of the desire. Did that help with your question? Yes. And when it is 51 or more percent, then we have greater frustration, greater difficulty with concern for we do not understand the time limit that we have created at the time we created the desire. Yes.

So if we're in the process of complaining about the responsibility we've incurred, that really means—

Well—

—we aren't putting God in it and carry all the weight upon our own shoulders.

That is correct. We have over-identified with our own creations. And through the over-identification of them, we are burdened with discouragement for we have denied responsibility of creating the desire in the first place, you see. Yes. Yes, please.

Does the mind ever trick you with the time frame of never?

Whenever we permit our mind to be the ruler of fulfilling desire that it has created, we do, indeed, trick ourselves, yes. Yes, I hope that's helped with your question. And [another student] has a question, too, please. Yes.

Is, is the awareness of a desire within me not a signal that I have—the existence of a desire is, is the indicator to me that I have denied responsibility and not accepting the desire because it seems to me that by accepting my desire it should shorten that time, mental time frame to zero because—

By accepting its right of existence, for you alone have created it. One can accept and should accept the right of existence for that is the law. The right of existence. And by the acceptance of the right of existence of a desire does not mean that you must fulfill it. Pardon?

OK.

Yes. You see, it is not an infallible law that by the acceptance of the right of existence of a desire, that you must fulfill it. Pardon?

If by accepting the desire, am I not fulfilling the desire in one either, either—

Yes, that is true. You can accept the right of existence of a desire and not be controlled by it, or you can accept the right of existence of a desire and fulfill it, you see? You see, total acceptance is the will of God. To deny the right of existence of that which is created is a house divided. A wise person accepts its right to existence and chooses, with his conscious mind, whether or not he wishes to fulfill it. If he chooses to fulfill the desire that his mind has created, then he must look at the law clearly to see what is necessary to keep God, the Divine Expression, in it or to go through the concern of the denial of the acceptance and the responsibility. Yes. See, one should not refrain from expressing desire, for to do so, one no longer can remain in the earthly form that they presently have. You do understand that, don't you?

Yes.

You desire to eat?

Yes.

Then you must eat. And if you choose not to do so, then you cannot long maintain your personal responsibility to the vehicle that you have merited in evolution. In other words, you deny the right of existence of the form that has been created by the laws you alone have established before entering earth. For it is the laws that you have established in evolution that has placed you in the house in which you now reside physically and mentally. Pardon?

Yes.

So, you see, to deny that you are responsible for creating that which you are, a house you are now in, is to go against the law. And to go against the law, to be tempted to go against the law, the law shall extract its just due. Pardon? Did that help you?

Yes.

Yes. Now someone else had a question. Yes.

What governs the time frame when we create a desire? How does that work?

Wisdom. Wisdom. For example, in the creating of a desire, if a person accepts full personal responsibility that they alone are creating this desire, and they consciously accept full responsibility for it, then they have the opportunity, they have granted themselves the opportunity to keep themselves freed from concern. And in the creating of the desire, to consciously create it and to declare the truth, "This desire that I have stolen from you (the Divine Expression), for I've brought it into limit, I return now to you for its fulfillment." And you free yourself from the fear, the frustration, the temptation, the concern, and all of the misery that the functions have to offer in reference to it. Yes. You see, time is an illusion.

Yes.

The limiting of the divine expression, known as desire, is an illusion. It is an illusion, a created illusion. So when one creates a desire, if one is blinded by the temptation in the creating process, then they are not awakened to the time ingredient that is in the illusion, known as desire, that they have created. Yes.

But—so if man is the creator and he's creating this time limit . . .

Yes, man alone creates that.

What sort of thing governs that—

Governs how long it will take?

Yes. So if he's the one creating it, how does that work?

The lack of concern is the fulfillment of the desire by the divine expression. The lack of concern. So, you see, if a desire is created and is not in its creating process of the mind, if God is not there, but the will of the mind is the predominant factor involved, the will of the mind, then man will pay the price of time element. The time element is dictated by 51 or more percent of the will of the mind over the acceptance of the Law of Goodness fulfilling it. Yes.

But if at the time the desire's created, if God is in it, it's—

If God is in it 51 or more percent—

Right.

—then man will not be plagued by concern.

But it still has a time limit on it, is that correct?

Yes, but that's in the wisdom of the Divine. That is, time is in this mental realm an illusion.

OK.

Yes.

So since it really doesn't exist as far as the Divine is concerned, does it just reveal how much obstruction we've place on it?

That's all it reveals. That is correct. You're absolutely correct. It's like, for example, the sale of this property. All it reveals—it is sold.

Yes.

All it reveals is the mental activity, the concern and the fear, the temptations and etc., that you, as students, are all learning about through the experience. Yes.

OK.

My channel has no concern whatsoever in reference to what we have instructed and told him. And we told him that many months ago and to this day he is not concerned. His work has been, and continues to be, to help my students to free them from their concern. Yes.

Thank you.

Yes, go ahead.

That makes sense.

Did you understand?

Yes. Thank you.

Yes. Now someone else had a question here. [That student] had a question, yes.

So then a desire can be fulfilled and not be manifested? It can be fulfilled and not have happened?

Now here is—what would you call that? I find two questions that are in direct opposite poles here. The right of existence—for example, you have a desire in your mind. You accept its right of existence. For you, that is its fulfillment. It does not plague you. You understand that?

Yes.

All right. You have a desire and you choose to fulfill it. That's another experience, isn't it?

Yes.

All right. Now desire is an expression of the Divinity. When it enters the minds of men, that divine expression becomes limited or bottled up. Man puts a cloak over it. Do you understand that? So you have this great power—you understand?—that the mind has captured. That's why we say, "God, I release to you this desire I have stolen from you." Because you are putting a great power into a very small vessel. Do you understand? Now the effect of this great power being bottled up by the human mind in its limit of the divine expression is a great force to the human mind for it has been bottled by the human mind. Do you understand that?

The form already created in the mind.

The mind has created the limit.

Right.

Now, for example, you have a desire for a house or you desire to move or you desire to marry or you desire money or you desire health or whatever you may desire, you are taking the divine expression and putting it into a vessel that you have created. It may be a very small one. Time reveals how small it really is, for the smaller it is, the less time has been given in the creating of the form that you have put this power into. Pardon?

Right.

You see? Now this is why, when you have a desire, accept the fulfillment of it. Do not permit the mind to dictate its expression, for when you put it into the dictates of the mind (What day will it happen? How long will it take? What are the dictates? What do you expect out of it? and all of that), then the vessel that you have put this great power into is very, very small. And you end up with frustration and concern and impatience and denial of the very acceptance of its own fulfillment. Hmm?

Yes.

Does that help you with your question?

Yes.

You see. You see, it's like a person who says, "Well, I'm hungry. Now I would like to have something to eat." And there are twenty grocery stores, [and they] all have the same food. Pardon? So does it matter if you quench your hunger from that grocery store or *that* grocery store? For your principle interest is to fill this hunger that you have, is that not correct?

Right.

Fine. However, that's just filling your hunger. However, if you've been to the twenty grocery stores and some people you don't like and some you do like, then you come up with a restriction that you're going to go only to that grocery store. You go to that grocery store, and you look at the door and it says "Closed for Inventory." Do you understand? So, you see, *we* create the limits. *We* create whether it's a very small vessel that we have put the Divine Power into or a very large one. Yes. And isn't it practical to give back to the Power that which we have stolen from it and limited in a small vessel? Hmm?

Yes.

Yes. So that it may be fulfilled in the way of goodness, for acceptance is the will of God, and the will of God *is* goodness. That's what the will of God is, is goodness. Yes. I hope that's helped with your question. And yes, please. Hmm. Be with you in a moment. *[The teacher addresses a student who is waiting to ask a question.]* Yes.

Do we steal the desire by declaring it as our own?

Yes. That's how we steal it. For example, as I said in reference to being hungry in the grocery store, you see, try to understand when you create a desire because you're hungry, there are other factors that put it from principle into personality. So you won't buy the same loaf of bread from *that* store because you like someone that's over at that store. Yet it's the same loaf of bread. That's the bondage of personality.

You see, it's like a person who's in pain, and they cry out for freedom from the pain. Does it matter whether it's a doctor they like or it's a healer they don't like or someone else? What does it really matter, if they are honest and pain is what they want to be freed from? Does it matter whether they're black, yellow, green, or blue? Does it matter? When you have pain (sufficient), then you want to be freed from it, isn't that correct? *[The teacher calls upon a different student.]*

Yes, indeed.

It doesn't matter if it's a mouse that comes and heals you. Does it matter?

No.

You see, that's the difference, children, between principle and personality. Honesty, the little light of honesty will reveal whether or not you are serving principle and the fulfillment of your desires or you are serving personality. For if you are serving personality, then you have many experiences to go through before it will be fulfilled. Does that help you with the question?

Yes, sir. Thank you.

You see, you see, you may not like a person, yet through that person you receive the fulfillment of your desire. Then you must overcome your adversity because, you see, the stone the builder rejects becomes the cornerstone. So it is what you reject. It's like the problem: the problem is the solution. It's waiting to be accepted. When you look and you say, "I have a problem,"—you make a change in attitude, and you have a solution. So a problem to one level is a solution to the next one. And if you think about a problem with a positive attitude, you move that much more quickly in making the change within and see, "Why, this was never a problem at all! This is a solution. I am so grateful for this experience. It is a solution." Do you understand?

Yes, sir.

All right. Yes.

You spoke of limiting the Divine into a vessel.

That is correct.

For a desire.

Yes, for its fulfillment in a mental world.

Well, is that the same thing as like when we identify initially, coming from the All . . .

Yes?

Is that the similar thing on a larger scale that through our desire and identification that we're put into a form . . .

Yes?

And then limit the Divine, the Power, turn it into a force and then have all this . . .

That is correct.

These so-called experiences in creation.

That is the error of ignorance, yes. Over-identification with limit is the true error of ignorance, yes.

And is that how we got into this form at, or any form in the first place, out of the formless and the free?

No, the purpose of the form, the purpose of the soul's incarnation into form is to evolve and to awaken form. That's its purpose. We have that responsibility. It's like building a house: putting windows in it so the light can shine through, you see? You see, a person does not live a healthy life in a house with no windows. You must have light, you see, to prosper. There must be light. The light is the sustenance, yes. The more light, the more sustenance. It is the over-identification with limit that is the problem. Yes. And also, the solution.

It seems that, as time is an illusion, that form, being a limit, is also really an illusion. Is that true?

Why, certainly it's true.

And if it's just an illusion—

It is an illusion. It is, however, one we've created. And because we have created it, we are bound by the belief of it. Yes.

My question was, since it's really an illusion, as time is an illusion—

It is.

Why go through this whole process of awakening it, if it really doesn't exist?

Through the love of that which we have created. It's known as the love of self. The love of self is the love of that which we create. Be it a desire for a cup of tea or a desire for a house or a desire for a place or a thing, it is the love of what we have created. We have fallen in love with what we have created, and the payment of that love is the bondage of our own beliefs. Yes. Yes.

So if we weren't in love with it—

If we weren't in love with our self, yes.

—then would we still incur this responsibility for raising the awareness of something that is only a delusion?

It is an illusion we have created. The illusion would not exist if there wasn't love to bind it together. It is our love that is the adhesive that binds it to our soul. Yes.

In the creative principle that . . .

Yes?

The one you taught years ago publicly, anyway.

Yes, and still do. Yes.

Then that first step . . .

Uh-huh.

The love, is—am I correct in understanding that that's really a bondage then?

Yes, because we limit it. You see, "Love all life and know the Light" is freedom, for it is truth. To take and put Love into a restricted vessel—do you understand, I'm speaking of the Divine Love that we are—to put it into a restricted vehicle puts us into all of the experiences that we have with the functions. The fear, the concern, and all the misery. Yes.

And was the belief that second step? Am I correct in remembering that?

Yes.

OK. Thank you.

Awareness, belief, become.

Thank you.

Hmm? So one becomes aware of oneself, and believes in their self-importance and the denial of a part of the whole. Yes. Well, it has, it offers to a person the balance between the positive and the negative, for the Divine is neutral, you see. The Divine is not the positive nor the negative. It is the perfect balance of the positive and the negative. It is the divine, intelligent, infinite Neutrality. Hmm?

Yes.

You see, Divinity, a neutrality, does not see difference. It just is, you see. And not seeing difference, for it has the one eye, the single eye of eternity, it does not see dual. So it doesn't see difference; therefore, it doesn't compare; therefore, it doesn't judge; therefore, it doesn't have the forty functions that have been listed. Did that help with your question?

Yes, a lot. Thank you.

Yes. Remember, if you keep thine eye single, you cannot have comparison and you cannot be bound by the creations known as judgments. It's not possible. For when the eye is single, you are not separated from that which you are. It is only when you see difference, you see duality that you have bondage. You cannot have bondage in that which is single and neutral. For that which is, is. There's nothing to defend for there's nothing to justify. It just is.

Well, friends, I see our time has passed. Well, one more question. Yes there, and then—

Thank you.

Yes.

With the difference between fear and faith, faith is from the heart, from the ...

When we direct that which we are to that illusion we have created, then we experience fear. Now we discussed that before in class. It is our choice either to direct it to the Source from whence it cometh—that's total acceptance—or to direct it to the limits of our mind, you see? So doing our part is freeing our self from concern, you see?

Yes.

Because when we have concern, we are denying acceptance, and therefore personal responsibility cannot express itself.

No.

You see?

Yes.

Yes.

Thank you.

Time, like things, are illusions we have created.

Thank you.

And so the mind calls that reality, a conscious awareness of passing events, though they may be, and usually are, shadows of yesteryear. That, to the mind, is reality. Yes. Or have you not heard the mind say, "Oh, in the good old days things were so great." Well, I've said to students before, "If things were so great in the good old days, why did you ever leave them? Why didn't you stay there? Hmm?" If they were so good, we wouldn't have left them in our consciousness, do you understand? Yes. Things that have passed or yet to be are always tempting and desirable to the uneducated mind. I do hope that's helped with your questions.

Remember, encouragement is like a coat of armor: you go through any storm as long as you remain courageous, and that's known as encouragement.

Thank you and good night.

OCTOBER 8, 1987

A/V Seminar 27

And welcome to Seminar One Eighty-Eight.

This evening we will discuss the chemistry of the human body and how to restore it to a state of balance, which is harmony, which is health. We know that we are Spirit, formless and free. We also know that whatever we think, and believe what we think, that we shall become, for we create the mental body in which the Spirit that we are temporarily resides. And so it is because we believe with our mind what our mind creates, we identify with the mental body and create a change in the chemistry of our physical body. So we see how critical and how very important [is] our attitude, which is our rate of vibration, which attitude is the expression of our belief in what we have created with our mind. For example, we believe that we are the sadness that we have created. We believe that we are the happiness that we have created. And in so doing we deny what we are and believe what we are not. By so doing we abuse, instead of use, the power that we are. We do so by an error of ignorance.

Remember that power is the expression of the formless, free Spirit that we are, and force is an expression of the mental body, the mental form, that we have created.

All chemicals known and presently unknown on your planet exist within the temple of God which is your human body. An attitude, which is the expression of intelligent energy directed to a judgment that we have created and believe that we are, has a direct effect upon the chemistry and the intelligent cells within the human body.

As I stated to my channel some time ago, heaven is where our heart is. Now one should always be aware of where their heart is. Their heart being an expression of their soul. So often we confuse our heart with our emotions. And in so doing we freely loan it, and sometimes have difficulty in reclaiming it.

The medical profession of your world is evolving in an understanding that an attitude of mind brings about a change in the physical chemistry of the human body, that it has a direct effect upon intelligent cells within the human body. And this is why, ofttimes, a person who believes that they are receiving a chemical that will improve their health, even though they are not receiving that chemical, their health will improve. For through their own belief, their own attitude of mind, they have brought about a change in the chemicals of their own body. For some people it does not seem to work; for some people it does seem to work. Of course, it is dependent on how much they believe, for their identity is with the body, the mental body, that they have created.

Now that which we create we are affected by. And so the mind, which we have created, and the body, which is controlled by it—the mind affecting the body; the body also affects the mind.

That which is controversial and disturbing to the mind is discordant and the direct opposite of health. Health being, of course, the effect of the Law of Balance, which is harmony.

Force, the king of the functions, is the realm of payment and attainment. It is indeed a costly realm for those who are tempted to control it.

Now we'll take a few moments for the questions that I see rising in your minds. You'll be so kind now to raise your hands. Yes, please.

How is it that the human—what are the laws governing the understanding that the human body contains all the chemicals there are?

What is the law governing the understanding?

Well, I'm interested in understanding how it came to be that our physical bodies contain all the chemicals.

Yes. Certainly. The physical body on your planet is the effect of eons of physical evolution. It has passed through all forms of your planet, known and unknown to your mind. In its evolutionary process, it contains in varying degrees all chemicals that exist upon your planet. For your body is, in its present stage of evolution, an effect of those eons of evolving. Pardon?

Thank you.

Yes. You're welcome. Yes, please.

Thank you. Would you please explain what you mean by controversial?

Controversial. For example, when a person expresses that which is not definite, then it is doubtful, would you not agree?

Yes.

Now that which is not definite and not specific is ever open to question. And that being open to question is open to doubt within the human consciousness. You are aware, I am sure, of the experience of indecision. Does it offer to your mind or has it ever offered a direction of positive encouragement?

No.

Fine. So the early stages of evolution offer controversy, doubt, and, of course, fear. Have you ever experienced question, doubt, and controversy without experiencing fear?

No.

Now what is fear? Fear demonstrably reveals that it is an expression of faith directed to the mental body; that it is a negative expression of the power of acceptance; that it is a denial. We fear, we fear what we deny, for what we deny becomes our destiny. And we fear our destiny from the error of ignorance. For example, a person may say, "I would like to have such an item. I would like to have a car. I would like to have a house or I'd like to have an apartment." A person says that to their, in their mind. When they do so, a thousand questions arise, would you not agree?

Yes.

Now of the thousand questions that arise, how many of the questions would you say, out of one thousand, that you experience a positive encouraging answer to?

Not a very large percentage.

A very small percent. Knowing that life and its experiences are nothing more and nothing less than an effect of our own attitude of mind, we can, with great assurance, know what tomorrow will bring us. Is that not correct?

Yes.

For it will bring us that which we have the greatest faith in. And if the greatest faith we have is in the mind, the mental body that we have created, then we know that it will bring us fear of not having what we desire or think that we should have. Do you understand that?

Yes.

And so, you see, by controversial vibration within the human consciousness we know what our tomorrows are going to be like. They're known as negative, for they are fearful for our faith is directed to that which we alone have created: our own attitude of mind, an expression of the judgments that we have made, and the fear that those judgments will befall us, which they do by what we know as experience. And so we are not lost, for we know the difference between believing, and the bondage of believing what we have created, and acceptance, which is the will of the formless, free Spirit that we are. Does that help with your question?

Yes. Thank you.

You're welcome. Yes, please.

Thank you.

Yes.

Would the beliefs affecting our chemical body, it's like a retraining and—

Pardon me. Our attitude of mind affects the chemistry of our body. Our attitude of mind is an expression of the believing that we are the thoughts of the mind that we alone have created. Yes. Thank you. Go ahead.

Thank you. And the retraining process, through this mental world inside of ourselves, the end goal is, like, through the doorway to acceptance, which is the will of God, and harmony within our mind and has the effect, then, in our body, our attitude.

You see, to love oneself is wisdom when one knows what oneself is. But to love oneself and to believe that oneself is the mind and the mental body that one has created, there is the difficulty, yes. You see, to love oneself is to love God, you see. However, it is an error of ignorance to love oneself and believe that oneself is the thoughts and the judgments that one alone has created. This is where self-love, like self-pity, which is an expression, of course, of self-love—self-pity is an expression of the love of the mind that we have created and believe that we are. That's what self-pity and self-love is. But if a person loves the [true] self, then they love the formless, free Spirit that they are. And the formless, free Spirit that they are is the Infinite Intelligence, for that *is* what we are. Yes.

Yes. Thank you.

You're welcome. Yes, please.

Did I understand you correctly to say that our Spirit resides in our mental body and—

Our Spirit expresses through our mental body temporarily. That is correct. Yes, indeed it does. That is the individualized Spirit which you know, of course, as the covering, which is known as the individualized soul. We are Spirit, you see, formless and free.

So we create the body; that is what we create. God does not create. God sustains. Man is the creator. We believe that we are what we have created, and in so doing our error of ignorance is indeed increased. Yes. We not only believe what we have created, we believe what everyone else has created because we cannot offer to another what we first do not offer to our self. And so by offering to our self the belief that we are what we have created, then we have no problem whatsoever believing what someone else has created. Does that help with your question? Yes.

That's why you say in your world that man is easily conned, you see. *[The teacher laughs joyously.]* You see, instead of an objective perspective that—you know, so often a person feels sorry for someone. Well, what we are revealing, of course, is that we feel sorry for our self, and we have someone else to lay the trip on. I think that's how you put it, you see. And because, you see, you cannot offer sorrow, feeling sorry, to anyone until you first offer it to yourself. Now the moment that you accept the goodness that you are, then you won't feel sorry for someone, you see. You will be happy in seeing the goodness that they are and how much brighter it's going to be because they're paying their dues, freeing themselves from the disasters they alone have created, you see. Pardon?

It doesn't mean you knock a person down when they're down, but you share with them an understanding, a demonstration of the Light of truth that they are not the situation that they believe that they are. They have created it. And as long as they believe that that is them, then it will take that much longer for them to get through it, whatever the situation may be, you see. Yes. That is known as the faculty of charity, you see. Yes. Yes, please.

What attitudes of mind are most beneficial, then, if controversy is . . .

Extremely detri—well, of course, acceptance is not only the will of God, it is the, it is the harmony, it is the perfect balance between the forty faculties and the forty functions. The Law of Harmony. And so what brings about the Law of Harmony? The various balancing of the forty faculties with the forty functions. [When] a person accepts—you see?—a balance starts to take place within the chemistry of the human body, and there's an attitude of mind that is changed.

And encouragement always makes a person feel better. One always feels better when they are encouraged, especially—you see, the divinity of disaster is encouragement. To see it for what it has to offer. Disaster offers to the human mind the opportunity of growing up, of changing, you see. And so one should not look at disaster without seeing the divinity that is within it, for seeing the divinity that is within it is encouraging. And encouragement is like an adrenaline to the system: one instantly feels better, you see.

Thank you.

Yes. Because if one does not feel good about themselves, then they are not, they do not have the proper perspective of what the self truly is. They believe that the self is the things they have created with their mind. So when one feels good about themselves, one is awakening to what they truly are: formless, free Spirit and not all the things they've created, you see? Yes.

Thank you.

Does that help with your question?

Yes, sir.

You see, oh, not that one is not responsible for what they have created and it is this weight of responsibility that is so discouraging and so disastrous, you see. Hmm? For, as I stated long ago, when the weight of responsibility exceeds the love of God, then one indeed has a burden in life, don't they? Hmm?

Yes, sir.

That's why the weight of responsibility, the belief that you are the things that you have created, must never exceed the love of what you truly are, which is formless, free Spirit or God. Yes. Yes.

We've always used responsibility in terms of personal responsibility, but in this guidance the weight of responsibility seems to be a burden of our own belief.

Well, of course, that's what the burden is. You see, disappointment, discouragement, and all of those negative things are only an identification with what one has created, you see. We create this with our mind; we create that with our mind by our belief that we are the judgments that we have created and have made, yes. For example, if someone says to you, "Your name is Robert," you'll have a problem right away. You will correct them and say, "No, my name is [Tom]." Is that correct? *[The student's name has been changed.]*

Yes, sir.

So what's in a name? What is in a name? Someone gave you the name that you have. Is that correct?

Yes, sir, they did.

Yes. Did you tell them that's the name that you wanted?

No, sir. I don't recall if I did.

Well, there you are, you see. However, you merited those parents who chose to give you that particular name for whatever selfish reasons that they had, correct?

Correct.

And so that's the name that you hold to. Yet you did not, by conscious choice, that you can recall, choose that name.

Correct.

However, you became attached to that name. You believe that name is you or you wouldn't have such a problem if somebody calls you John. Pardon?

Yes, sir.

You see? Yes. And so we see that very early in life we believe in this special, unique form that we have created, you see, very, very early in childhood. And we become very defensive and extremely emotional if someone chooses to call us by some other name, for we have already accepted and we have judged and we believe that's who we are.

Now what is the name? The name carries what? It carries all of the emotions, all of the feelings, and all of the experiences since your early days. Correct?

Correct.

So if someone takes that name away from you, they don't just take a name. They take all of the things that you are dependent upon with your mind for identification. Pardon?

Yes, sir.

Because you have created that under the umbrella of the name that you have become attached to and believe that you are. You are not attached to the name [Tom]. You are attached to what the name [Tom] means to your mind, the good, the bad, and the indifferent. Do you understand that?

Yes, sir.

Very well. Now you know, perhaps, why they don't give you any name. So many students of mine over the years have said, "Why don't you have a name?" I don't need a name. That's the last thing that I do need is a name. *[Many students laugh.]* Yes. Perhaps you understand a little better now why I don't particularly need a name. I have no need for it. I had one long ago. I don't recall that. Yes. So it's not the name. It's what it means to *you* or anyone else, you see. Yes, please.

Thank you. Could you talk a little on encouragement and when is it appropriate to encourage yourself and encourage others and when is encouragement simply a mask of the, of the levels or the forms?

Yes. In reference to encouragement—and you may be encouraged right there *[The teacher addresses the church's dog, Reddy, who is trying to nuzzle the teacher.]*—in reference to encouragement, first of all, one, in order to be effective in encouraging anyone, must first enter that state of consciousness within themselves, you see.

Yes.

Now ofttimes it is used by the mind—you're very encouraged there *[The teacher again addresses Reddy, who has just laid down on his cushion.]*—ofttimes it is used by the mind as it is even with a child to, as you say, a mask to receive a fulfillment of its own desires. We understand that. Therefore, a person knows within themselves if their encouragement, their own encouragement, is dependent upon what someone else does or doesn't do, you see. So a sincere encouragement is not dependent on anything that it cannot, by the Law of Personal Responsibility, control. So you can control your own mind, correct?

Yes.

Pardon?

It's possible, yes.

Why, certainly. And ofttimes you have demonstrated that, especially when you decide that you want something, correct? Pardon?

Yes.

Yes. And so when you decide that you want something, and you go through your mind that it is within your right and you can accomplish it, you encourage yourself—is that not correct?—and then you get it.

That's correct. [The student speaks very quietly.]

Pardon?

That's correct.

But, you see, you're not dependent on what someone else, you understand, does. You are dependent on what you by your own choice do. Do you understand?

Yes.

So you are not trying to manipulate something outside of your own just and rightful domain. In other words, you're not trying to manipulate another person who also has the divine right of their own encouragement.

Yes.

And so that is encouragement. And a person, when they encourage themselves in anything, takes a look at what they're encouraging themselves in, weighs it out whether or not it's depending on someone else, and then they go ahead and they do it, don't they?

Yes.

And they reap the harvest thereof. So if you want to encourage a person in anything, first be aware whether or not the person you are working to encourage is working through the laws of personal responsibility and it does not interfere with the divine rights of another individual. Do you understand that?

Yes, I do.

So because, otherwise, you have, you become the victim of the error of ignorance, and you have a mask or false encouragement, and it will fizzle.

Right.

Do you understand?

I understand.

You see. So if a person understands that and is aware of the person that they are trying to help, through the Law of Solicitation, you understand—yes. Because unsolicited help is ever to no avail, extremely detrimental to the one who is tempted to help. Pardon? And so through the Law of Solicitation, definitely, be well aware of whether or not that person is doing it within their own divine right and not interfering with the divine rights of another.

OK.

Within the law, you see, the spiritual laws and the mental laws.

OK.

Did that help with your question?

It does. Can I ask another question?

Certainly. You go right ahead.

So if, if the person isn't making the effort and they still solicit encouragement . . .

Then you will pay the price of the depression of self-pity, which you have exposed yourself to within your own consciousness, for it's a deception.

I see.

You see, they don't want help. They only want it "subject to:" there are stipulations in how they will accept help. Do you understand that?

Yes.

And so as long as you have these conditions, you understand—that means you would have to meet those specific conditions of the judgments of the human mind in order to help them. And remember, you would have to meet those judgments within your own consciousness, your own set of judgments. So that is conditional encouragement and is not sincere encouragement, which is a soul faculty, because it does not carry with it the lamp of reason or the light of honesty, you see?

OK.

It's deception.

Yes.

Because the encouragement is solicited with conditions, which is contrary to the spiritual law, you see.

Yes.

Did that help with your question?

Yes, it did. Thank you.

Yes, certainly. Yes. You know, that's kind of like saying, "God, I will do this, if you will bring me that." You see, it's a bartering type of thing. Anything that is conditional is controversial. And anything that is controversial is not healthy for it is not specific. That's the law that's involved.

Thank you.

Yes. You see, ofttimes our minds are tempted to help another; we are tempted, and we must ask our self, "Why am I tempted, when I see clearly they are not willing to make the necessary changes to help themselves?" You see?

Yes.

And that is when a person lets go of the temptation of their mind or pays the price for they must enter that realm of consciousness of condition and controversy. Now remember that when you're helping a person, if you are so inspired to do so, and you become aware of that, you can easily become aware of the mountains of justifications why they're not moving ahead. Do you understand that?

Yes.

There's always a defense of a judgment. Now that's what a justification is. It is a defense, the first line of defense of judgments. And a person who believes they are the judgments they have created has many excuses, many justifications, and has an extremely controversial vibration or attitude of mind.

OK.

Yes.

Great. Thank you.

You're welcome. Also, you will find there's always something wrong outside; that they're in a helpless state of victimization. You will also find that.

Thank you.

Yes. Yes. Good evening.

Good evening, sir. When we feel our self getting into a level that we're—our health is not feeling good. We feel our self starting to feel bad physically.

Yes.

What techniques or steps should we do to reverse that process, sir?

Definitely. That is a very, very dangerous realm to enter for it's extremely detrimental to one's health. One has exposed themselves to a controversial vibration, which is negative. Extremely negative. And one therefore begins to feel, without conscious awareness, a pity of the self, an over-identification with themselves. Now an over-identification or thinking of the self, you understand, will bring about a chemical imbalance within the human body. It is extremely destructive. The body affects the mind, and the mind affects the body. One should then make a drastic change within their consciousness. They must make the great effort to think of something else. Do you understand that? Still take care of their responsibilities, but they must make greater effort on doing their breathing and on awareness of their thoughts and feelings. Otherwise, their health will continue to deteriorate. Yes, absolutely.

And we must remember that it works through the water center. We are magnetically pulled through the centers of emotion, you see. And also, we have a tendency, you see, to think of events that have passed. And, you know, guilt is rejected desire. And so we must—that which has passed has passed and has served its purpose. So why call it forth again? Isn't that correct?

Yes.

Pardon? You know, because you cannot evolve that way, you see. What's gone down the river, let it go down the river. It'll drown in its own way under its own weight, you see. You know, it's kind of like a child, you know. They may sometimes burn their finger before they learn how to properly use a match. Isn't that correct?

Yes, sir.

So if they burn their finger a few times, it won't be too long before they learn their whole hand will go if they don't make changes. Now if we interfere, through emotion, we become responsible for postponing the lesson that was due them at the time it was due them. And then we become a part of that, and we pay our self. So, you see, it's not the path of wisdom. Would you not agree?

Yes, sir.

Yes. You see, ofttimes when you tell a person, "No," it's the kindest thing that you could possibly do for them. You know within your own heart that no is no and ofttimes no is God's direction. If they cannot see the goodness of that at that time, it's simply because they haven't evolved yet to that state of consciousness. Someday they will, you see. Don't hold your breath in the process, though. *[The teacher laughs joyfully.]* Does that help there?

Yes, sir.

Do your breathing. And remember, it is the mind. You just close the door, the magnetic door that opens up, you see, from shadows of the past, you see. And, you know, rejected desire is a very destructive thing. It's known as guilt, you see. It's created by the mind, you see. And we don't have to believe in it if we don't want to. Especially when we see how destructive it is to ourselves, you see. Yes.

Thank you very much.

You're welcome, you're welcome. Yes, please.

Thank you.

Yes.

I believe it was said the divinity of disaster is encouragement.

Why, [if] you see the Divinity there, then you cannot help but be encouraged. Why, certainly.

And I think at one other class encouragement was said to be, to be courageous?

Of course.

And is that, in that moment to—in the middle—or to see the disaster, to—

To be aware of the disaster and see the Divinity.

To see the Divinity by separating . . .

Your emotions—separating, you see, your own—you see, it's our mind, you see. We believe that—and we see something and we say, "Oh, it's a terrible disaster." It stimulates our senses, you see. And then we become the victim of what our senses represent: force. And I just finished, I think, explaining to you that force is the laws of payment and attainment, you see. You know, a lot of people, you know, if they, they see a so-called road experience there—several cars all smashed-up—and they always look to see how dismembered the victims are, you know, because it's stimulating, you see, to the senses. It's so stimulating, yes. You know, or they say, "Oh, I can't bear all that blood," and they look right at it, you see. So they can become more stimulated, yes. I hope that's helped with your question.

Can I ask another one?

Yes, certainly.

And the courage is the separation at that moment from the form, then, [to] who you truly are?

Why, of course. Certainly. Absolutely. Yes. If your hair turns white overnight, will you be encouraged or discouraged? Now if you see the Divinity in it, you will be encouraged: you got a different color.

Right.

Pardon? And it happened overnight! Well, now, there you are.

Well, it's so nice to be with you again here in this seminar and I look forward to seeing you, then, next month. Yes. Good night.

JANUARY 14, 1988

A/V Seminar 28

Good evening, class.

Our class this evening—we will discuss the chemistry of thought. If you will think for a moment that each and every cell of the physical body is an intelligent entity. Whenever we entertain the thought of dependence on anything beyond the rightful domain of the intelligent cells of our being, those cells are denied the true purpose of their being. And in so being denied, we experience an upheaval within our emotions. We know that as frustration. That is a manifestation of denying the cells, those intelligent cells, the true purpose of their existence.

And so we find that an attitude of mind that does not deny the right of the cells of our being brings about harmonious action, and we experience what is known as the joy and fullness of life.

We all realize what it is like to be denied what we believe is our right. We experience what is known as a rejection, little realizing that we have, through an error in thought, set that law into motion by our own dependence. And so we cannot feel rejected without feeling dependent. So it is so very important for us, in order to experience good health, the harmonious expression of these intelligent cells, it is so very important for us to realize the purpose of their being and not to deny them their right of existence. For to depend upon anything that is not within our rightful domain is to establish that law of denial, destiny, rejection, and frustration.

The manifestation, the chemistry of thought, its manifestation, is known to us as experience. We often wonder why we have the varied experiences that we have. Yet we really do know that we have set those laws into motion in order that we may take full responsibility for what we have earned at any point in time in our evolution.

To worry or to be concerned about what someone else does is to deny the intelligence for which you are responsible. No one can afford the luxury of worry or concern about what someone else will or will not do. Everyone should enjoy the practical experience of what they, by their own choice, will or will not do. For if we accept responsibility for our ship, we will not have to be concerned about what the crew will do, for our crew is the intelligent cells of our own being. Remember that to concern ourselves with what someone else will or will not do is to deny one's own responsibility to the intelligence that they are responsible for and, in so doing, by that denial, to experience rejection through dependence and, therefore, live a life of discord, known as frustration.

Now we'll take a few moments for questions along the line of our present discussion. If you'll be so kind as to raise your hands. Yes, please.

Yes. I'd like to know how do you not be dependent on that which you follow.

One follows, in reference to your question, How does one not become dependent on that which one chooses to follow? One becomes freed from dependence on what they choose to follow by accepting that they are the follower, and in so being, they are following that which is within them. You see, a person looks out and they will see a person and they will choose to follow that person based upon the demonstration, the experiences that they have had with that person. Now if a person, in accepting personal responsibility, reminds themselves that what they are following is what they have created in their own mental world—in other words, the form is a manifestation of what they have created in their mind. Now, for example, a person looks out and they say, "Well, now that appears or seems to be something worthwhile to follow. Now that something that I see is what I have created. I must not forget that I have created that. Because I have created that, it cannot go until I choose it to go. It is not out there. It is what I have created in here." *[The teacher points with all the fingers of his right hand toward the center of his forehead and then moves his hand downward, parallel to his spine.]* So, you see, therefore, it does not leave until one chooses it to leave in their consciousness. In other words, if a person follows the manifestation of another person, it does not matter whether that person is in the physical flesh or not, for they have created that person within their consciousness and that person will remain within their consciousness as long as they choose to keep that person there. Pardon? Did that help with your question?

You see, therefore, a person is not dependent. You see, it is the illusion that it is out there. That is the—that is the trap. That is the trap of dependency and frustration, denial, rejection. That is not where it is. It is manifested out there to those who believe there is only a physical world. To those who understand that a physical world is a manifestation of a mental world, which is, in truth, another manifestation of a higher world, to those people, they know that it is something they have created within their consciousness. Therefore, it cannot and will not leave until they themselves choose to replace it by creating something to take its place within their consciousness.

So it's not dependent upon the physical, only to those who believe there is nothing but the physical. Does that help with the question? Yes.

And could you discuss, please, a little bit about when a person goes to change it in their thinking? How would they know if that's a beneficial change in accordance with the Light and their progression or if it's a self—darker level?

Yes. Well, now, there is one sure way of knowing: that is, to winter it and summer it, that is, before one springs and falls it. Now that is—let the seasons pass. Now a person usually understands the seasons to be a spring, a fall, a winter, a summer. It is the seasons of the consciousness. There are eighty-one levels of consciousness. And if a person winters and summers, springs and falls anything within their consciousness, they will see the various changes that they go through in their consciousness. When they have gone through all of them, if it is a progressive step to the next step, what they will find is there is no problem with it going in any of the levels of consciousness, you see?

Yes.

You see, we must not forget that whatever we follow is something inside of our self that we have created within our consciousness, you see.

Yes.

And if we will remember that, it doesn't matter where the physical being is or is not, because it is what we have created, and therefore *we* can let it go and replace it. It doesn't matter because that's where it really is.

Yes.

First of all, it's created by the consciousness, and the form is filled by the physical world. Does that help with the question? You see, you see, first [of] all it's created by the, in the mental world. That's where it's created. And when a person is convinced in the mental world that that is what they want, truly convinced, and has accepted that within their consciousness, then it is filled by the physical world.

Yes.

You see. You see, it applies to everything: people, places, and things. It applies especially in the material world to money. You see, if a person—because it's created by the mind and is filled by the physical world. Everything is created by the mind, then, by the law, filled by the physical world. So if a person has the chemistry of thought of ever, always a shortage of money, they will always have that experience. They will have the physical manifestation of a constant shortage because that's what they've created with their mind. Now if a person creates an abundance of that in their consciousness, you see, and they are consistent with their creation, like creating anything, then they will always be abundantly filled with it in a physical manifestation. You see, the physical reveals the chemistry of the mental that we, by our own choice, are constantly setting into motion. Yes. Did that—yes.

May I ask one more in regard to that?

Certainly.

When we winter it and summer it . . .

Yes?

How are we aware that we have gone through the whole cycle and that we're not interrupting it partway, through our own judgment or desire?

Yes. Well, for example, a person, when they winter and summer something, they go through the worst of the storms: the worst of times and the best of times. And then in their consciousness that's looked at—both sides—and they have no desire, no desire to replace it and no desire to keep it. That's when they know they've gone through it and the next step will manifest itself. Yes.

No desire to keep it?

Why, no. No desire to keep it and no desire to let it go. You see, because desire cannot exist in the light of reason. You see, you're asking about, When does a person know when they have wintered and summered something and not established a law of judgment to make a change within the consciousness? When they no longer desire to make a change, when they no longer desire to remain where they are, desire no longer exists, you see. And when desire no longer exists, the light of reason reveals itself. There is no desire concerning it.

OK.

You see, because the moment there is desire, then there is concern. And that establishes, in the chemistry of thought, another creation, you see.

Yes.

Do you see? Because, you see, creation does not exist without the Law of Desire. Do you understand that?

Yes.

You see, when there is no desire, there is no creation. Desire's the divine manifestation, you see; the law—that's the Law of the Divinity. And when that is absolutely balanced, a person doesn't desire what they have; they do not desire what they do not have; and therefore, they are freed from it. Did that help with your question?

Yes. Thank you.

Yes. Because the moment you desire, you are in the process of creating. Now when you're in the process of creating and you create something, you understand, the cup may overfloweth. So something has to go to make room for what is coming. Do you understand that? You know, a person, I think, best relates it, perhaps, [to] time and time-pressure. And when the cup is overflowing and there's so many things to do and there's so many things to fit in, you see, and the cup is overflowing. You see? And so you can only get another drop in, perhaps, if you're fortunate. And you've got to squeeze it into the glass. Because something has to go. And then one must weigh out, "Now just a moment. What has to go?" Then, you see, one says, "Well, let's see, now I've had this jacket long enough, I'll throw that out. And I've had this, I'll throw that out." And the next thing you know, one is making room for all these new creations. Do you see?

Yes.

Yes. Does that help?

Yes. Thank you.

Certainly. And, [that student], please.

Thank you. Could it be likened to planting a seed and then that would be, you plant the seed, but then you don't keep—with one's consciousness it wouldn't be wise to keep digging up the seed. And then in the fall, then, you won't see the harvest of, I mean, could you—

Yes, of course. Indeed. Because, you see, when you create something and you keep looking at it to see how it's growing, you begin, you start to become frustrated because it doesn't seem to be growing at all. Do you understand that? And then you become impatient, you see. You know, it's like a person who says, "Well, I want money," and they keep looking to see where the money is, and the money does not manifest itself in the physical world. Because, you see, the more you look at it, you interfere with its growth process and cannot see the growth at all, you see. It's [like] looking at a baby every five minutes to see if it's ready to walk. No, it's not ready to walk. Yes. Yes.

Are the same chemicals in the thought as are in the physical when it finally manifests?

Oh, yes. Absolutely. Definitely. You see, each and every thought in the chemistry of thought affects a part of the mental body, which, in turn, is manifested into the physical body. Yes, definitely. And I think many of you students are aware that the neck is will, and it's also a very critical part, of course, of the physical anatomy because it is directly responsible for several types of problems with health, you see. Yes, absolutely. You're welcome. Yes.

Flowers offer us a healing. How then do the flowers and the intelligence of our cells communicate then? Or do they communicate?

They do communicate. To the human mind it's known as a feeling, you see. A person looks at something beautiful and—a person may not want to take care of flowers, but to look at them, they have a good feeling, of course. Because, you see, they manifest the beauty of nature. Yes. So they communicate through what man knows as a feeling, you see. He looks and says, "Well, they're beautiful," and then he feels for a moment—some for several moments—they feel good at that moment. Yes. Yes.

What is—is it the thought, then, that's being adjusted or it is the chemistry?

We, by our physical view of beauty, we are adjusting the chemistry of our thought, which is changing the cells of our body at that moment into a state of harmony. For example, a person looks out at a dawn or a sunset [and] says, "Oh, that is so beautiful," in that moment they are adjusting their own chemistry. Do you understand that?

Yes, sir.

You see? You see, attitude, which, of course, is the effect of thought pattern, which, of course, is the effect of thought that we entertain at any moment. Thought is very critical to the chemistry and the good of life because it is the vehicle that is controlling the physical world that our mind believes that we are. Do you understand?

Yes, sir.

Yes. So it is extremely critical to have a good thought because from a good thought a person feels good. And it is a good thought that is a free thought, not a dependent thought, you see. You see, for example, you can look at the sunset and not feel dependent—do you understand?

Yes.

And not be concerned of what it's going to do or will it be there tomorrow. It is through an error of ignorance of permitting the mind to feel good—do you understand—and in feeling good to become dependent, you see. Now I don't think any of you would say, "Well, if I don't see the sunset, I'll feel terrible." No, no because our intelligence tells us, "This is ridiculous," because we may not see the sunset every day from experiences. Therefore, we are not dependent upon the sunset. Do you understand the difference?

Yes.

You see. It is when we permit our self to feel good and we add to that a dependence on something we cannot control and do not accept its divine right of expression—like the sunset, that you may see it one night and the next night you may see it again and it's different, you see. See, there is the difference between freedom and bondage. You look at the sky and you see a cloud. And you tell yourself, "That is just beautiful." And to you it is absolutely beautiful; to someone else it, at that moment, it doesn't matter. But to you it is beautiful. But you don't have with that a dependence that that cloud must be there again tomorrow at this same time for you have already accepted its divine right of expression, which brings about an entirely different chemistry of thought in your body, you see?

Yes, sir.

Yes.

Thank you.

Yes. You're welcome. [Yes], please.

I'm, I'm wondering whether mental substance and mental body are two separate, are both separate or are they one and the same?

A mental body is created from mental substance, yes, yes. Yes.

Could—I was thinking in terms of reacting to others. So if, if—

Reaction, of course, you understand—Excuse me—is dependence. *[The teacher may be excusing himself for interrupting his student.]*

Right.

Yes, yes.

So that would be the—it would be—that would be the same—you're speaking of the same thing if you're dependent upon other's reactions to you.

If you are dependent on other's actions.

Actions. So you react to their actions.

Then you are controlled by them. But because, you see, you see, a person when they permit themselves to become over-identified with their personality, with their own being, then a person, when they fall into that, becomes very, very dependent, very dependent on what others think about them. And in so doing they destroy their health, you see, because they enter the realms of discord. Because you—on a dependence like that, the mind is very fickle. And a person says to themselves, "Well, why did they say that? Why did they look that way? Why didn't they say good morning?" Do you understand that?

Yes.

And everything is taken personally. You lose objectivity. Now the clouds don't say that to you. Neither does the sunset, you see. Yes.

Thank you.

You're welcome. Yes, please.

Thank you.

Yes.

In the last class it was said that the heart is an expression of the soul.

Yes.

And sometimes we confuse our heart with our emotions.

That is correct.

OK. Specifically, if we, if we love something or care for something outside of ourselves—we were just speaking about the sunset and so forth.

Yes.

Anything.

Yes.

Be it something or a person. How—you may have answered this already—How do we know this is an emotional response or it's a response of the heart?

Yes. Because, you see, love is not dependent. You see, that's the difference with love and desire. Love is not dependent. You can love the sun, the dawn, and the sunset, you can love the ocean, but you're not dependent upon it. Now that's love.

OK.

Now that which you find yourself dependent upon is desire, and it becomes very confused. Do you understand that?

Yes.

You see?

Yes.

[It] becomes very confused, you see. But if you'll remember that love is not dependent (desire is dependent), then you will be able to understand the difference between love and desire.

Yes.

Yes.

So if you don't—if you find yourself not desiring something, but feeling great compassion or love or whatever—

Yes?

That, that type of feeling.

Yes.

Then that's when you're coming from the heart and you're not emotional on that.

That is correct.

OK.

That is correct. And the mind has no concern, interest, or dictate of whether the cloud's going to pass or not.

I see.

Because, you see, it's not dependent. That's love.

So it's really for the moment.

Oh, yes, of course, it's for the moment, for that moment.

Yes.

Yes. Because, you see, it carries with it the full understanding of the divine right of the expression. Do you understand?

OK.

You see, the cloud may be this shape today and that shape tomorrow, but it's still a cloud. It wears many faces.

Yes.

Yes.

OK. Thank you.

You're welcome. Yes, [another student] has a question at the moment.

If we have angry thoughts and they're not expressed, what happens to the, those chemicals that we've churned up with those angry thoughts?

They go to, they go to war. They go to battle. And they start fighting each other within the body. And depending on which, which of the—the water center, the fire center, the air center, etc.—the various centers of the body represents the chemicals, a person can become very ill. Especially if their resistance, their good health is broken down. Now remember, we break down our good health by an over-identification with our water center, with our personality. And so when our resistance or our basic harmony or good health is broken down and we permit ourselves to be angry over something—or even when it isn't broken down—the cells go to, they go to war, is what they do. They go to war within our own chemistry. Yes. Yes.

So the angry thoughts are not fulfilling their purpose? Is that what you meant?

Yes, well, the angry thoughts—now remember, the feeling of anger is a defense of a judgment that a person has made. You understand that?

Yes.

For example, you know, if we believe we are the thought pattern, the judgment that we have created and someone offends that, our child, we become angry and for some reason do not express that anger, then the war, the battle goes on in the chemicals within us. Therefore, it is very important that we should express that. We do not necessarily need to express it to the person that we thought offended our judgment. We need to express it to ourselves because we created the judgment and we created the second judgment that judged that they had offended our first judgment. Does that help? So—but we do need to verbalize it. We need to give it life-giving energy to bring about a balance within our own being. Because remember, we now have two children fighting. We have judgment number one and then we have the second child, judgment number two, who has risen up, which is a judgment that the first child has been offended. And so these two judgments go to war inside, which are chemicals, you understand, and affect our chemistry of our body, you see, and also our experiences, for they create them. So we have these two, little, spoiled children fighting each other: the first one, who made the judgment, the second one that made the judgment that somebody offended the first one. Now this is all created within our consciousness, and that's where the battle and the war goes on. It's within our own consciousness. Did that help with that question?

Thank you.

You're welcome. And [another student] has been waiting, yes.

Yes. Thank you. I'd like a little more understanding about every cell is an intelligent entity.

Indeed, it is. It has a purpose to serve. You have the earth center, fire center, water center, air center, electric, magnetic, and odic, all right?

Right.

And ethereal, of course. Now there are cells in the physical body. They know what to do. They have a job to do. You do understand that, don't you?

Right.

Yes. Now when the work of those cells is interfered with, you understand?

Right.

You experience what is known as a disruption in your state of harmony or health.

Right.

Do you understand?

Yes.

All right. So what was the question? You don't understand that you have cells in your body that are intelligent, that have been created, that know exactly what their job is?

Which has been created by our mind, each and every one of their jobs.

Man is the creator. God, the Divine Light, is the sustainer.

Right.

Yes.

Right.

You see.

Thank you.

You understand you have red corpuscles and you have white corpuscles in your blood?

Yes.

And you understand when they go to war and if the red corpuscles gobble up the white corpuscles or the white corpuscles gobble up too many (by killing them off) of the red corpuscles that you have a health problem or a discord or disease?

Yes.

Pardon?

Yes.

Well? Those are intelligent beings. They—just because they are microscopic to the physical eye—they are intelligent. They know what their job is, and they try to do their work. And whenever you have a thought, by the very creating of that thought, you use intelligent beings to create that. Do you understand that?

Yes, yes.

Well, you know, a person thinks, they say, "Well, I have this thought of a pink rose. Well, I just had this thought, you know. I mean, that didn't take anything." It did. It took a great deal. It affected various chemicals in your body in order to create the thought.

Yes.

Now if you have a thought that uses and affects too many of one particular chemical in your body, then you find there is a shortage of that chemical. And when there's a shortage of that chemical, then there's an increase of another chemical. Now what people must realize is that there are various chemicals in the physical body. If there is a shortage of one chemical, then there is an abundance of another chemical.

Right.

You do understand that, don't you?

Yes.

Yes. For example, if you take, artificially, into the system, because, you understand that you have a shortage of certain chemicals in your body—

Right.

And you put those into your body, you do so at the expense of a reduction of other chemicals in your body. And so you have various reactions that you are aware of in your physical body.

Yes.

Do you understand that?

Yes.

Well, for example, it's like going and, you know, you have the, what do you call it, the flu or something.

Right.

So you go and you get some kind of an immunization, you know, that you don't want to have it again next year. And so what you do, you are taking a small amount of that germ and that virus into your body, measured so that your body will build up a resistance to it. Do you understand that?

I do.

All right. So if you—if it isn't measured properly, then you find you have the virus, because it was improperly measured. Your resistance was down and you were not able to battle off the small amount of the poison that went into your system. Do you understand?

Yes.

Yes. So now relate that to the chemistry of thought. You have a thought of dependence for feeling good.

Right.

That thought is dependent on something or someone you can't control.

Right.

So when they do something that you judge they should not be doing, they have an effect upon you. By your own chemistry of your own thought, you experience what you know as a frustration. Correct?

Correct.

Well, each time you experience that frustration, the chemistry of your body has gone to war. Do you understand that?

Yes, I do.

Well, that's what happens with everyone. Yes, yes.

I have one more question.

Yes.

With each of these various centers, is there, like, a chemical, I know it's made up of different chemicals—

Why, certainly.

The air center is predominantly one chemical. The water center is—

Oh, absolutely. Absolutely. Definitely. In all of nature.

Right.

Certainly, yes. Yes.

So in one particular case if one has become too magnetic, let's say, how then, in relation to what you just said, does electric, does the introduction of electric, how does that help?

Well, for example, if one, from the error of over-identification with self, one finds themselves drowning, which everyone is destined to find themselves drowning who thinks of self too much (over-identifies), then ofttimes one becomes sufficiently angry with themselves that they bring about a balance. When you, you know, when you become angry, what you do is increase the intelligent chemicals in the fire center. Pardon? But, you see, you must do that—if you do it with emotion, then you just get worse. You do that with intelligent reason. You make a conscious choice. Now a person will say that "Well, I've had enough of that." Right?

Yes.

In anything. Now when a person says, "Now I've had enough of that," and they're talking to themselves, the next thing that rises up, and should rise up to the mind, [is], "How am I going to change it?" Well, the first thing they have to say is, "Now how am I going to change it? Well, I created it." You see, they must free themselves from the dependence on something they can't control, because if they don't free themselves from the dependence on something they cannot, by divine law, control, then they cannot be freed within the consciousness, you see? So one must say, "Now I have created this person in my mind. *I* created this situation in my mind. And because I created it in my mind and I am its creator, I can do something about it in my mind." You cannot do something about it in someone else's mind. You can do everything about it in your own mind because only in your own mind has it been created. Do you understand? It hasn't been created in someone else's mind. In someone else's mind, something else has been created. Do you understand?

Yes.

So you can do everything with what, by the divine law, you alone have created. But you've got to do it where you've created it; can't do it out there, because out there, they're creating something else. And you're not responsible for what they're creating. You're responsible for what you're creating. Yes.

So you're saying first you have to break the dependency on thinking it's out there.

Oh, yes, because, you see, if you do not move in evolution to that step, you can't do anything but end up constantly frustrated. You can't make any changes. Yes.

OK. And then you apply, then it helps to apply anger to . . .

Inside oneself.

Inside oneself.

To what they've created and haven't made a new creation, you see.

Oh.

See, man is the creator, as I've said to my students here for many, many, many years. Man *is* the creator, you see. We are not, only in ignorance, the victim of experiences. It's only in ignorance we are the victim because of our belief and dependence on something that is not within the realm of our control, you see. Yes, yes.

So is—could one say that's actually a three-step process: first the breaking of the dependency . . .

Well, now, first you have to become angry in order to see that in error of ignorance you believed it was out there when it was always in here. *[The teacher points with his finger to the right side of his head.]* Yes.

OK. So anger's first. And then—

Yes, that usually, that comes first.

. . . tendency, like, just becoming aware that you have this dependency. [The student speaks simultaneously with the teacher, which makes accurate transcription rather difficult.]

Oh, yes. Yes, that helps with the anger.

OK.

Because, you see, an intelligent mind does not want to be dependent on anything they can't control. I know of no intelligent person that ever consciously said, "Now I would like to find something I can be dependent on that I can't control." Pardon? No, no, no, no, no. No one says that. No. No, because, you see, no one really wants to be a victim. So why would they want to say to themselves, "Now I'd like to find someone I can depend on"? Yes, yes.

So then, would the next step after that be creating the new experience?

Why, of course! Absolutely. Because the last one, and all other ones, have been created by one's own mind. And so one can choose at any moment to create something new. But, you see, in creating, it's like creating money, because that's—it's created by the mind.

Yes.

You cannot desire it and then deny it. You see, because, you're—you see, you can't create an abundance of money and then every few moments take a look and deny that you have it. You see, you must accept it in your creation. You can't create what you don't accept. You couldn't create this vase, if you did not first accept it. *[The teacher refers to the vase of flowers on the table at which he is seated.]* It's not possible to create it, you see; you have to first accept it. Yes.

So that would be like growing spiritually, if you keep denying the growth, if you . . .

That is correct.

Harping on oneself . . .

Absolutely.

Then you won't, you just . . .

Certainly. Because whether we realize it or not (and ofttimes we don't), when we desire to create something, we constantly look at it and deny that it's happening. Don't you understand, you see? It's like a person who wants to go someplace and they keep looking: are they going to go on vacation or they're going to go on this or go on that. And they keep looking and looking and looking and looking. And it seems like it never happens. And usually for a person that's overly concerned with it, it doesn't happen. Because they have created the direct opposite of what they think they desire. Do you understand?

Yes.

You see? Because—how has that happened? Because more attention (energy follows attention) has gone to the opposite of what they desire. You see, it's like a person who says, "Well, I would like to have my own place." All right? All right. And they keep thinking about it, and they keep desiring it. Yet they spend more attention, more time, more energy on that they don't have it yet than on the creating of it. Don't you see? Yes. Or like a person that wants money. They keep thinking about wanting it, and every time more energy goes to wanting it, which is an expression of denying that they have it, than creating it. Yes. You're welcome. Now [another student's] been waiting with her question. Yes.

If one is, had a lot, been in lack a lot and that's the, you know, dependence . . .

Yes.

And they wish to grow into abundance, how—so, so rather than keep looking at the fact that it's not there yet, what do they do?

Well, they accept that it is! They accept that it is, and they direct all of their energy that it is. And stop allowing their own mind to create that it isn't!

Well, do they say, "Well, it is here. It just hasn't manifested yet?"

No, because then they'll be waiting for the next ten centuries! You see, you see, the mind always wants to dictate a day and an hour and a time and a place, you see, but we haven't reached that state of evolution that we snap our finger and then it appears. When we reach that state, yes, then we— *[The teacher snaps his fingers.]* There it is! Yes. Yes.

In regards to making a change or establishing a law, it appears that, you know, we're going full force and then there's, there seems to be a period where nothing is happening. Is that because of our mind dictating a lack of patience that there's, like, a stillness? Kind of like moving forward and with a direction and pushing forward, then all of a sudden there's like a stop.

The best—

Or appears to be.

The best times in life are when there's no thing, like you say, happening. That's the best times in all eternity.

Thank you.

Yes. God manifests in the silence of the Light.

Thank you.

Yes. Yes.

A little while ago you spoke of when we follow, we are actually, that's a manifestation of what we've created inside.

Yes.

And I'd like to ask about our responsibility to ask, then, where we're going without trying to be in control of it or be in the mental about it.

Well, you see, when one thinks of where one's going, it reveals—and this is very important, you understand—concern of the future.

Yes.

And denial of the present. See, [the] power of God and the Light is in the present. Yes.

Well, what if, what if you find yourself questioning the present?

If one finds themselves questioning the present, it is from the perspective that they have chosen to view it. Yes, go ahead.

And in that regard, may I ask one more associated with that?

Certainly, certainly.

A couple weeks back you were speaking of the heart.

Oh, yes.

So I'd like to ask, What is the best way to make sure our heart is where we are, if we find it somewhere else?

Well, now remember, if we find our heart anywhere that we do not choose it to be, then we want to remember that it is the heart of our desire. We understand that, of course.

Yes.

And so it's the heart of the desire instead of the heart that we are. And because it is the heart of desire and not the heart that we are, it will winter and summer, and spring and fall; it will come and go. It always does. Because, you see, it's desire; it's not heart. And it is not, it does not, and never has, and cannot, weather the test of time. Yes.

Well, then am I to understand, then, any separation is really just the desire heart and we really aren't separated from our real heart? Is that what you're saying?

That is correct. It is desire. You cannot separate the true being and the soul from the heart, which is its expression. It's desire that separates. It's desire that moves all over the universe. The heart is the heart. Yes.

And you spoke a minute ago about perspective, about not understanding or being able to deal with the present. How does one best correct that perspective?

Yes. Well, now, first of all, one has to understand how one has placed oneself in any perspective. Now the present is a moment of conscious awareness. Only a moment. So because the present, where power is, is a moment-by-moment experience in consciousness—it's not the moment that just passed.

Yes.

It is not the moment that is waiting to come, for that is not where power is. So in this very moment, one must ask themselves, "What is my perspective? Because if I am aware of my perspective, then I am also in the light of the Power that I am." But you will find, you see, when a person thinks of the present, it includes chapters of yesterday and tomorrow. *[Many students laugh.]* Ofttimes many volumes. So that is not the present of which I speak. The present of which I speak is this moment.

It's not the moment that's a minute from now. And it's not the moment that has just passed. But it is this very moment. That's where the power of God is, in the very moment.

So in perspective, let us not forget that the present is the very moment in which we are consciously aware. Only that moment is the present and only that moment is the power. All others are chapters of the past and ofttimes encyclopedias of those yet to be. Does that help with your question?

Yes. Thank you.

Certainly. Yes. Yes, [another student] has a question, please.

[The student clears his throat.] *Excuse me. At the last seminar, I believe you said that the divinity of disaster is encouragement.*

Oh, yes, indeed that is the divinity of disaster.

So—

An incentive to move out of it. I would certainly call that a great divinity. Yes.

And at what point of the situation do these intelligent cells recognize encouragement?

At what point to they recognize encour—when we hit the bottom. You see? You see, when do we hit the bottom? We hit the bottom when we finally, usually from poor health, exhaustion, and many other factors, and of a breaking down the system, and sometimes it takes longer for others and sometimes it takes a short time, and finally we accept what we already know: "That's enough! I'm the one that has to change. I have exhausted myself from trying to change someone else." You—do you understand?

Yes.

You see, you see, give what you have to give and care less what they do with it. You see, when you fall into the trap of trying to change someone else, and you become frustrated, then you realize how dependent on someone else you are. That should certainly infuriate a person, and that certainly is the divinity of disaster. Does that help with your question?

Yes. Thank you.

All right. Yes. Yes.

When we're in the moment of now and the power hits these thoughts with their chemicals . . .

Yes?

What happens?

When a person is in the eternal moment of now, in that moment, in that very moment they have control, in that moment. You see, but if you consider the moment of now the moment that just passed and the one that's waiting to come, that is not where the power is and that is not where the restoration of health is or any other good. Did that help with your question? Yes.

Yes.

Yes, you see. You see, you cannot permit your mind to think that this is the eternal moment while you allow the mind to think of a moment that just passed. Yes, please.

When a person is considering making a total change of occupation, which is something different . . .

Yes?

And you hold that vision in your—and you're creating that vision.

Yes?

You were speaking about not, not putting your attention upon it or—

Oh, I didn't say not to put the attention upon it. I said not to keep the concern over it. It's like a person—

Oh.

—that's creating the abundance of money and they keep looking at it and directing all of the energy that it hasn't arrived yet. Yes, yes.

So you can keep your attention upon it and keep building it and, and thinking about it without the concern.

And feeling good about how it's building and how it's growing. Yes?

And then eventually—

But that takes honest, conscious awareness. Because, you know, when a person's looking to see if the seed is growing— "Where's that sprout? That should have been up by now. Something must be wrong." I know how the mind works. Yes. So be very alert to that, you see.

OK.

Then after the sprout comes up, "Well, when are those leaves going to open? I can't even see a leaf there." Yes. Yes, someone else had a question.

So you—one has to actually tune in to the moment consciously, tune in to the moment so that—is that true?

Yes. Yes, you don't have to tune in. The moment is. Just accept it. See, everything else is gone. This is the moment that is. Is that not correct?

Yes.

Not an hour from now. Not what you're going to do tomorrow and not what you did yesterday. This is the moment that is. Now in that moment you can feel very good, if you choose to. Is that not correct?

Yes.

And so this *is* the only moment. That's where the power is. So when you're creating something, you create it in that moment. Now it's like [the other student] over here, sitting back there, said, "Well, can you look at it?" As long as you're in the moment. You see, it takes power to create something in that moment. You see, if you look, if you plant the seed and you go back to look at it and you have the type of thinking, "It's growing beautifully under there, just beautifully!" if that's the type of thinking that you have, then, you see, you are helping it to grow. Do you understand?

Yes.

Well, that's the difference. That's where the power is moment by moment by moment. You can't go, as like [another student] was saying there about spending a lifetime of lack, that's—you see, it doesn't matter if you spent twenty eons of lack. What matters is, Do you want to use the power that is your just and right, your divine right? Do you want to use that power? Then in so doing you don't think about you spent a lifetime of this or you spent years of that or what you might spend tomorrow, because the power is not there. When you move out of the eternal moment of the now, you enter the realm of force. Don't ever forget that, children. Your choice is between power and force.

And so when you plant a seed or you put a penny aside to multiply, if you permit yourself to leave that moment when you look at it, that new moment, that eternal moment, then you've entered the realm of force and are controlled by all the variables of a mental world. Yes. Yes, please.

I'd like a little more understanding of magnetic and electric energy. Is magnetic energy of the water center?

Yes, it is.

OK.

It is. And it is controlled by force.

Controlled by force.

That is correct.

And then what controls the electric?

Power.

What is the corresponding center?

Power. And you know, our time is up. And so we will carry on with this at our next seminar. Remember that Light is power and it is electric, and magnetic is force. Hmm?

Thank you. Thank you.

Yes. Thank you very much. And have a nice evening. And good evening.

FEBRUARY 11, 1988

A/V Seminar 29

Yes, now are you prepared there now?

Yes, sir.

Very well. This evening's class, as I stated, is "Contradiction and The Law of Control." And we are fortunate to have had that experience to prepare us for this evening's class. *[The technician recording this class had some difficulties initiating the recording when the teacher first began speaking.]*

Now, the acceptance, the application of acceptance is the experience of our life as rejection, being review, is our destiny. Now we find in our daily experiences in the world that ofttimes we believe that we are very happy, that everything is going very well, only in the next moment that everything is a disaster. It reveals to us—this contradiction reveals to us our degree of control of which level of consciousness that we are perceiving our life from. Now we all know that we alone choose on what plateau of consciousness that we will stand. We do not often have the awareness, consciously, that we have made those choices. And because we do not often have the conscious awareness, we do not accept that we have made those choices that we may have those distasteful experiences. Yet we have made those choices for man is a law unto himself. And when man believes that experiences are life, then man is indeed affected by them.

That which is contradictory in consciousness is opposite to the Law of Harmony and the Law of Abundant Good. So whoever permits contradiction to flood their consciousness willingly chooses, in fact, desires to be controlled. Now anyone who desires to be controlled is a person who has permitted themselves to believe in need and, therefore, becomes dependent.

We ofttimes hear the mind say, "I do not like responsibility. I have never liked responsibility. It is a heavy burden and a cross to wear in life." But the choice of liking or not liking the Law of Responsibility is one of desire to be dependent on something, somewhere that, of course, we cannot control.

Now when our minds face what we believe we cannot control, we begin to feel a satisfaction, a satisfaction of dependence. A heavy burden of the emotions is lifted for we do not feel the weight of responsibility. And we feel how much lighter and brighter things are when someone, somewhere, something, somehow will do it for us. It's like going to a doctor. We've established laws of contradiction within the consciousness, discord and disease has taken over, and we feel a temporary relief that someone else, somewhere, something is going to bring about this miraculous change and do it all for us. We won't have to make any changes within the consciousness. There will be some pill, some miracle drug, somewhere, something the doctor will find, and therefore no changes within our consciousness are necessary; no effort need be made; no possible acceptance of responsibility and all of its weight. That's how we become dependent.

But in that dependence, we deny the most precious thing that we have earned in our entrance on the planet Earth. We not only deny it, we deny its very existence. So we deny, we reject that everything, everything in the universe is taking place within the consciousness that we truly are. To move from dependence is to move into responsibility. It is only a great move to those who have wandered so far from it for a time.

Whatever change that we desire waits for us. It is waiting for us. We will meet it when we accept the law that fulfills it. And, of course, we know that the law that fulfills it is taking charge of this little ship of destiny, and taking charge of anything, be it ship or shoe, is known as responsibility. So responsibility isn't something, when we look at it in the light of reason, responsibility is not something that is a heavy weight or a burden. It is a freedom that we know inside is that precious something that we truly are.

We have no problem with accepting our right of responsibility when someone tells us to do something we don't want to do. And usually the first thing our mind says is, "I'm exercising my divine, individual rights!" So we do demonstrate at times, we do demonstrate the awareness that we have a divine right. That divine right expresses through what is known as responsibility.

Now it's your opportunity to ask your questions of this evening's discussion. Yes, please.

Sir, when we feel our self falling into the level of dependence, which, I suppose, fear comes in that same area—is that correct?

Yes. Fear is used to secure us. It is a security mechanism of the mind. For example, when we become dependent on anything and we entertain in our consciousness the possibility of making a change within our consciousness, then fear rises so that we will not make the change because we feel secure in making less effort in what we have decided is our security. Our emotional security, our financial security, which, of course, is in truth emotional security because we have made it so. Yes.

Thank you. When we feel our self falling into that level . . .

Yes.

On a given situation, what can we do to stop it at that point and reverse that, that feeling and rise to a higher level of consciousness?

Well, of course, the first thing in weaning oneself away from dependence, the first thing to do is to go along the path of dependence, for the mind has become habituated to it, you understand, to go along with it with a different perspective: to be consciously aware of what you are doing and lessen the feeling, the experience that you have emotionally from the dependence. I do hope you understand what—a conscious awareness of following the habitual path of dependence is the first step in weaning the mind away from the dependence on something that one cannot control. Because the alternative of continuing on with dependence on what one cannot control is a frustration path for the mind and for the emotions. It indeed does take its toll. Yes.

Thank you, sir.

Yes. You see, so often a person says, "Well, of course, we're supposed to be dependent on God." We're not dependent on God. Without God, the Divine Intelligence which we are, all this other, our forms, wouldn't even exist. That's not a matter of dependence. That's a matter of absolute truth and demonstration, you see. See, I'm speaking of dependence of the mind: making a judgment how much better it will be if such and such and such happens. You understand that.

Yes, sir.

So what the mind does, it sets itself up by the denial of personal responsibility and becomes dependent on so-called, what do they call it, luck? Pardon?

Yes, sir.

Yes. The loser's excuse for a winner's efforts—is that what they call it? I think it's something of that nature. Yes. Did that help you?

Yes, sir.

Yes, certainly. Yes, please.

Thank you.

Yes.

Is the contradiction the flip-flopping between the beliefs of the different forms that we've created in our minds, that's the contradiction in this—

Well, you have to understand that which contradicts controls. *[After a short pause, the teacher continues.]* No, you don't understand. You don't understand. You know what contradiction, what I mean by contradiction.

Yes.

That which is contrary. That which is discordant. That which is not unified. That which is not harmonious.

Right.
Pardon?
Yes, I do.
All right. Now if you walk into a room and everyone seems to be happy and very pleased, and you come in and you speak to someone and you establish a law of contradiction, you soon have the opposite of the harmony of the people that are in the room. Would you not agree to that?
Yes.
Have you not had that experience in life? Yes. All right. So through the contradiction, the Law of Contradiction, there is a change with all of the subjects that are in the room. Is that not correct?
Correct.
Usually with most all of them, if not all of them.
Right.
Is that not correct?
Correct.
Now what happens within the room once you establish the Law of Contradiction? *[The teacher continues after a short pause.]* There is a change, isn't there?
Yes.
Who's responsible for the change?
I would be.
You were the one that established the Law of Contradiction.
Yes.
Yes. That puts you, then, in control. Now you understand the Law of Contradiction and the Law of Control. That's how the mind is controlled by the Law of Contradiction. Not by the Law of Acceptance. Not by the Law of Harmony. But by the Law of Contradiction, you see.
OK.
You see, if a wife wants to control her husband, what does she usually do with him? She makes sure that she contradicts

him so that she can change him, and vice versa. It is a rare person who involves themselves with another person who doesn't make great effort to make a clone. Pardon?

That's true.

Yes. We're speaking, of course, of a mental world. As a mother tries to make her child a clone of herself, a father, a husband tries to make his wife, and a wife tries to make [her] husband. And so they have control through the Law of Contradiction. Because that's how they are controlled inside of themselves. Do you understand that?

Yes.

You see.

Yes.

You see, you will find it usually with little children, you know, little children that are used to having their own way. And if two or three children are playing with a toy and the little child that's used to having its own way comes in and he sees he's not getting the attention, he very quickly, very quickly establishes the Law of Contradiction, becomes in control, and now he feels better.

Yes.

Pardon?

Yes.

Well. Does that help with your question?

Yes. Thank you.

Yes, certainly. Yes, please.

So if one set up the Law of Contradiction to control, then inevitably that returns to one.

They are controlled by it. Indeed, indeed. You know, some people, they say they're like [a] duck to water: you see, nothing really seems to bother them. Then some people, they go down only to bounce right back up again, and you never know when they're going to bounce up again. And then some people go down and they stay a very long time and you think they're going to pass on because they've been down there so long. Does that help you? You know. You see, some people can stay under water longer than others. It depends on how much experience they've had on going down under there. Pardon?

That's right.

Oh, yes. So everyone has a different tolerance level based, of course, upon their own experiences and their own efforts in evolution, you understand. Yes. Yes.

Thank you.

You're welcome.

Would reminding oneself, continually, that one is responsible for everything help in . . .

Well, as long as they remind themselves of the good things that they judge are good as well as the opposite. Yes, because, otherwise, all they do is feed their own discouragement, which [the] only thing it does is cause a person to go down even deeper. And some people can't stay under water too long, you know. What I mean by under water is in the water center of emotion, over-identified, yes. Pardon?

OK.

You're welcome. [Yes], please.

Yes. Say, for an example, if a person walks into a room and there's a predominant vibration that's being emanated in the room.

Who judges the predominant vibration, may I say? From whose perspective is the judgment made, or decision made that there is a such and such predominant vibration?

OK. Well, let's say, we walk in—

Because that's important. Yes.

And a bunch of people are smiling and laughing.

And then we make a judgment that that's a happy vibration, is that correct?

Right.

All right. Fine. Now I want to understand clearly here what we're speaking about.

OK. And, and the person walks into the room is not in a smiling, laughing vibration.

Yes?

Can't they just as easily make a conscious choice to get out of whatever level they were in and choose a smiling, laughing—

Well, if they want to, yes. If they want to, they can.

I mean, if they want, I'm, I'm saying as opposed to a person walking into a room in a lower level—they judged in a lower level—

Yes?

There's a higher level, they judged there's a higher level going on.

Yes?

And so, I mean, in other words, just, even though there's a predominance, they judged there's a predominance of a higher vibration, I'm trying to see how—

I understand. But it depends on how far under water you are. Sometimes, you know, a person needs incentive.

OK. Yes. But I'm saying that—OK.

Yes.

OK. There—I mean, in order for the person to change the vibration that's in the room to the vibration they're in . . .

Yes?

I mean, I mean, I'm, I'm asking how is that, how is that to happen or as to you being in control. I mean, I would feel like—

If a person—may I say this?

Yes.

If a person walks into a room and they are not in harmony with the predominant vibration that is being emanated in the room, if they, if they insist on expressing—and we express in many ways. You know, people think that expression is limited to open the mouth and to have the words come out. Expression is an emanation.

Right.

You understand. And if they emanate a vibration which is not conducive to the predominant vibration that is in the room, then something has to change.

Right.

And here [at the temple] it usually does.

Yes.

Pardon?

I mean, yes, it does. I mean, OK, it does. But what I'm saying is, even though, OK, even—Why does the predominant, if, if the vibration is predominant, why does it have to change to a lesser or different vibration than the—

It doesn't *have* to. If those involved accept and apply personal responsibility, it doesn't have to.

No, it doesn't have to. But, OK, that foreign element that comes in there with, that foreign element that comes in there, as long as the people that are in, that are in the room do change their vibration, that foreign element that's in there, it's going to just stay in that level or . . .

Oh, no. No, no, no. It doesn't work like that. You see, the predominant vibration is the controlling vibration. So the discordant vibration cannot take over a sustained and maintained predominant vibration. No. Mathematically the numbers are against it, no matter what it is.

OK. Good.

Pardon?

Yes.

Did that help you with your question?

Yes.

Yes. But we must understand that we are so—if we permit our self to be—you see. Easily influenced people—try to understand this about the human mind—are people who do not readily accept personal responsibility. People who are easily influenced are people who still desire someone else to do it for them. Those are easily influenced people. Did that help with your question?

Yes, sir.

You see, if a person wants some good and they look around and quickly make the judgment, well, they can get the good there, there, there, there, or there; they don't have to make any changes whatsoever, you understand. Those are people who are easily influenced. Especially, I think, your world is filled with that awareness now during your election year, you see. You'll see a great deal of that. It's known as easily influenced people. I think you call [it] buying the votes or something. What it means is people who do not desire to face personal responsibility easily, easily sell and give away their votes so they don't have to make the effort, yes. Yes, and [another student], please, is waiting.

Thank you.

Yes. Certainly.

[The student clears her throat.] *Excuse me.*

Certainly.

Thank you. On the other hand, what if you were involved with a group of people—let's say you attend a seminar or a conference...

Yes.

Or something like that.

Yes.

In which the group of people is in a lesser vibration and you're in a higher vibration.

Yes.

Uhm ...

Then the law must be applied: to be with a person, place, or thing and never a part of a person, place, or thing; to be in the world and not a part of the world. And so a person in a situation of which you speak should make the effort to constantly flood the consciousness with that demonstrable truth: to be with a person, place, or thing and never a part of a person, place, or thing. Because, you see, what happens there—you know it as personality—what happens there is, through the lack of responsibility, we become dependent upon how someone else looks, thinks, speaks, and acts. And so, in so doing—for example, say that we were going to a school and we were going to learn about computer graphics, for example. And we were in the school studying these computer graphics and the person next to us, we didn't like something about them. That tells us immediately that we have lost perspective; that we are not there for the purpose of what we thought we were: learning computer graphics. We are there for the denial of personal responsibility and the dependence upon what other students are doing or not doing. Does that help with your question?

Very much.

So, you see, what that reveals, the situation of which you speak, that reveals to us, personally in our own being, what our motive truly is. It tells us, without anyone ever saying anything, where we are, where we have put our self. And then we can make an intelligent decision whether or not we want to continue to put our self in that type of level of consciousness within our self and lose out all of the benefit that we are going to the computer graphic schools for.

Yes.

You see?

Yes.

You see, we must understand that it is something that we've permitted to take place within our mind. Pardon?

Yes.

And so often students go to various types of schools, and after the first six months or even a few years—depends on the individuals, you see, as everyone has a different state of evolution—they don't seem to benefit from their study courses. They don't seem to get much out of it, as much as they used to get out of it. Well, try to understand, they get less out of it because they put less into it. But the mind deceives us that we're putting more in when we're actually putting less in. We're putting less of our self in, do you understand?

Yes.

You see, because we've become distracted with what someone else is doing. Pardon?

I see.

You see?

Yes.

You see, it's like this evening here. On contradiction and control. Now we had this lovely little experience here with the microphone—pardon?—which gave all of you the wonderful opportunity of whether or not you were in control, through the Law of Personal Responsibility unto yourself, or the experience that you were having, during the waiting for the changing of the microphone and etc.—that had not been checked out, obviously—whether or not you were in class for the purpose of the spiritual awakening or you were in class and had lost that perspective and had entered the distraction of personality.

Yes.

Does that help with your question?

Yes.

You see? You see, everything, every experience offers to us a revelation of the law that we set into motion and what we are doing with that law at any given moment. Do you understand? You see, so, therefore, if a student, like here this evening, began to feel emotionally bad, they are doing no benefit to themselves if they feel guilty as being responsible and not having checked it out, you understand that? Then they're on the road to awakening, as long as they carry it on through. Do you understand?

I see.

You see? So that law that declares the truth that we get out of a thing what we put into a thing and never one iota more should always be foremost in our mind, especially in classes of spiritual awakening because so often our true perspective, our true motivation is being distracted, you see. On the spiritual path of awakening, as I said so many years ago to you students, many, many things will distract you, many things. How someone else looks in school, what they are doing, what they are not doing, why they are not doing it, many things—those are all created things, you see—many things will distract you.

Now, you see, those are the lessons to learn in a spiritual school, because when you leave your physical bodies, all these things in the universe of your experiences will call to you along your way to the Light. They will all call out for they are echoes; they are shadows that have been created. Do you understand? And so they will call to you. If you listen to them, you will be distracted, and it will take you longer to get to your destination so that you can move on in your evolution.

Yes.

Pardon? Yes, you go right ahead, yes.

So am I to understand that what you're saying is to stick with the principle?

Definitely. Absolutely.

. . . consciousness. [It is difficult to accurately transcribe the student's words.]

With that.

With that.

Because, you see, it doesn't matter what someone else does. It indeed does matter what we do in life, you see? Because, you see, we take ourselves with us. Wherever we go in the universe, we must never forget, we take ourselves with us. And fortunately or unfortunately for us, ourselves include many, many trunks of experiences. It takes a very large ship for the little pinhead, so-called, size of a soul to move in the universe. Because that ship is filled with all of the baggage that we've held on to, you see?

Yes.

You see, each time we permit our mind to think of what has been, we just add more weight on our ship of destiny that we must sail through the universes. Now the more weight there is, the slower the ship moves. So if we have permitted ourselves to hold on to many, many things in our consciousness, our ship continues to move, but it moves much more slowly, *much* more slowly. Yes.

That's very nice.

Yes. You're welcome. Now [this student], please.

Thank you.

Yes.

I believe you began to speak about incentive . . .

Yes.

About that we could offer others or ourselves in keeping closer to the path of personal responsibility rather than yielding to the desire to operate as an agent of experience.

Yes, indeed. You see, when we look at the alternatives, when we look at the alternative, when we look at what our mind has tried to insist that responsibility is such a weight, when we look at the opposite, [we see] the denial of responsibility adds the absolute slavery of dependence, you see. Now, try to understand this: dependence causes our mind and our attention to be extremely active with what's happening to what we're dependent on, you see? Say, for example, a person is dependent upon the stock market, for example. That's only one thing now. Just one little thing. So every day the attention is placed on there, whether it's gone up or it's gone down. Do you understand that? Now that consumes a great deal of energy, of vitality of the human being, a phenomenal amount of energy. Do you understand? All right. Now that's only one thing in a person's life.

Then a person also adds to that a dependence on their wife or on someone they are involved with. Do you understand that? Now, then the mind is flooded with, "How did they say hello this morning? What are they doing? Where did they go? Have they spent too much money? Are they spending any of mine?" And that is taking energy from the consciousness. Do you understand that?

Then, included on top of that is where they live and how long will they live there? And will they buy the place and will they won't? That is taking energy.

Now I am speaking about energy being utilized constantly, daily, without any conscious awareness. Now you add all of these things that a person permits their mind to depend upon and you will see a phenomenal amount of energy is being dissipated from the consciousness. Now that same energy that is being dissipated [is] flooding our consciousness over [a] habitual pattern that we are no longer consciously aware of it.

For example, a man is involved with a woman and he is dependent upon her and even though he doesn't think of her, if she is upset, energy is drained out of him. Do you understand that? There is a transference because they're a law; the chain of attachment has been established. Do you understand?

Yes.

Now that girl may leave his life and his universe, and another replace her. Do you understand that? But the one that has left is still draining energy. Do you understand that? Why? I'll tell you how and why. Because he has replaced the one that has left because of a similarity within the consciousness because he never let the attachment go. Do you understand that? Pardon?

Yes.

So now he doesn't have one wife to support; he's now got two. Do you understand? That one leaves, and he now has three. That one leaves, and he now has four. That one leaves, and he now has five. Now you stop and think of how that works. All of these changes and all of these people or all of these things, they are replaced because of similar similarities. Do you understand?

Yes.

Now remember that similarities and familiarities are one and the same. They are one and the same. They're spelled a little different, but they are one and the same.

Yes.

Hmm? So all of that energy dissipated in those many different ways is not then available for a person's fullness of their spiritual awakening. And so they look and do not pierce the veil. They open their ears, they hear, but they do not listen, you see? Because the energy is being siphoned off constantly to all these things. Hmm?

Yes.

You see, and so, for example, say that you go to the store and you take your friend with you, and she stops and looks in a window. At that instant, at that very instant, every experience you've ever had with any other woman who stopped at a window while you were with her is now draining energy. Do you understand that? Oh, why, certainly. So a person stops and they look in a store window and they see a red coat. Every experience of every woman they've ever seen, of every experience in their own life with a red coat is immediately, instantly siphoning energy from the person. Do you understand that?

Oh, yes.

And so that's what happens all the time. So a person must be aware, awake, and alert; do their daily concentration and meditation or they will not survive in a physical world. Certainly not on the Earth planet. Because, you see, all of this is taking place at all times. All of these things and experiences and these energy drains are taking place. So a person must choose very carefully within their own consciousness what, where is their mind. "Where is my mind? What is happening to my mind? What am I doing with my mind? Or what is being done with my mind?" You see, that's the question a person must ask themselves. "If I am not aware of what I am doing with my mind, then something somewhere is doing something with my mind, and I don't like the experience." Pardon?

Yes.

Do you understand?

Very well.

Yes. No one likes someone else to take control and play with their mind, you see. You know, for many years I have refrained from discussing thought force and things of that nature to any great extent, until my students would flood their consciousness more and do their flooding-their-consciousness exercises so that they can prepare themselves and be more aware of what's going on inside of themselves.

If a person feels badly, when they feel they have the awareness that they feel badly, they're not feeling good, then they should be able to take a look and see what is happening within their universe clearly and to see if there's any dependence. If there is dependence, then there are problems. For whoever is dependent is a person who has many problems. Do you understand?

Yes.

Yes. Does that help with your question?

Oh, absolutely!

Yes.

Thank you very much.

You're more than welcome. Yes, please.

Thank you.

You're welcome.

Then how can we consciously get rid of our baggage of our past history?

Well, through flooding the consciousness daily.

Yes.

Through more effort to conscious awareness. Through more effort to conscious awareness. To be aware when someone does or says something, what kind of feelings you have inside of yourself. Because, according to the feelings that you have, whatever they say, reveals how much dependence you have upon them. And, you see, you will find that when you make that effort to be aware of how you feel when someone does something or doesn't do something, you, at first, will not like the revelation that you could be so dependent upon them, you see?

Yes.

Yes. Remember now, the law clearly reveals that which disturbs us controls us. So let us be fully aware of that which disturbs us. And by being fully aware of that which disturbs us, we can start to wake up and say, "Well, thank you, God. This is what's controlling me. I have created all of this to control me. What kind of a life have I made for myself? I know I have made this life that I have. I alone have made it. Life is as we make it, and just the way we take it. So I know that I have made this in my mind, I've made this life myself. For me to permit myself to say someone else has made it this way, that reveals my dependence and my bondage that I alone have created by denying responsibility." Do you understand?

Yes, I do.

You see? You see, if a woman doesn't like the way her husband is acting in her home, you see, she first comes to a decision: well, whose home is it? "I declare it my home. Therefore, he goes." And then she moves him. Is that correct? Sometimes she puts all his clothes, even goes to the great effort of packing his suitcases and things, you see. It depends on the individual, you understand. First, they have to make a decision of whose home it is and what they're going to do. Isn't that correct?

Yes.

Well, there you are. Yes, yes, indeed. And so it is with all things in life. And, you see, when we go to let go of something, especially a thought, a judgment that we cherish, you know, in our consciousness, and we go to let it go, then we should be consciously aware of the experiences in our mind that we are having. Once we make the decision to let it go, do we let it go easily? Or do we let it go begrudgingly? And ofttimes, you know, when we let something go and we let it go begrudgingly, it doesn't go at all: it just stretches on a rubber band and hits us back periodically. *[The teacher and some students laugh.]* And we wonder how come it's bothering us again, you see. "Why, I gave that away some time ago." [We] didn't give it away at all. We loaned it, you see. We loaned it because temporarily other things had priority. Do you understand that?

Yes, I do.

Hmm. That happens so often in marriages, you know, and divorces, you see. They think they're divorced. They never did get divorced. All they did was just loan it and periodically, you know, every so often, it bangs them back on the head. And they wonder how come that person's back. "What happened? That got back in my life. How did that happen?" You see. Yes.

Thank you.

Yes, you're welcome. [This student], please.

My mind has a judgment that—you were speaking of some people have a tolerance for being under water for a long time.

Yes.

Others have the, what my mind judges, is the ability to let it just flow off them. So I have a judgment in my mind that those who can be under water longer, that that's more, that it's better to let it flow off you. Is that so?

No, I would say one, in reference to that of which you are speaking, to remember, one who loves their judgments more than they love the Law of Responsibility is one who is in deep trouble. Pardon?

All right.

Yes. Because by reminding oneself of that truth, it's indeed helpful.

OK.

Yes.

Thank you.

You see, we always get what we really want, but we have to face the judgments we created that are in the way. But we always do get what we really want, you see. You see, the only thing that stands between us and this fullness of life are all the judgments that we've created and, by creating them, believe that we are them. That's all. You know, a person says, "Well, I want to go here. I want to do this or I want to do that," all these many things that they say they want. But they want their judgments that stand in the way more than they want that, you see. So because, you see, you always have to give something to gain something. Because our cup overfloweth. And because our cup overfloweth, we must empty a little out, so that what we think we want can get in there. It can't get into that cup, because the cup overfloweth, you see.

And what is it that, that empties the cup? Those judgments that we believe that we are, we've got to empty some of them out so that what we think we want can get in there. Oh, it gets all around it, but it doesn't get in there because it's full. It's overflowing, you see. See, our mind is overflowing with our judgments. So more have difficulty getting in. They can't get in. Does that help you?

Yes. Thank you.

Yes, certainly. Whatever it is you say you want, just remember, empty your cup just enough to let it in.

Thank you.

You don't have to empty it completely. I don't know of anyone that's completely emptied their cup. But you could empty, perhaps, a sixteenth of it and let those in, you see.

Thank you.

You're welcome. Yes, please.

Are distractions, then, a form of disturbance or contradiction?

Distractions, for example, that which, of course, distracts us from what it is we want, we have to understand we already have set those into motion. You can call them temptations, you can call them disturbances, but in truth they are temptations. Now not all temptations are satisfying. Many temptations end up as very, very controversial, contradictory, and discordant in our lives. We're tempted to many things. The child is tempted to light the match until he burns the house down. But, you see, therefore, once he has the experience, he's not tempted to use the match so foolishly, right? So, you see, we're tempted into many things. We're tempted by what we believe, *we believe* brings us what we want. We're tempted to it.

And remember, we can never be tempted until we first deny responsibility. You see, we must first make the judgment we don't have it to be tempted by it. Now you cannot be tempted by anything, you cannot be tempted by *anything* you do not first judge you don't have. You must first judge you don't have it. You may judge you used to have it. You may judge many things about it, but you must first judge you don't have it in order to be tempted by it. You cannot be tempted by that which you already have and are responsible for. Do you understand?

Yes.

Now if you have something, you already have it, and you deny responsibility for it, then you could be tempted by it out there. Because you're denying responsibility for it, you see. In other words, "That's a better coat. Well, I got last year's, but that's a better one." You understand? But you already have the coat. You already have it, you understand?

Yes.

You're tempted by it because you're denying responsibility for the one you got. So, you see, you go through the process, "Well, this is better, this is newer, this is this, and this is that." Those are all temptations, you see. They appeal to the senses.

It's known as appearance. It appears, you see, in the consciousness. You cannot be tempted by that which you are responsible for. You must first judge you don't have it, and you must also judge that you must have it. Then you must justify why you must have it in the mind. You must therefore go back into your past into the shadows that tell you, "Well, you had this, you had a good time, you had that and etc." That's the only way you can be tempted. You can't be tempted any other way. You can't be tempted 'til you first deny responsibility. Pardon?

So the justifications are all, just the way the mind works, then?

Well, of course. It, it is defending—the excuses and justifications, they are supporting the judgment that you created that you believe that you are. Even if you created it twenty years ago, it doesn't matter. That's all taking place within the mind.

You can't walk down the street and be tempted by anything or anyone until you deny responsibility within your consciousness. You must deny responsibility in order to be tempted, yes. Now responsibility is a soul faculty. And temptation is a weakness. It is when the faculties and the functions are out of balance and this flow, this light of reason doesn't flow anymore within the consciousness, you see? See, your functions and faculties have to go out of balance before you can deny personal responsibility. You cannot deny responsibility until you have created an imbalance between your forty faculties and your forty functions. It is not possible. It is contrary to demonstrable law. And you cannot be tempted until you first deny responsibility.

I see that our time is up. Thank you very much and have a good evening.

MARCH 10, 1988

A/V Seminar 30

Good evening, class.

Let us be still and be aware for the joy of living is the Law of Care. This is a very important understanding to have in one's evolution for so often in our life we believe that we must make changes in order to enjoy life. And that is true, demonstrably true. And sometimes we believe that we are doing everything necessary to bring about those changes. And yet somehow the changes that we desire seem to escape us. We must understand the only reason they seem to escape us is because we have left out an indispensable ingredient necessary for the change that we desire.

We have spoken many times on the life-giving energy of the spoken word. We must try to understand that life-giving energy is the giving and the creating of life. When we speak and give forth this vital energy into our atmosphere, into our aura, and into our universe, we sometimes fail to remember what we are giving life to. To support by the process of life-giving energy the obstructions in the way of our heart's desire is, of course, a path of failure. For example, we awaken in the morning, are we still? And by so being, become aware? Or do we permit without monitoring in our consciousness the giving forth of energy and creating obstructions to our own desires? It is a matter of constant vigilance. It is a matter of constant effort.

Ofttimes we hear, "It'd be so nice to retire." But we must ask our self the question, What will we put in the place of what we are presently doing to serve the purpose of our life? That which does not move in a constructive way to accomplish the purpose of its being moves, by the very laws, in a destructive way and destroys that which is not serving the purpose of its own being. That destruction is known as self-destruct.

Let us remember, life isn't better until we first accept that possibility. That step, number one—that is not the only step.

That's only the beginning step. Accepting that life is better is the beginning step. Giving it energy to manifest itself by the spoken word is step number two. We cannot speak forth how miserable life is and wait and expect it to get better. It will only get worse for the law is being fulfilled. Life is better when we are inspired to make it so. Life is better this moment, if that is what we choose. Life is worse, if that is what we choose.

It is up to us, as students of the Light, to demonstrate the fullness and the joy of living. Not to do so is not to apply what you are working in life for. To know the way to a mountaintop does not place us on the mountaintop. There are paths that we must walk upon. There are many detours and there are many distractions. To remind our self by flooding our consciousness how good life is—for all of life is in our own perspective. Each moment we make. Each year, each century is what we make it. To lose sight that we are making our own life is to walk upon the path of self-destruct.

We look around here at the world and we question and we wonder why so many people work so hard in their efforts to deny themselves the goodness of life. We wonder why they do it. We wonder why they choose the path of self-destruction. We would wonder less if we [would] pause to see if, in any way, we are doing that to ourselves. Are we telling ourselves and the universe how beautiful our life is or are we telling the world and the universe how bad and how miserable our life is?

Be aware. Be still and be aware. Some time ago I spoke to you on being still. Let the body be perfectly still and be aware of what is calling you. Be aware. Do you first sense the foot? The toe? The hand? The ear? Be aware. Be alert. And be awake. For each part of the temple of God, which is our physical body, represents these forty faculties and forty functions. Be awake and be aware. Take a moment, one moment. There are as many moments in consciousness as we choose to make.

Let us not forget, we make our minutes as we make our hours; we make our years, for we make our life. We make what we have named as time. We make it. We create it. Some of us have made a long span of the illusion of time. And some of us have made a very short time for our life. If we have chosen, through errors of ignorance, to make a short time (for we alone create this illusion called time), if we have chosen to make a short time, then we will find ourselves ever chasing, ever working, trying to fit all of the things that we desire into the short span of the illusion of time that we have created. A wise man realizes that time is something that he alone has created. He realizes that he has created it. And by realizing that he has created it, he is not controlled by it. When we remember that we have created it, when we remember that God sustains what we alone choose to create, when we remember that, then we can start to change when we desire to change. We are not helpless for we know the way. Whoever knows the way is not a victim, only by choice through the error of ignorance. We know the way. Therefore, we are not victims of time and space until we choose to make ourselves so.

To speak on the joy of living and the Law of Care is only an awakening. It is only through the application of that law that we have the experience.

So often in our lives we know we must make changes. Let us never forget, when we become aware that we must make changes, that changes take place within our consciousness inside of ourselves and have nothing to do with the world beyond it. Let us not forget that.

And when we find ourselves upset, frustrated, and emotional, let us apply what we know: the cleansing breath is exactly what it means, a cleansing. Let us apply the cleansing breath that we all know as religiously as we apply our baths and brush our teeth. Let us clean inside and we won't have to worry so much about cleaning outside. For it is when we clean our house inside—and I speak now of the house, the temple that we are responsible for, known as the human body and the human mind.

To be discouraged is a denial of the very Law of Life. We, as students of the Light, have no right to that luxury for we know better. To permit our minds to give life-giving energy to that which is contrary and a denial of the truth that we know in our heart, we, as students of the Light, are not allowed such a luxury of ignorance. No one is without all the tools necessary to bring about within their own mind the changes they desire to accomplish their purpose of being and the goodness of life.

It is not so easy for many in evolution to wrench oneself free from dependence. But wherever there is dependence, there is not the fullness of truth. Wherever there is dependence, there can only be half-truth. For dependence is a denial of the demonstration of life that each and every soul has entered whole, complete, and perfect. To deny that demonstration cannot bring the goodness of life, for it is a denial of what is.

Now it's time for your questions. So if you'll be so kind as to raise your hands. Yes, please.

You mentioned earlier—if I understand correctly, sir, that changes take place inside of us and have nothing to do with what is outside of us?

That is correct. The changes take place inside of us, and once the change has taken place, the manifestation reveals the change that has taken place within our consciousness, for outward manifestations or experiences are revelations of inner attitudes of mind. To bring about an attitude change takes effort. It takes consistent, daily effort. And one of the things necessary in bringing about a change in one's attitude is a daily shower, a daily cleaning inside. It's known as the cleansing breath. You were given it many, many, many years ago. And it requires—you see, as you awaken in the morning, it is a rare person that fails to brush their teeth. It is a rare person that will go a week or a month or six months without taking a bath. And therefore, if you are as religious with cleaning inside as you are with cleaning outside, that is, the temple, the house in which you live, then the changes will come about. You will gain control over what is going on. You know, ofttimes a person says, "Well, suddenly I have a terrible attitude. You know, I'm like a barking dog, running around biting everyone." Well, it's a lack of effort on the part of the biter to take his daily shower or brush his teeth and clean inside. Does that help with your question?

Yes, sir.

Certainly. Yes. It is true it is tempting, certainly it is tempting, if someone else is willing to scrub you and shower you and brush your teeth for you, it is tempting to a certain part of the human mind. That is correct, yes. And there are people who will have no problem letting someone else brush their teeth for them. Yes. Yes, please.

Thank you. Would it be possible to have an explanation of the cleansing breath? I've never been given that.

You haven't? You haven't. Oh, very well. Now, first of all, you should sit as comfortably as possible. Try to keep the spine erect. Now you should purse the lips so that you can just inhale through the mouth. Now the entire purpose of that is to inhale slowly, rhythmically, to hold the breath as long as comfortably and to exhale through the nostrils. Do you understand?

Yes, sir.

All right. So we'll just take a moment here, and all of my students—and I accept that you had not been given that, though all of the other students—is there anyone else—perhaps [that student]—who hasn't been given the cleansing breath?

I've been given the cleansing breath. [The student responds.]

I see. All right. So let us do our cleansing breath and let us take a bath inside where it really counts. *[The teacher demonstrates the cleansing breath, which takes approximately 51 seconds.]*

Now you should be aware, awake, and alert of the energy moving throughout your body, from the tip of your toes to the very top of your head. Now that should be done at least a few times in the morning and whenever you find yourself a little bit disturbed, as people do, in their work ofttimes, to do the cleansing breath. You see, it's like taking a shower. You clean yourself inside, you see. Does that help you?

Thank you very much.

It should be done daily, every day. One should not go through a day—and then, you see, you will find, slowly, over time, through consistency, control of the mind and to be able to be in the world and not to be a part of it, do you understand?

Yes, sir.

You see, to be able to be aware and to be objective and to see these various different levels expressing themselves without becoming trapped by them within one's own consciousness. You're welcome. Yes, please.

Would you speak more on, on dependence and there can only be, with dependence there can only be half-truths?

Well, certainly. Because every time we depend on something outside, we deny its existence inside. And whenever one denies the existence of something inside, then they cannot have the fullness of life nor the joy of living. Because, you see, to depend on something outside of yourself, you are denying the existence of it inside of yourself. And by depending upon it outside, you place yourself as a victim of another person, place, or thing, for you have denied it within yourself. Either a person is whole, complete, and perfect or they are not. Now God did not place, the Divine Intelligence, half-souls on the planet Earth and whole souls on the planet Moon or Mars or some other planet. That is absolutely [a] ridiculous type of thinking.

So if you really permit your mind to believe that you are a half a person, then you can only experience half a goodness; there will always be something missing in your life. No matter what it is you'll desire, it will always come short of the mark. It will always come short because you have denied it inside of yourself. Do you understand that?

I, I realize that I've denied it, but I, I don't . . .

But you don't have to deny it. You know, a person can accept what they have denied for they alone are captain of their ship. Say, you deny—you've denied that. Because you've denied something in time past, there is no law that says you cannot in this moment accept it. Is that not correct?

That's correct.

You have the power to deny, and by the law of demonstration of the power to deny, you have the power to accept. So if your life has not been what you'd consider it should be, in the fullness of life and the joy of living, then all you have to do is to accept the fullness and joy of living not dependent on what someone else does. It is when you depend on something that by the very divine law you cannot control, that's when you become half a person and have half a life. Always falling short of the mark, hmm?

Thank you.

You know, it's like, perhaps, a girl or a boy constantly engaged and never getting married, you see? It never—it always comes short of the mark. Do you understand?

Thank you. Yes, I do.

Always short of the mark. Because you're dependent on that which you cannot control. Now you can control yourself; that is the Law of Personal Responsibility. So what you can control offers you the fullness of life and what you can control is yourself, you see?

Yes.

Does that help with your question?

Thank you very much.

Yes, you're welcome. Yes, please.

Is it recommended to do the breathing exercise before meditation in the morning—

Definitely. Definitely.

Or after?

Before. The first thing should be done is to take a shower and clean up inside.

OK.

Absolutely. You see, brush the teeth, take the shower outside after. You have to start from inside. Inside out and you'll never be rotten to the core. *[Some students laugh.]* You see, it's the core that we must be interested in. So start with the core, you see. So if everything's right with the core, if the core's had a scrubbing and a cleanup, very first thing when you open your eyes, you see, then the rest will shine.

OK.

Yes.

OK.

Because beauty and the harmony and goodness is inside. It shines through, you see. Yes.

OK. Thank you.

You're welcome. Yes, please.

Thank you. May you, please, speak a little bit on the joy of living is the Law of Care?

There's no joy to be experienced in anything that we don't care about. You know, one cannot, one cannot, in our thinking, say, "Well, I don't care about that." Well, how can you get any joy out of that? You see, the law reveals that we get out of anything, *anything*, whatever we put into it. So if we don't put any care into it, we certainly aren't going to get any joy out of it. You know, it's like, you see, man is married to the universe he's in or it's like a marriage. You see, you're married to life on the planet Earth, right?

Right.

So you're marr—you're married to the planet Earth at this time.

Right.

Because that's where your identification is; that's where you're evolving through the planet Earth. So you're married to the planet Earth. So if you don't care about the planet Earth, you can't expect to get any joy out of the planet Earth, then, can you? Because you can't get joy out of anything you don't care about. Do you understand that?

Yes, I do.

You see? See, if you don't care about the temple of God, if you don't care about your body, then you can't expect any joy to come out of it. If you don't care about your thinking, if you don't care about your attitude, then you can't expect to get any joy out of it. Because you can only get out of anything what you put in. And if you're not getting something out of anything that you think you're putting something into, stop, pause, become alert, aware, and awake, because the truth is you're not putting anything in because we get out what we put in. So if you're not getting joy out, you're not putting care in. You see.

It's like a person, you know, perhaps they have a pet. They have a dog, a cat, or something. They have a little pet, and they say, "Well, this pet has become a burden to me. It's getting inconvenient. It's a constant hassle. I got to take care of this. When I want to do something, I got to look after my pet." All right?

Right.

You no longer experience any joy from your pet because you're not putting any care into your pet.

Right.

You see, that's the thing about life. We really do get out of life what we put in. As we put less in, we get less out. Do you understand?

Yes, I do.

You see, it's like a marriage. If you really put something into a marriage, then you get something out of a marriage. But if you don't put anything in and you wake up one day and say, "I'm not getting anything out of this contract, this institution I've created," then you've got to get a different perspective because you really, you're not putting anything in. Now you may have put in something during the honeymoon, you understand?

Sure.

But the mind is thinking about those two months, or three, or six or whatever it was.

Right.

It's not thinking about the daily process of putting something in.

Right.

Do you understand?

Yes, I do.

So often the mind, we permit it to deceive us. We tell our self, "Oh, you know, when I first got married it was such a wonderful experience, etc." And then years pass by and it's miserable. There's no joy in the marriage. There's no joy in the relationship. There's no joy of any kind. There's only a drudgery and it's a real effort to even go home. Right?

Right.

But the person thinking that way, with that type of an attitude, keeps reminding themselves of how much they're putting in. But they are deceiving themselves because they are thinking about their effort during the early stages. They're not thinking about the day-to-day effort that is required.

Right.

Do you understand?

Sure.

It takes day-to-day effort.

Right.

Because you are working not just with yourself, hopefully with yourself, you're constantly being tempted, you see. Convenience is a trap that a wise man doesn't tempt himself into. You see, without conscious awareness, you find yourself becoming more and more dependent. [You] don't even think about the dependence. Well, the person [says], "Where are they? Five minutes past and they're still not here!" And all of these various patterns of mind, you see, these habits, they start growing very strongly, and they reveal the dependence that is taking place. Yes.

Right.

And so a person becomes, in a situation like that, much more aware of what the other person is not doing than what they are really doing themselves. You see?

Yes.

So they stop and say, "Well, they're not doing this anymore. They're not doing that, that, that, that, that, that." But you have to understand that during the early stages, you see, what is known as the romancing stages, all of the energies and efforts were going in to please the other person. And the other person was putting all their efforts in to please that person, because, you see, they want something out for they have denied what they have.

Right.

They've denied it all exists within their own consciousness. Do you understand that?

I do.

Does that help? Does that answer your question?

Yes, it does. Thank you.

Yes. You see, they lose their individuality. They lose their individual—remember, whatever you begin to depend upon, you do so at the sacrifice of your individual freedom.

Thank you.

Yes.

Yes.

Yes. Yes, please.

Thank you. Following that, when is—how do you know when it's appropriate to break that contract? In other words, grow— 'they grow or they go' kind of thing in any relationship—a job or—

Oh, yes. Yes. You see, when a person makes the change within their own consciousness, the person they are depending upon will either grow in that changing or they will go. The law fulfills itself. Absolutely. Because, you see, as a person's making an effort to free themselves through that dependence with another person, what happens [is] the other person begins to sense that.

Yes.

Nothing has to be discussed.

Yes.

You see? And so they are sensing something not right with their own dependence. They are sensing that which they are depending upon and have become dependent upon is doing something different.

Yes.

And that threatens their dependence. Do you understand?

Yes.

That threatens their dependence, yes. Does that help with your question?

Yes. That helps. I, I still have part of the question.

Knowing when the timing is right?

Ah, it will come to me.

Oh, indeed. Indeed, it always does. It comes to everyone. You see, usually a person awakens from a dependence rather irritated.

Yes.

That's not the wisest way. That's not the best way.

OK.

No, no, no, no, no. A person should awaken as an adult.

Yes.

And they should say to themselves, "Well, in my errors of ignorance I became extremely dependent. I put someone or something in place of God, truth, and freedom—"

OK.

"The light of reason. Now this is what I have done. Because I have done it doesn't mean I can't change it. By the law of doing it, I can undo it." But a person, in that awakening, should be very honest with themselves and then communicate with that which they have become dependent upon.

Yes.

You see?

OK.

Now one must be very careful with an awakening because there are times when we think we are awakening but we are tempted and distracted by something else.

Right.

You see?

Yes.

So one must winter and summer those changes before they spring and fall them, you see.

Yes. OK.

Yes, winter them and summer them, yes.

OK.

Because that's a sign of growth. It's a sign of responsibility. It's a sign, of course, of honesty, and then only good can come out of that.

Yes. OK.

Yes.

Am I, am I understanding it correctly, when—so in other words, allow the other person to change. Don't continue to look to your past efforts and their past efforts, and so forth. Look at the present.

Only at the present.

Right.

That is the only place, the only place in consciousness you have power.

Right.

All the past must go.

Right.

You see? Because they are filled with justification, which is the first line of defense of judgments.

Yes.

And the experience and the discord is the effect of those judgments that have been made.

Yes.

So all of those must not be allowed to enter the consciousness. That takes great effort of self-control. And start with the moment which all the change of goodness can take place.

OK.

You see? No shadows can be allowed in making an effort to make a change in evolution. All shadows must go. Now that will take great effort [by] a person. It will take conscious awareness constantly. Which is a shadow and which is a new created form that one has created? Hmm?

OK.

Because, of course, shadows do not let go easily. Only because we allow ourselves to be dependent upon them. It's known as, some people like to call it, the good old days. Well, if they were so good, why did we leave them?

Yes.

That's the question that I've always had, you see. Because I've heard many, many students along the path say, "Well, things used to be so nice." Well, if they were so nice, why did we leave them? We could have stayed there in consciousness, you know, but we didn't. Isn't that true?

Yes.

Yes. You see, each moment is better than the last if we want to make it that way.

OK.

Each moment is. And so—but it depends on what we want to do. Now if we want each moment to be only a reflection of all the moments that have gone, then we must face those experiences, you see. It's like a person going for a job. Depends on one's attitude. The experience they encounter is only a reflection of the attitude or vibration they have taken to it. Now if they take a good attitude, then they will have a good experience. And if they will only accept that what we experience in life is reflecting an attitude, an attitude that we nourish inside of our self. See, the moment that we accept and apply that wonderful truth—"All of life is reflecting to me only my attitude; the attitude that I alone create, moment by moment."—do we change our attitude. We change our attitude, [then] we change our spoken word; [and] we find our experiences filled with the joy of living, yes.

OK. Thank you very much.

You're welcome. *[The teacher then addresses another student, who is a four-year-old child.]* Well, it's nice to see my youngest physical student here. And how are you this evening?

Good.

Did you have a question? *[After a short pause, the teacher continues.]* Not at this time. When you do, you raise your hand. *[The teacher then calls upon another student.]* Yes.

When we become aware that fear about anything has registered in our consciousness, what is the wisest path to follow?

Well, we must not forget that fear, based upon the judgments that we have made in our life—they use many devices so we won't make changes. And fear, of course, is one of them. Fear is one of them. It controls the senses. Now, you know, it's like a person, they take a look and they say, "Well, I'm afraid, I'm afraid what's going to happen tomorrow." If you want to experience the fullness of fear, listen to your daily broadcast. Listen to your newscast, and you won't want to breathe the next moment. You see?

Now we must also remember that fear has a way of exciting the senses. So when we permit our mind to say, "Well, I'm afraid of what's going to happen," we get a certain negative excitement [that] takes place within us, you see. "I'm afraid I won't have enough money for tomorrow. I don't know what's going to happen to me when I'm sixty. God forbid if I make it to sixty-five." And so you fill your mind with all of this, but you must ask yourself the question, What good comes out of that?

Fear is something that you alone, you create it. You create it, you see. You create it with your own judgments.

So ask yourself, "What is it that I fear?" Some people fear being alone. Some people fear the lack of money. Some people fear poor health. Some people fear going to the doctor. Most people fear going to the dentist. What is it that they fear? Hmm? What is this? It's an expression of judgments they've made in their own mind. That's all that it is. They made the judgments. Some people fear catching a cold. Some people fear that their marriage won't work out. Some people fear that they won't get married at all. So, you see, there's no limit to what people choose to fear because there is no limit [to] what people choose to create.

So if you say, "Well, I have this terrible fear," well, face the fear. It is something you have created with your judgments. Face it, and you will see it has no substance. No substance whatsoever. That help with your question?

Yes, sir.

See, all you have to do is do it. You see, ofttimes we permit our mind to say, "Well, I'm trying. I've done everything." No. There's something that we haven't done. If we desire change and the goodness of life and we are not experiencing it, it is because there is something that we haven't done. There is something that we know that we haven't done. Yes.

You know, to look at our life and to say, "Well, if that wasn't that way, then I could make this change. If this wasn't that way and that wasn't this way . . ." you must realize that is absolutely contrary to the demonstration of this philosophy. It is absolutely a denial of its, of its truth because it is a dependence on what someone besides our self will or won't do.

What is important is what *we* do. And when we are more interested in what we do, we will find our self less concerned with what they do. We must be interested in what *we* do. What are *we* doing to fulfill the purpose of our being? What are *we* doing? That is the question to ask our self each day and during the day and evening. "God, what am I doing? I don't feel real good this moment." Ask yourself the question, "Now what am I doing?" Forget about what he's doing or what she's doing or what someone else is doing. Ask yourself the question, "What am I doing?" Because that's the only place you can make any changes at all, is in what you're doing. But you cannot make changes if you are not aware of what you're really doing. So we must be more interested in what we are doing individually so that we can see whether or not we are applying what we are well aware of in our life.

Then you will have no interest in fear. You will have no interest or concern with discouragement and all these many things that build obstructions in our life. We must not permit the mind to use the mouth and feed the obstructions, and then cry because we experience the obstructions! *[The teacher laughs joyously.]* You know, you cannot, *you cannot* speak forth one thing and manifest in consciousness by attitude the opposite and expect success no matter what you choose in life. There has to be a unity between what the mouth says and the mind thinks. There has to be a unity in order to experience what you are seeking in life. Yes. Does that help with your question?

Yes, sir. Thank you.

Use this energy and be interested in what you desire and forget about the obstructions you've created. And then you will find life greatly improving. Yes.

You know, there are so many, so many different writings and books and tapes and all kinds of things on positive thinking. They don't work until you feel them in your heart and apply them with your mouth. You know, long ago there was a man who said, on your planet, "Every day in every way I'm getting better and better and better." Well, if you say it enough times, you'll begin to believe it; and when you begin to believe it, you'll begin to accept it. And when you finally accept it, then you'll experience it, you see. You must accept. We accept so many things. We accept all kinds of obstructions and rarely accept the ways. Hmm? Well, the joy of living is the acceptance of the way. You want something? Stop seeing the little pebble on your path which you make a mountain out of in order to get there, you see?

You see, it's like going for a job. A person wants to go for a job and they say, "Oh well, let's see, this is going to take two hours. I've got so many other things that I wanted to do. No, no, no, no. Let's see if there isn't another job I can look for that will only take twenty minutes." And then they cry about not having a job? Well, that is ridiculous. Ridiculous. It's a ridiculous type of thinking.

You see, when you feel sorry for people who aren't working, remember, you're feeling sorry for the ignorance inside of yourself. Because there's work for every honest worker. You see, to accept all of this other foolishness—when we really want to work, there is work for us. It may not be the work that our little minds want at the moment, [but] work is work, you see. So if it's work that we want, there is no shortage of work available for all workers. God has work for every willing worker, you see.

So if you start off with something that you don't like, you face your adversity before it becomes an attachment and then you move on. Well, a lot of people get married for various reasons when they don't like the person at all. Then, years pass on by and they become quite attached to them, depending upon their own adversity. Hmm, yes. Then when they find out they've become dependent on what they were originally adverse to, then they become adverse again and the next thing you know you have a divorce. Oh, yes, that's the human mind. *[The teacher and some students laugh.]* Yes, indeed. Yes, please.

Could you speak a bit more on the statement that you made...
Which one?
When we wake up to a dependence sometimes we do so irritated.

Yes. Well, what happens is our mind, which unfortunately sometimes believes it's absolutely perfect, cannot accept that it has made such an error. *[The teacher laughs joyfully.]* And then it begins to feed off of all of the energy that it's given and all of the time (months, days, weeks, or years) and it becomes very irritated that it was, in its judgment, so stupid. *[Many students laugh.]* That's not really wisdom. It's something else, but I certainly would not call it wisdom. That's usually how a person awakens, yes.

You see, that's not the way to awaken. That's when one does their cleansing breath, very calm, and then they say, "Now just a moment here. I'm not going to feel sorry for myself"—because, you see, it's an expression of feeling sorry for oneself. One says, "How could I have been so stupid?" Of course, it's the morning after, you see. You know. And one says that to themselves. That's not the way for things to mature and to grow. No, that's how children awaken. Children in mind, they awaken that way, you know. "I thought I had a good deal and look what happened to it." *[The teacher again laughs joyfully.]* You see, that's not, that's not the kind of thinking at all. No, one says, "Now just a moment. In my evolution I chose to deny the truth and I became dependent on something outside. And I have now woken up that it didn't work out the way I thought it was going to."—All right?—"Because I didn't care enough to make it work out." Now remember, you see, that Law of Care is very important. When a person no longer is getting something out of what they think they're putting time into, they must remember the Law of Care is diminishing. Pardon?

Yes.

All right. Now we must also remember that the moment we permit our mind to say "I need something," and we do not find it inside, from errors of ignorance in our evolution, then we experience within our emotions what we know as need or lack, that something is lacking. Do you understand that?

Yes.

All right. Now when we do that, we establish this Law of Dependence. Now man, when he is experiencing need, he uses great care, the Law of Care, to put something in to what is fulfilling his need. Do you understand that?

Yes.

All right. But we all must also remember that need, it's like the waves of the ocean: they come and they go. You see, we experience need for certain spans of time. Then we don't have need. Then we do have need. Then we don't have need. Now stop and think. I have need right here. *[Reddy, the church's dog, sits down right between the teacher's legs and many students laugh.]*

A person, a person feels, "Well, if I had this, then I wouldn't have this feeling of lack. I would feel better." All right, they make the judgment, and they deny that it exists—they deny that it exists within them. So they create this situation in their mind that they need something. So they go out. They follow that law of their own judgment, and they find what they judge is a fulfillment of that need. And they don't have that feeling anymore. They now have—the need is filled, all right? Time passes on, and what they found is not filling the need like it used to. But they don't say the truth to themselves, "Just a moment. My need has been so filled, the cup overfloweth. I'm not experiencing this need like I used to. Something's wrong." Well, the first thing the uneducated ego does is blame the person they're depending on that used to fill their need. See, the person gave too much. Filled their need to overflowing. And so now they have a need, they think, to be alone. Do you understand that?

You see? Not to have anyone around. All right? And so they go through that phase. And they go through that phase so long and the next thing you know, the need rises up again. Because they're not looking at it clearly: that it's all taking place within their own mind. It doesn't exist anyplace else. Does that help you?

Yes.

It never did exist anyplace else. Man has not come to Earth a half a person. Man has come to the planet Earth whole and complete. If he chooses to judge he's half a person, then half a person is what he is as long as he chooses to make that judgment. Pardon?

Thank you very much.

Yes. Why, certainly. Yes. Be with a person, place, or thing; never a part of a person, place, or thing. To become a part of a person, place, or thing denies what you are. And when one denies what they are, they cannot experience the joy and the fullness of life.

Thank you. I see our time is up and good evening.

APRIL 14, 1988

A/V Seminar 31

Good evening, good evening, class.

When understanding dawns, difficulties disappear for understanding is the revelation of the laws that govern difficulties. So often in life we want so many things, more of some things and less or none of others. And in our thinking, they cause us difficulties. It is because in our thinking we do not understand, and not understanding, the laws are not revealed to us. For if we did understand, then the revelation of the laws that govern those difficulties would inspire us to make the necessary changes within our thinking that we may remove those difficulties. No one that I have met has been freed from what is known as difficulties, for no one that I have met has arrived to the state of absolute perfection.

We ever seek perfection for without that seeking, we do not make changes; we do not grow; we do not evolve; and that is contrary to the law that is. Without seeking perfection, we are not inspired. Without seeking perfection, we do not change. And so everyone seeks perfection. Every mind wants something different. Every mind wants something better. In our days of ignorance we seek for that something better, and we seek for that perfection outside of our self. Ofttimes we think we have found it, only to find, in time, that we have not, for we look, of course, where it does not exist for us. For us, for each and every individual, it only exists inside of us. It is only difficult to find because it is, as we well know, the last place that we're willing to look. It is the last place that we're willing to look because we do know inside of our self that it is a threat to what we believe that we are. Therefore, that which we judge is a threat we keep, certainly, at arm's distance.

However, hope is eternal, as we know, and truth is inevitable. And life's experiences, revealing our own attitude and our own thinking, slowly but surely brings about the changes necessary for our own personal growth.

We are all well aware of the bondage of dependence. And yet we are often tempted to it. We enter dependence each and every moment that we permit our mind to think that the cause of our experience is beyond our control because someone else has done, is doing, or is about to do something to us. And if they haven't done it yet, our worry and concern shall indeed guarantee it. Let us be more aware of our attachments that we may better understand our dependence and, in so doing, truly understand what we choose, though ofttimes in errors of ignorance, to control us.

I spoke to you a few classes ago on the chemistry of thought. Remember, without thought, without attitude, there is no experience. The control of thought is the control of attitude and the control of experience. For whatever thought that you create and then control by conscious choice is the control of the experience you are about to encounter. You control your own experience until you permit your mind to judge and be dependent from that judgment on what someone else will or will not do.

Remember, the someone else, the something else, the world about us is in truth our own creation. The acceptance of that demonstrable truth places you in control through your own effort in control of your life, the reflection of which is known as experience.

We know that the thing or things that disturb us have control over us. They demonstrate their control by what we know as disturbance. So let us be aware of what disturbs us, and in that awareness remove it from our consciousness. Do not ask or expect someone else to do that, for that, once again, places you into the dependence; for whatever you ask someone else to do for you, you weaken yourself and your own abilities.

Now it's time for your questions in reference to this evening's discussion. Yes, please.

Thank you. By asking someone else to do something for you, you are asking that they help you become more productive in so far as the two of you together can accomplish more than you could individually.

Yes?

I believe.

You'll always be disappointed. Because two—there are no two minds that have the same thought or attitude in reference to anything. Therefore, there is a guarantee in creation in this respect: there will always come a time—because you have two perspectives looking at the same goal. There are differences; they are destined to appear. Does that help with your question?

Yes.

Now *if* a person is willing to adjust and take a differing, slightly differing path to the same goal, that is known as the success, which comes from tolerance. Tolerance, of course, comes from understanding. So that is dependent therefore upon one's understanding, which is a revelation of the laws, [and] one's tolerance, [which is] not being attached to the way to get to something as long as they know they're going to get there. Did that help with your question?

Yes, very much.

So it takes a great deal of tolerance, depending on how distant the goal is, for those who are working towards it. Yes.

Thank you very much.

You're more than welcome. And, of course, the closer—if you have two people or more working towards the same goal, the closer you get to the goal, the more aware you will become of the difference, differences with the other people who are involved in reaching the same goal. And therefore, tolerance indeed is stretched for many people, and they surely do quit before the victory. Pardon?

Thank you.

Yes, you're welcome. [Yes], please.

You said that difficulties disappear when we have understanding.

Yes, yes.

Are you referring to mental understanding or a, or a soul faculty?

No, understanding, the very foundation of the soul faculties. Because when the understanding is dawned over any experience, the first thing that takes place within the mind is an acceptance of personal responsibility. The law is quickly revealed from the dawning of understanding. That places a person in a position to make the necessary changes that are required to free themselves from the difficulties that they are experiencing. Pardon?

Thank you.

Yes. You're more than welcome. Because let us not forget that the difficulties, the experiences are self-created. They are self-created. All struggles, all difficulties, all experiences are self-created. Now when we move in that step in evolution and accept that great truth—all struggles, all difficulties are self-created—we are then in a position in consciousness to do something about it. Yes.

Thank you.

You're more than welcome. Yes, please.

Thank you.

Yes.

We are constantly seeking perfection.

Yes. All people are.

What's, what's happening inside when we allow seeking perfection to control us?

First of all, it is the very nature of the being to seek perfection. That is the nature of the being. It is our very nature. If seeking perfection creates a difficulty for a person, then the seeking of perfection is not in balance with their soul faculties. Duty, gratitude, tolerance, understanding, they're not in, it's not in balance. And there is a denial of the Law of Personal Responsibility. You take a person who has a priority of seeking perfection, though it is very natural and it is a natural process of the being to seek perfection, the evolution of the being, a person with difficulties in seeking perfection is a person who is looking for that perfection in someone else, usually someone they are attached to. Because whatever we are attached to is in truth a mirror reflecting back to us where we are at the time of the attachment. Did that help with your question?

Yes, it does.

Pardon? Yes.

How does that relate to seeking perfection in a thing? Say you're making something, you're creating something.

Well, the making or creating of something is a birth that you are giving, and in other words, it is the attachment of the creation. It is the attachment to the self, and it is an extension of the self. So the person is seeking perfection in themselves—you understand that?

Yes.

Which is a natural process. And in the creating of something they want that perfection to manifest itself. Do you understand?

Yes.

Pardon?

Yes.

Now, you see, like anything in life, it's good or bad depending on one's own perspective. So one can create something and not be particularly happy with it. You understand that?

Yes.

And they want to improve it, but there comes a time to let it go or it'll never get finished. Isn't that true?

Yes.

Pardon? And remember this, everyone is on a different rung of the ladder in evolution in perfection. And so what is not quite perfect to one's perspective is indeed perfect to another's.

OK.

You see, it's like looking up or looking down. So if you're on the rung of the ladder seeking perfection and you're looking up for perfection and there's someone else on the rung of the ladder and they're looking down for perfection, you have two different perspectives. So to one, it's perfect; to the other, it's far from perfect. Correct?

Yes.

Yes.

OK.

Did that help you?

It does.

Yes.

Thank you.

You're more than welcome. Many things in creation have come close to perfection. And those who have created them have long passed to our world. And they did not in any way think that it was even close to their quality standards of perfection.

Hmm.

Yes.

Thank you.

You're welcome. And, yes, [you] had—excuse me, I'll be with you in a moment. [Another student] had a question there, yes.

So we accept our difficulties that we have created—if we accept our difficulties, then we—

Well, to battle them, may I say, to battle our difficulties only leaves us in a constant state of frustration. Yes, to accept our responsibility for creating them, certainly.

Then understanding will have a more—you'll have more receptivity to—

Understanding will reveal the laws that were set into motion that created the difficulties by our own choice. Pardon? Well, it's like a person who wants to go two places at the same time. They must make an intelligent decision. They either decide, "I'm going to go—I cannot split myself in two"—do you understand? So they sit there and they must make an intelligent decision. "I'm going here or I'm going here, but I'm not going both places at the same time."

Yes.

Pardon?

Thank you.

Does that help you?

So make the choice to, to—in other words if you make reasonable choices, you won't have as many difficulties.

No, that is not the—no, no. Many people make what they consider reasonable choices. All right? But they do not understand the laws that govern the choices that they have made. Pardon?

OK.

And so not understanding the laws that govern it—you see, understanding would bring the revelation of the laws. You see, first is understanding, the revelation of the laws. Then a person, with that revelation, makes an intelligent decision of whether they're going to go on that path or they're going to go on *that* path. So the first thing is to understand. So the laws that govern what you're about to choose, you can understand. A person usually, when they go to a store, they take a look to see what the price tag says before they buy the garment, don't they?

Yes.

Pardon?

That's true.

So in making a choice, a person wants to understand, to have the laws revealed to see, "Now it's going to cost so much if I take the left path, but it's going to be more economical for me to take the right path. However, the right path is not going to get me there as quickly. And therefore, I choose to take the left path because I find that my desire cannot wait that long." Does that help with your question?

But sometimes wouldn't it be wiser to, to educate your desire and . . .

Oh, certainly. Certainly. But you find if you tell someone, "Well now, you just educate your desire," the experience isn't usually a pleasant one. Is it? Pardon?

Right.

Yes. Does that help you?

It does. Thank you.

Certainly. Yes.

Sir, if desire is of the form and aspire is of the soul, why is desire one of the principles of creation?

Now let us not forget that desire, desire is the divine expression. Desire *is* the divine expression.

But you said it was of the form.

Certainly. Certainly. All soul faculties and sense functions, when they're out of balance you have what is known as a function of desire. For example, you have a function of understanding; that's known as knowledge. Isn't that correct?

Yes, sir.

You see, understanding reveals the laws. Now when you put that into the mental world you have knowledge, correct?

Yes, sir.

So when you take the divine expression and you dictate to that, you enter it into the mental world. And so you have a desire for something, but it has limits, you see. It has left principle and it has entered personality. Now, for example, you don't just have a desire that you would like to go eat, correct? When desire for hunger rises within the consciousness, your mind registers that you want to eat. Then your mind dictates, based upon its own experiences, where it will go, how much it will spend, whether it'll go with someone or without someone. So the limits of the faculties take place in the consciousness when the mind gets it. Do you understand that?

Yes, sir.

You see. You see, it doesn't mat—the moment that the mind gets anything, the mind limits it by its belief that it is the experiences that it has already created. For example, you have a desire for something and someone hands you a slice of bread and you say, "No!" because you want a beefsteak. Correct?

Yes, sir.

All right. But, you see, you've lost the principle of the hunger. It's entered the personality of the mind and is therefore dictating exactly what will fill its hunger. Not the principle of food. Only certain kinds of food. Does that help with the question?

Yes, sir. Thank you.

You see, all of those details come from the dictates of mental substance because when you say to yourself that you, say, for example, that you want a drink. Say that you're thirsty and you want a drink. The moment you register thirst in the mind, immediately all experiences that you have created that govern the quenching of thirst enter in the consciousness [and] bombard the consciousness for priority. Did that help with the question?

Yes. Thank you.

You see. *[The teacher drinks from a glass of water.]* A person could register thirst and they can see a gallon of water. And it won't even register in their mind because they want a beer. Does that help?

Yes, sir.

Or a glass of wine. Now what is actually happening is that all of the things created by the mind in its past experiences all rise up. They all want their way of quenching the thirst. Now the ones who win out are the ones who have had the most energy given to them over a person's life. Pardon? Did that help with that?

Yes. Thank you very much.

You're welcome. Yes, please.

In regards to what was just said, that doesn't necessarily mean it's the best way in your interests, though, because of those things winning out.

Well, no, but, you see, that depends on how much a person, in their experiences, [is] attached to their experiences that they have created. Pardon?

Past experiences, like the, the past experiences that they have fed.

Well, you know, if we ever forgot the past and stopped worrying about the future, we would live a life of beautiful joy. Pardon?

That's right.

So, you see, you must remember, here we stand. There's the shadow of the past.

Right.

Here's the foreshadow of the future. And here we stand, looking at both of them. And so when we stand here and we're looking at the past and we're looking at the potential future, we fall down here in a constant state of concern and worry. Pardon?

Yes.

You see, you see, we've left the moment.

Yes.

We believe we are what we are looking at.

Right.

See, step outside of yourself for a moment in consciousness and place [Jane] right there. *[The teacher uses the name of the student with whom he is speaking. The name has been changed.]* And stand—sit back and take a look at [Jane]. Well, when you look at [Jane], what do you see? What floods your consciousness? All of the past experiences come rising up and the possible future experiences. And so you end up with all of this concern and upset and you lose the beauty and the power and the energy of the moment.

Yes.

So now your future is dependent upon looking at two things: what has been [and] what possibly will be. And what has been is constantly battling to win out.

Right.

Pardon?

Right, right.

Now we understand that in this philosophy, the Living Light, we understand and know that as temptation. See, the temptress is what we are looking at that has passed that we believe that we are. That's the temptress of creation. Pardon?

Right. Although even though they could be appearing [as] similar experiences, our perception has changed. So therefore, they're not the same experiences.

Why, certainly not. You see, for example, a person, when they're, when they go to look at something, they look at it from their own perspective. Their perspective is clouded by what has passed and what is yet to be. Hmm?

Right.

Now say that a person wants to feel good. Well, feeling good is a necessity to survival. I can assure you of that. All right. So a person says to themselves, "Well, I want to feel good. I don't feel right. I want to feel good." Now the moment the mind makes that statement—"I want to feel good"—in that instant it goes immediately to everything past that it has created; that's all of its experiences. And all of those things rise up in the consciousness that they believe that they are that made them feel good.

Right.

All right?

Right.

Now the other I is looking over here at tomorrow or the next minute or the next hour. Do you understand?

Right.

And so here we are, split. We're looking here, and here are all of these things we've created. We believe that we are those things. And they tell us they made us feel good. We believe that they did because during those experiences we made that judgment. And so they're all up there screaming for priority. And then the mind takes a look at tomorrow, and it tells those things—not consciously, you understand. This is all going on within the water center. It tells those things, "No, no. I've got to make some selections here. There's 500 here and I can only, I can only service, maybe, 3 of them." And so then there's all of this upset and then the next experience in the mind is "Well, I've picked the ones that gave me the greatest good in the past." You understand?

Right.

"So I must fit them in." And so the mind goes to work to fit those things in.

Right.

Then, worry and concern enters. The energy becomes drained from [you] because worry and concern utilizes a great deal of the vital energy. And perhaps you end up with only half of one of them getting any feeding at all.

Right.

You see?

Yes.

So you ask for goodness; you know that it is necessary for life itself.

Right.

[Goodness] is absolutely necessary. And you have all of this process going on.

Yes.

You see?

Yes.

But now if you take another look [and] you say, "Now just a moment. I understand that. I've had years of, years and years and years of that taking place in my consciousness."

Yes.

"I choose to create something new in my consciousness, not dependent on anything that has been."

Right.

"And because it's not dependent on anything that has been, there's no possible concern of what is going to be because it's all new."

Right.

You see? It's all new. "I am creating it this moment all new."

Right.

"There's no dependence outside of me. I am personally responsible. Doesn't matter what someone else is doing or isn't doing. I'm creating this all new." Make sure it's not—that it is all new and it isn't one of those shadows that snuck in with a new garment on him. Yes.

Thank you.

All right. You're welcome. I hope that's helped there.

Yes. Thank you.

Yes. Yes, please.

What is the law governing the dawning of understanding?

The law governing the dawning of understanding is the full acceptance of personal responsibility. When we stop and say, "All right. So? I feel this way. I'm personally responsible. I've created this. I don't like it, but I know that I have created it. I know that it is something that I created in my mind. I don't like it. Now I'm going to create something else." That requires energy. You understand?

Yes, sir.

You see. You see, it requires more energy because that that has risen up and is flooding the consciousness has a great deal of energy from many years of energy being directed to it since the day it was created. So you find that when you start something new, it takes a strong effort of your will to get it accomplished. Pardon?

Yes, sir.

You see? Because it's something new, and you have all of these other things that demand that you give energy to them for they're used to receiving energy from it since the day that you created them.

Thank you.

But we do change and we do evolve. And life reveals that to us moment by moment by moment. Regardless, we do make changes. And when we permit our self to be off guard in consciousness, those things of years past they rise up through the laws of association. Wouldn't you say? *[The teacher addresses another student.]*

Yes, sir.

You see, you know, suddenly a person, they're out into the world and they hadn't thought about something for years, perhaps. Then all of a sudden it rises up, doesn't it?

Yes, sir.

And we say, "Well, now why this and why now?" All we have to do is pause. Stop in consciousness and look around. And we will see that it snuck into our consciousness when we were off duty through the Law of Association of what our ears hear, our eyes see, and our senses feel. Is that not correct?

Yes, sir.

It happens to all of us all the time when we're off duty. So let's get on duty.

Yes.

And enjoy life. Those on duty enjoy life. And those off duty, they can fill the rivers with their tears. Yes. Yes.

I've no more questions. [The teacher then addresses a student who had previously asked a question.]

Well, did that bring a little clearer understanding for you?

It did. I was, I was thinking about a shadow wearing a new—I'm not sure of the exact word.

A new garment.

A new garment.

Oh, ofttimes they, if they can't get in with their old garments, they'll put on a new one.

Right.

You know, let's try to look at it like a salesman. *[Some students laugh.]* You know, if he comes to the door [and you say] "No, I don't want to buy anything." [He] goes out and changes his jacket and comes back again. [If] that jacket doesn't work, go try another jacket, you see? Because we all realize that it's a salesman's world whether we like it or not. Pardon?

Yes, it is.

Well, why is it a salesman's world? Well, I think that a salesman would say there's a lot of suckers out there. I would say that we're easily tempted. *[The teacher laughs joyfully.]* Call it what you like, but I would say that we are ofttimes easily tempted. And so it's a salesman's world.

Right.

Pardon?

That's right.

Yes. Absolutely.

Thank you.

And a good salesman, the first thing he learns is what tempts you.

Right.

What do you, what do you think is the first thing that tempts the mind? Pardon?

Convenience?

Well, of course, convenience is involved.

I mean . . .

The mind is tempted by anything possibly it can get for nothing or almost for nothing.

Right. Right.

Little or no effort is a salesman's paradise. *[The teacher and some students laugh.]* No reflection on salesmen, but that's the first thing that they learn if they're a good salesman. Because, you see, they must tell you what they're going to do for you.

Right.

And then you must judge, "Is that all it's going to cost me? And you're going to do *that* much? My goodness' sakes, really!" *[The teacher laughs again.]* Yes, that's known as a good salesman. I think you call it, "I'll get it for you cheaper," or something like that. Yes. Well, isn't that what that word means—*sale*?

That's right.

You know, below the price you judge it is or should be of something—

Right.

—is a sale, right? Why, certainly. So you have sale and person, salesperson, or salesman or saleswoman. I think you call them now salespersons. I don't know how well a salesman would like to be called a sales*person*. However, let's move on with our class. *[Again, the teacher laughs joyously.]* Seems to have an identity crisis problem with some people. *[Many students laugh.]*

Thank you.

You're welcome. So a person asks themselves if they're easily sold.

Yes. Right.

And if a person's easily sold, then they know right away that they're easily tempted. Hmm?

Yes. Thank you.

Yes. *[After a pause, the teacher continues.]* Are there any other questions this evening? Yes.

I wanted to know if what you were saying is that it's the laws we set into motion by the choices that we make—is that correct? That we set certain laws into motion by the choices that we make and that creates our experiences.

You put it into a little different wording there. Of course, we alone are creating all of the experiences that we encounter. Why, certainly. Now if we want to change those experiences, if we decide that we're not happy with them, then through an acceptance of our responsibility for the experiences that we presently have, then we will gain understanding and the laws governing the experiences that we desire will be revealed to us. Yes. But, you see, if a person doesn't get discouraged, disappointed, or disgusted with the experiences that they're having, then they have no incentive to bring about a change. Would you not agree?

Yes.

Yes, you see. You see, so if a person truly wants a change in their experiences, if they truly desire a change in their experiences, then they go through the necessary steps. Number one: "This experience and these experiences I personally have created. Like it or not, and I don't like it, but I have created it." That's the first step, is the acceptance of the law. Because if you do not accept the Law of Personal Responsibility, you do not place yourself in consciousness in a position for the laws to be revealed to you that govern what it is you desire to have in life. You see, you first must accept that you alone are creating them in order to gain the understanding, which is the revelation of the laws that govern the experiences. Pardon? So if you permit the mind to deceive you and tell you that your experiences are caused by what someone else is doing, has done, or didn't do, then, you see, you will not be able to bring about the change, because the laws within your own consciousness will not be revealed. Do you understand that?

Yes, I do.

Certainly.

Thank you.

You're welcome. You see, you cannot permit the mind to deceive you and to deny that your experiences are caused by something or someone else. You will not gain understanding that way. The laws will not be revealed within your consciousness, and you will not have the incentive to make the necessary changes to bring about the new experiences. Hmm?

It's like we were just discussing salesmanship. Well, you know, if a salesman is in a certain attitude of mind and then he attracts what he calls, I guess he'd call them hard sells instead of soft sells or whatever, and he blames the person that he went to see, then he's denying the very Law of Personal Responsibility so he can bring about the necessary changes so he has more soft sells and less hard sells or whatever they call those things, you see? You see, that is a terrible error in the mind, and it gives all of the power necessary for the changes of the experiences to the person that they've had the difficulty with. Do you understand that?

Yes.

Yes. Yes.

Thank you. Back to the salesman thing.

Yes.

I was reading something from a famous psychologist this week that said we are all manipulators. We all manipulate each other.

All, all—yes, definitely.

All the time. So if—since that's true, then we should manipulate for the good.

Absolutely.

I thought that was kind of curious. And I was wondering what we, as students of the Light, you know, how we should take that.

Well, all minds manipulate. It is the very nature and the principle of the human mind. They manipulate because the human mind believes in need.

Yes.

Need is the effect of denial. The human mind has denied its own sustenance.

Yes.

The human mind. It believes it is a separate entity in the universe; it is unique, special, different, one of a kind. Pardon?

OK.

That's part of the ingredients of the separation from the Source itself. Now, first of all, the human mind denies, you understand?

Yes.

And by its denial, it experiences need. Now need is something that will do anything to fulfill itself. We understand that, don't we? That's known as manipulation.

OK.

Yes.

So while we're in need, then we will always manipulate.

Yes, whenever, whenever we permit our mind to believe that we are in need, we will do whatever we believe is necessary to fill the need. And that is known, in psychological terms, as manipulation.

Yes.

Definitely.

So there really isn't such a thing as manipulation for the good. In other words, are we capable of even knowing what manipulating for the good is?

No, because, you see, manipulation is based upon the belief that we are separate entities.

Yes.

And good is not a separate entity. Good is a universal principle. Do you understand?

Yes.

Therefore, one does not manipulate to experience good. One manipulates to fill need. And the fulfillment of that need, by the mind, is known as good or good feeling.

OK.

Did that help?

Yes.

You see, you know, when they spiritualize psychology, they will indeed have the world by the tail. You see, they do have it right about the human mind.

Yes.

And its constant effort of manipulation.

Yes.

But they must understand the human mind would not manipulate if it did not experience need, and the human mind would not experience need if it did not first deny.

OK. That explains it.

Yes.

Thank you.

Yes. And so, you know, you'll notice with children, very early in life they learn the techniques and the devices of manipulation to get what they believe that they need.

Yes.

You see?

Yes.

Because a person does not live very well with a mind filled with too much need, you see.

Yes.

You see, need and the talent or ability of manipulation must be kept balanced in the human mind, you see.

Yes.

And then a person sooner or later in evolution, they get weary of the games the mind plays because they become the very victim of the manipulation.

Yes.

You see? It's a never-ending, vicious circle, you see. You see, need, and then there's the fulfillment of the need; and then there's need again; and then there's fulfillment. It keeps going round and round and round and round, you see.

Right.

Yes.

Thank you.

But the mind, of course, its instinct, of course, naturally, is to fill the need, you see, that it keeps creating.

Hmm.

The more manipulation, the more need; the more need, the more manipulation. Yes. This is why, you see, you cannot fill, you can never fill need. You can never fill need. It's a constant effort, and a person gets weary of the manipulation to keep the cup filled, you see. There's—it has no bottom to it, you see, because it's based upon the very principle of denial. Do you understand that?

Yes, I do.

You see, if a person—if you say to the mind, "Well, I'm just like everyone else. I'm a human being." You see? And if you say that to the mind, the mind doesn't take that very kindly. You understand that? You see? Because a person looks at their reflection and says, "No. I'm different. There's not another being exactly like me." Is that not correct?

Yes.

Well, to put one's total faith on the variety of creation at the denial of the wholeness of the universe that they are a part of is what creates so many, many problems in life. Yes.

I see.

Yes. You're welcome.

Thank you.

We have a few moments left if there are any other questions. I noticed that my youngest student has done very well this evening. Do you have any questions? *[The teacher addresses his youngest student, who is a four-year-old child of two other students.]*

No.

You don't?! You know everything, hmm? Do you?

No.

You don't. Well, maybe tomorrow or the next time you'll have a question. I'll say good night. Thank you very much. Good night.

MAY 12, 1988

A/V Seminar 32

Good evening, class.

This evening we will discuss, for our class, shadowlanders or, more properly known as, inhabitants of the shadowland. Between adversity and attachment lies the neutrality of spirit. The wind blows and the tree bends, and we find ourselves disturbed or controlled. The question is, Is it our attachment to the tree? Is it our adversity to the wind? We know that it is neither. It is our resistance to the Law of Evolution, known as change. This so-called karmic wheel of illusion, known as reality or physical substance, is merely an effect of the Law of Resistance. Creation is an effect of the Law of Resistance. We find our self in life not controlled by what we accept; we are controlled by what we resist. And we are tempted to resist anything and everything that we believe we cannot control.

And so we find in our life a constant panorama of creations, which we know as experiences. They are the direct effects of our resistance. As we awaken from the shadows and we turn to what we are, by refraining from resistance to what we are, we will have less experiences to control us and more acceptance to free us.

Resistance is an obstruction to life. Life is not creation. Creation is the shadow created by the obstruction or resistance to what is. As we awaken to what is, birth and death no longer exist for we move, born in adversity and attachment, we finally move to the neutrality of being, that which we truly are.

We cannot control the natural laws of life. We can and are responsible to move in harmony with them. When, through our error of ignorance, we resist the Law of Evolution, which is a demonstrable law of life, then we are controlled by the creations which are the effect of our own resistance. We resist the natural Law of Evolution by resisting change, which is indispensable to evolution. We resist change only in the illusion of time and then we cry for change.

Remember, students, we are controlled by that which we resist, and we are freed by that which we accept. It is our resistance that creates our experiences. It is our acceptance that frees us from being controlled by them. Now in many classes you have been given that as the Law of Personal Responsibility. Resistance of the Law of Personal Responsibility permits us to believe what we are not. We believe we are an experience that we have created. We resist it when we judge it is not pleasing to us.

We fear what we know as death, that only exists in our mind by our own resistance to life. Without that resistance, that illusion could not, for us, exist. Our belief in physical substance is ever dependent upon the tenacity of our resistance to that which is.

The law of physics applies to all form. Without resistance, creation, as you believe you know it, does not exist. Think of a few of the things you have experienced, an effect of your own resistance, and think of the changes that have taken place the moment that you accepted them. When we accept what we have resisted, for what we resist we create, then we are freed from it. Remember, we can only be controlled by our resistance. And we can only be freed by our acceptance. When we resist the possibility of anything, we create the obstruction necessary for the experience. When we look at what we have created, we turn our back to what we are (the Light) and we see the shadow known as creation and believe that we are it. That in our world is known as a shadowlander, an inhabitant of the shadowlands: one who sees and believes in the illusion they have created by resistance to what they are.

And so creation, the shadowland, is a playground of things in which only children should play. Many times in our life we don't want to grow up; we want to be a child. But when we're a child, we want to grow up and be an adult. We got what we wanted: we wanted to grow up and be an adult, and then we resist the experiences that we create and want to return to the innocence and the ignorance of not knowing that we alone are the creator.

Now it's time for your questions. Yes, please.

Sir, is it possible to ever reach the state of total acceptance in our present form of evolution?

Momentarily. For moments, for fleeting moments, yes. Fleeting because it takes a constant, moment-by-moment effort to flood the consciousness with the awareness, which is an effort to turn to the Light and not to see the shadow. You see, when we turn to the Light, we do not see the shadow, which is the effect of the obstruction that we are making. Others may see the shadow and see that because they see from the shadow world. And so for moments at a time, in the present evolution on Earth, yes, it indeed is not only possible and probable but many do, do that, yes. Yes.

Sir, would the, the exercise that we've been taught thus far help us accept more and create less?

Yes, indeed it does. It certainly does. It is designed for that purpose. However, one must ever be conscious and aware that resistance to reentering the shadowland of creation is not helpful in remaining free from it, for the resistance is the cohesion of creation or the shadowland. Yes. Well, for example, one has moments of going along and feeling good inside and freed from many things; then one stumbles and trips, and then they become very upset. The upset is an effect of their resistance to having tripped in the first place. Did that help with your question?

Yes, sir. Thank you.

Yes, certainly. Yes, please.

It seems to me that resistance must be magnetic and acceptance electric, is that so?

No, it is not.

It isn't?

No. For example, you may call adversity magnetic and attachment electric. You see, resistance, resistance, to resist—What does that mean, the word *resist*, to you? Does it not mean a refusal to accept?

Yes.

Pardon?

Yes.

All right. What one resists one suppresses.

Oh.

Yes, unfortunately people think, "I resist that. Therefore, it does not exist for I resist it." Their effort to resist it places it in a suppression within the consciousness. For man is an inseparable part of a universal whole. What exists for one exists for all. Do you understand that?

Yes, I do.

So, you see, our teachings have always been to educate, not to suppress; to accept the divine right of expression, not to resist it. For the moment you resist it, you create it within the depths of one's own consciousness, guaranteeing an increase in the adversity to it. And remember, an adversity is only a developing attachment, as an attachment is only a developing adversity. Does that help with your question?

Yes. Thank you.

You're welcome. Yes, please.

May I ask for a clarification in the last part that you said about creation is only a playground in which children should play? And then you said—and I'd like a correction on this, if necessary—and then, we wanted to grow up to be an adult and then we want to go back to the innocence of that childhood ...

What does *innocent* mean to you? Is not innocent ignorant?

Yes. And then you said that we are not the creator. Did I understand that correctly?

I think [if] you will check the tape, [you will] find a correction there. We are the creator of our experiences.

Yes. And so I'd like to ask, Is the child part the innocence of not knowing that we're the creator?

A lack of awareness is correct.

And—

The child is not aware that his experiences are effects of his own resistance. *You* are aware.

Yes.

The child is not aware.

Then why should only a child be in creation if he's still—

Because he's still ignorant.

OK. Thank you.

He is still ignorant or, as you may say, innocent. As a person grows up, they become aware they are responsible for their life. They personally are creating it moment by moment. A child's mind does not yet know that. Pardon?

Then what would be the adult role in creation?

To free themselves from the shadow of their own creation.

Thank you.

Yes, I do hope that's helped with your question.

Thank you.

Yes. You see, this is our discussion this evening, *Shadowlanders, Inhabitants of the Shadowland*. For the shadowland, as I have said, is the illusion. We believe this is physical. We believe ever in keeping with the degree that we believe we are the physical body. The more we believe we are physical, then the more we experience physical as our reality. Our reality is dependent upon our resistance to what we are. Pardon?

Yes. Thank you.

Yes, you're welcome. Yes, please.

Thank you. Am I correct in understanding that we, that we repress what we resist? You mentioned—

Yes, indeed we do. You see, whatever we resist within our consciousness, we suppress it.

OK.

Now in that suppr—in other words, we are no longer consciously in control of it. Would you understand it that way?

Yes.

You see, that which one suppresses, they are not in conscious control of. You know that as the subconscious mind is now in control of it.

Yes.

You see, adversities and attachments, you see—

Yes.

—are controlled by what is known as the subconscious. Now a person doesn't go walking down the street or to work and suddenly have an experience and say, "I'm adverse to that." They are adverse at the instant of experience. They do not have a conscious decision to say, "I am adverse to that." Do you understand that?

I see. Yes.

Pardon?

Yes, I do.

You see, that is controlled beneath the conscious awareness.

Yes.

And depending on the resistance to the experience in their lifetime will show to them how much they are controlled by it.

OK.

For they, in their subconscious mind, what you know as the subconscious mind, they have created a phenomenal resistance. That resistance, the effect of that resistance is a created form which now controls them. It works the same way with an attachment, of course, for, you see, attachment and adversity are one and the same thing.

Yes.

They're both the same.

Yes.

You see. You see, between this duality of creation is the neutrality. That's what you are. Everything else is what you've created. Pardon?

OK. That brings up another question.

Yes.

You said adversity is magnetic and attachment is electric.

I did not say that. I do feel that one of my students just got through saying that.

OK. So then that—

I did not say that.

OK.

Yes, we will leave that for another class.

OK.

That'll help my students here. *[The teacher laughs joyfully.]* I—you see, it's what is known as a catchall. When, you see, at the present stage of evolution if I should tell you that adversity is electric and attachment is magnetic or if I should tell you that attachment is electric and adversity is magnetic, it would be used and abused instead of wisely seen for what it all is.

OK.

Do you understand? You see, therefore, I will not answer that question—

OK.

—at this time. Because I know what the mind does. Pardon? I've spent much time with it. Yes.

OK.

My own mind, yes. Go ahead if you have any other question.

OK. Yes, I do. Thank you. And then in that you mentioned expression, you know, that, that expression was a part of, I guess, bringing up, the way I understood it was bringing up what we're resisting. In other words, we have to express.

Well, you see, the moment a person communicates—you see, the effect of communication is understanding.

OK.

You see. And so all of man's so-called problems are his, through error of ignorance, his constant effort of resisting. Pardon?

OK.

You see? You see, a person says, "Well, I cannot live in creation and be a passive person because they will mow me under."

Yes.

Pardon?

Correct.

Is that not true? Is that not how the mind thinks? Of course, it does. A person can be extremely passive and the world would know it not. Do you understand? You see, it depends on how much you believe you are a shadowlander. If you believe you are the shadow, known as creation, because that's what creation is, a shadow, a shadow of what is—creation is not life. Creation is a shadow of life, you see?

Yes.

So if you choose not to believe that you are a shadow of life, but that you turn to the Light, that you are Life, for that's what you truly are—

Yes.

—then you can be very passive—

Yes.

—very accepting and not be mowed under.

Thank you.

Do you understand?

Yes.

You see, you see, it's a matter of making a turn to that which is, [away from] the hissing hounds that are calling you. You turn around—you first know that they are shadows. And in order for you not to be mowed under, you understand, if you're still attached to a part of your shadow, you turn around and you do what is necessary, but you know that that is not you.

Correct.

You know that you are in creation, but you are not a part of creation. That is something known as flooding the consciousness. To flood the consciousness with that awareness will keep you free from all of these experiences of disturbance. You will know that you are responsible, but you will know that they are not you. Does that help you?

That helps with my question.

Yes.

Thank you.

You're more than welcome. Yes, please.

Is, is that what you mean by separating truth from creation?

Well, the separation of truth from creation is the awareness, the awareness that you are not the shadow; that creation *is* the shadow, but that is not what you are. You see, as long as you believe that you are the shadow, you will have all the experiences, for experiences exist only for shadowlanders. They do not exist when you turn to the Light that you are. Do you understand?

Yes.

Does that help with your question? Yes, go ahead.

It does. Thank you. And let's say you're in the midst of an experience and because it seems, to my mind, in a poss—you're in experience and it's like you're in creation—

You don't mean that you're inexperienced, but you're in the process of an experience. Is that—

Right.

Yes. Fine. Yes.

Like you're, you're living in it, so to speak. You're in form—

Well, it depends on what percent you're living in it.

OK.

Because a person is in form, in the illusion of physical matter and substance, in no way guarantees they have no awareness of where they are. Now people who believe they are creation have

lost, temporarily, an awareness of who they are. Why, certainly. For they believe they are the shadow that they look at. Pardon?
Yes.
Does that help you?
Yes.
Pause in the midst of creation; pause and accept who you are. Not what you are. Who you are. There's a difference between who you are and what you are. Who you are is the Light of freedom, acceptance, the world of goodness. What you are is resistance, the shadowland of old creation. Pardon?
Thank you.
Yes, please.
Yes. Thank you.
You're welcome.
What is the relationship between—or when I'm, when a person is in a state of neutrality...
Yes?
What is the function or relationship of the subconscious mind at that moment to the state of neutrality? And also, to the conscious mind.
The subconscious mind is a shadow and not a part of what you are. The subconscious mind is nothing more nor less than a computer bank of experiences, effects of resistances in your life. Pardon?
Thank you.
It is not what you are—it is not *who* you are. It is what you are, but it is not who you are. Would you understand that? It is what you are when you identify with the shadows. All right? It is not who you are. Because the subconscious, as I have said, is nothing but a computer bank, a data bank of ex—of resistance, the effect of which is experiences. The conscious mind is the only place where the soul faculties express. Not the subconscious. The subconscious—the job of the subconscious is the control of the functions based upon its own resistance. You hear? That's

its job. The work and job of the conscious mind is the awakening of the mind through the faculties of the soul. Yes.

Is it, is it possible to, to discipline the conscious mind to filter out the, the . . .

The influences of the—

The influence and the information provided by the subconscious mind?

Absolutely. Definitely. And it is the purpose of all these classes and has been for many, many, many, many centuries. The control, *not the suppression,* you see, the education and the control. You see, you begin by acceptance of its existence. The acceptance that there are certain functions that you're familiar with. The acceptance that they are a part of the shadow or what you call creation. Do you understand? And that all of the experiences contained therein, in the subconscious realm of consciousness, all of those experiences are effects of your own resistance. That's all that they are. They're nothing more and they are nothing less. They are ever subject to change and are in a constant process of reevaluation and change.

Survival is the domain of the functions. The faculties have no concern, for life is. You see, birth and death are the domain of the subconscious mind who has a database of experiences created from resistance in times of errors of ignorance. Would you understand that?

Yes.

There. So it is your conscious mind that must remain the master in a mental world. Your conscious mind. Conscious choices. Yes.

Then I think I have a judgment about the word neutrality *in relationship to the conscious mind. The conscious mind being an active, an active entity. An active and, and . . .*

Active in the sense of resisting anything that is not already in its computer bank. Do you understand that?

No.

Well, for example, the purpose of the subconscious mind is to store all experiences. That is its purpose. And to resist anything that is foreign to the experiences it has already created. Do you understand that?

Can it resist if it's not, if it's just a storehouse of experiences?

Because it's not only a storehouse; it sends a message to the conscious mind. It's constantly sending messages up to the conscious mind. Now those messages entering the conscious mind—you understand that?

Yes.

The conscious mind then takes a look at all of its experiences. Would you understand that?

Yes.

As the conscious mind looks at all of its experiences, it resists the change that it is facing.

Yes.

The conscious mind is the active mind. Do you understand?

Yes.

It is the messages that come up to the conscious mind from the subconscious mind that cause the resistance. Do you understand?

Yes.

And that resistance supports what already exists within the storage bank. Pardon? So it is this interrelationship between the functions and the faculties that's going on all the time. Pardon?

Yes.

So, you see, the conscious mind says, "Well, if I accept this, then I am going to experience that." That judgment is made by the conscious mind. Pardon?

Yes.

What you are really doing is supporting what already exists. Fear does not exist in the conscious mind. The conscious mind is not what resists change. It is the messages from the subconscious mind to the conscious mind that cause the resistance to the laws of evolution. Do you understand that?

Yes. [The student speaks very quietly.]

Pardon?

Yes.

Because the subconscious is the magnetic. And the conscious is the electric. Do you understand? The conscious mind is the electric. So resistance is taking place by the conscious mind based upon information fed by its magnetic counterpart. Pardon?

Yes.

You see? But man has the right of choice. He does not have to resist and create more experiences and be continuously bound on the karmic wheel of illusion. He has the right of choice. He usually chooses, however, *usually* chooses what the subconscious, in its own fear to protect itself, sends up as a message. Pardon?

Yes.

Did that help there?

Very much.

Yes, please.

Could one say that the subconscious mind, is it below the conscious mind?

Consider—considering that it is the victim of its own fear, yes, I would consider it below, certainly. I would certainly not consider it above. If you must have an above and below, the conscious mind is where the right of choice truly exists. It does not exist in the sub—the right of choice does not exist in the subconscious mind. The right of choice exists in the conscious mind, yes. Yes.

Could, could you say that it's, it not only is below but be—is it behind, like . . .

Well, it serves the purpose for which it is designed: survival, you see. As long as a person believes they are the shadow known as creation, their subconscious computer banks are serving their purpose. Pardon? Yes. If you ask a person if they want to be without feelings, you'll hear an instant reaction of no. So remove the subconscious and remove the sensation of what you know as feelings—pardon?—and be freed. Remember now, you cannot have feelings without a subconscious mind, and you cannot have the need for feelings without it. Hmm? Because the dependence, then, no longer exists, you see. Yes.

But don't, don't we—those feelings are necessary. That's what you just said, right?

They are necessary as long as you believe you are a shadow. As long as you're a shadowlander, if you are a shadowlander, then, of course, they serve the shadowlands, known as creation. Of course, they do. Certainly. They're necessary for that, for the shadow world. Why, certainly they are. Yes.

You could act—are you saying that you could actually be here . . .

Pardon?

Without the feelings?

I have said for many, many, many, many centuries: be in the world and not a part of the world. Be with a person, place, or thing and never a part of person, place, or thing. Dependence only exists in the shadowland. You must understand that dependence is a denial of what you are. When you stop resisting or denying what you are, then you will not have feelings of dependence. Pardon? Dependence only exists for people who believe that they are what they are not. Hmm? Dependent people know birth and death, yes, and experience and the shadowland known as creation. Yes.

Thank you.

For they deny. They resist. They resist that which is: themselves. Yes, please.

Thank you. Would you please speak more on the law of physics and how it relates to resistance?

Well, for example, would you understand there is no cohesion without resistance? Would you understand that?

Yes.

Pardon?

Yes, I would.

Fine. All right. Is experience a cohesion?

Yes.

It's an effect of resistance.

Yes.

Without resistance, it does not exist. Your physical world only exists as an effect of resistance. When you resist what you are, you experience what you have—what you are not, you experience what you have created. You are not what you have created. You are what you are. You have created what you believe is a physical body, a physical substance.

You see, your body is an effect, an effect of what you have created in evolution. It is the culmination of all of your experiences in evolution. Without resistance to life, you could not experience. You only experience by the Law of Resistance. That's how you experience. You do not experience by the Law of Acceptance. You experience by the Law of Resistance. So when you accept the possibility of something, you establish the law through which, by your own resistance, you experience it. When, for example, you accept the possibility of something happening, your mind begins resisting everything contrary to it. Surely, after these many years you understand how that works. As you resist everything contrary to it, you bring in all of those necessary experiences. For—I'll just put it more down to the mundane. You accept you're going to have a lot of money. All right? And time passes and you don't have a lot of money. And you ask yourself the question years later, "Why don't I have a lot of money?" Because you have been resisting—you understand that? Not resisting you have a lot of money. Resisting you don't have any money. And by resisting you don't have any money, you create more of the experiences. I do hope that's helped with your question. Does that help you?

Yes, sir. Thank you.

Yes. Hmm. *[The teacher laughs joyously.]* And so we are here in these classes to take another look at our ourselves and see, "What am I and what do I believe I am? I am what I am, yet I believe what I am not." You see, belief is not necessary to truth. Truth is. See, truth needs no defense because it has no belief, you see. See, belief is bondage. Truth just is. You cannot defend truth. It's falsehood that requires defense. For what is defense? Wouldn't you understand that it's resistance? Pardon?

Yes, sir.

Well, certainly. So that which requires defense or resistance is not truth; it is the opposite of truth, known as falsehood. The mind is not truth. Such a fickle thing could not possibly be truth. There's no fickleness in truth. Truth is. That which is fickle is and it isn't. Then it's known as fickle. No. Yes, please.

When you're, like, on the path of the straight and narrow and you have the adversity and attachments, and the subconscious is feeding things to the conscious mind, the only way to, like, to stay on the straight and narrow and to keep that neutrality . . .

Well, may I say one thing?

Yes.

As long as the mind judges that freedom is straight and narrow, it won't be tempted to work for it. Yes, go ahead with your question.

OK. When it's feeding—the subconscious is feeding the conscious mind all these, all these thoughts, the way through it is the awareness of them, the acceptance of them, and the communication of them and the responsibility for them. Is that correct? To stay . . .

And the lack of concern over them. We must not forget the lack of concern.

OK.

The business of good living is the lack of concern. Yes.

Thank you. Yes.

Yes.

Thank you.

You're welcome. If you want to be controlled by something, make great effort to stay concerned over it. You see, concerned people are controlled people. I didn't say they're in control. I said they're controlled.

Right. That's good. Thank you.

Because concerned people are constant resistors.

Right.

That's why they're so concerned. Do you understand that?

Yes, I think I do.

Well, a person [says], "What's going to happen tomorrow? Is this going to take place? [Is] that going to take place? How am I going to get through this? What's going to happen yesterday? Oh, what did happen—I forgot what happened yesterday." *[Many students laugh.]* That's a concerned person.

Right.

They're controlled. They, you see, they are attached to the fruits of action. People who are attached to the fruits of action are very concerned people and very controlled people. They are haunted and hounded by past experiences. And so each time they go to make a step forward in evolution—and as we all know, without change, the Law of Evolution is not possible. Change is indispensable to evolution. Concerned people have great difficulty in evolving. Great difficulty. Because they resist. They resist change. You see.

Right.

See, to resist change is to create more of the very thing you want to move out of. Like I said long ago, if things were so great in the good old days, why didn't we stay there? Well, none of us stayed there, now did we?

No.

No, we move on, you see. So they really weren't that great or we never would have left them.

Right.

Pardon?

That's right.

You see?

Yes.

So the more we're concerned, the more we resist, the more, the more we lose the joy of living, you see.

It's true.

Now a lot of times our mind will say, "I'm a responsible person. Therefore, I'm a concerned person." That's justification of the ignorant. Pardon?

Yes.

Yes. When one accepts personal responsibility, they are freed from concern. Through the acceptance of personal responsibility, concern disappears. You do what you have to do, you give what you have to give to the best of your ability in your evolution and you're free. Especially when you're corrected. *[A few students laugh.]* Yes. That help you with your question?

Yes, it does. Thank you.

Very good, very good. Don't look at freedom as the straight and narrow or you'll never make any effort to get there.

OK.

That's not a bit tempting to the mind. You see, the mind likes things crooked, not straight and narrow. Not straight period. Crooked. Why does it like things crooked? Yes.

There's more bends for there's more shadows.

More shadows? Of course. The mind is tempted by difference. Now if everyone is straight and narrow, there's no tempting to the mind at all. The mind likes things different.

Yes.

If the mind does not have distractions and it has not had the necessary self-discipline of some type of meditation or self-control, the balance of the mind will be lost within seventy-two hours. Seventy-two hours. The only thing in your day of space travel and things that is permitting your pilots [to] go into outer space is a disciplining, through a type of meditation or some type of self-control, or they lose their mind. Because without that effort, the mind is in a constant state of having to be distracted. That's an undisciplined, uneducated mind.

I see that our time is up. Thank you and good evening.

JULY 14, 1988

Seminar 33

Good evening, class.

This evening we will discuss the energy fields of the universe that your scientists are so interested and so baffled in your world at this time. Some of you, I'm sure, are aware, from what you might consider your current affairs or news, that a seemingly strange and baffling energy field in the universe has been physically detected by the finest astronomical instruments available to your world. For our class this evening, we will share with you our view and our understanding of this seeming strange phenomenon. First of all, it began, this movement of energy in the universe, not in this year of its detection by your instruments in the year of 1988. No, it began back in what you might consider over thirty years ago of your earthly time. We see from our records that could well have been what you call the Aquarian age.

How does this energy field affect you as students of the Living Light of Spiritualism, the light of reason? Well, it affects you directly. It affects you indirectly. It affects all beings, human or animal, on the planet Earth. It has been doing so for over thirty years.

Some time ago we brought to you a small booklet. We had it printed in your world and we gave it to you, as students, freely. Many of you have not bothered with its simplicity. It has always been available to those who are simple and child-like in their consciousness, waiting for you, as students, to understand and to apply. To your world it was known as the "Celestial Marriage," a simple, little, so-called fable, properly studied and understood would have prepared you for what your scientists now, in this year of 1988, are informing you on your own so-called news media. It is still available in this the Serenity Church. *[Please see the appendix.]*

However, the so-called big bang of the universe that began what you understand as planets and solar systems is not like what you might consider a shotgun and suddenly everything appears. That's not how planets and solar systems are born. That is not how they die. It is a very natural process.

We are recording everything for your benefit, although it will be some time before you receive a copy, for that is another factor. We're still waiting on what you call our copy machine. *[The teacher is referring to the distribution of the audio tapes of this class to the students.]*

Now let us return to this great energy field that is coming towards your solar system and specifically the planet Earth. When a solar system is born, it gathers unto itself energy from surrounding solar systems. It does this in keeping with natural law. As it draws this energy from surrounding solar systems, those solar systems, by natural law, are in the process of their decay or death.

There are many solar systems. There are many universes. And so we will speak from this moment of only one. The one that is directly related to this great field of energy that is being released. Whenever form begins the process of what you know as death, there is a release of energy that is indeed measurable. And so this great energy that your scientists have detected, and little more will be said on your news media, is an effect. It is a solar system that is changing. It is dying. The energy is being released planet after planet after planet, as it goes through its transformation and returns to the source from whence it had been born. All things, all form, all planets, all people, all animals, all things, all limits return to the source, to their sustenance, are transformed and renewed.

Many times there is much confusion in reference to that scientific and demonstrable, [what] in your world you call fact. Confusion because one then is tempted to believe: they are born, they grow, and they die; and they return to the planet again and again and again. It's known in your world as reincarnation. Our understanding and our view for so many, many centuries is evolutionary incarnation. Everything that is born and returns by the process known as death to the source that has given it birth is refined and evolved. As above, so below. Solar systems are solar systems within, and they are solar systems without.

Some of you students are well aware and waiting to study Atlantean astrology in an intelligent, humble, and simple way, given to you so very many years ago. Not Babylonian astrology. We are not interested in confusion and regret. We're interested in demonstrable, scientific demonstration.

And so our class this evening of which all of you have been, at times, so concerned about: energy. Without it, you have no health. Without it, you have no wealth. Without it, you have no joy. Without it, you have no understanding. And without it, there is no wisdom. Now it's going to take what you call light years before the effects of this dying solar system, returning to its source—and what is the source of all solar systems? There's one Light. There's one sustenance for all solar systems. Well, you know it in your world as the Sun.

Many very intellectual people for centuries on your planet tried to insist it was the planet Earth. What is the center of all universes? The source from whence all the children have been given birth. All children return to their parents. All things return to their source. And so let us take this great phenomenon that has been happening in your world for over thirty years, that you are now slightly, just slightly aware of. For the mind accepts more readily what it respects than it does what is not respected, and the mind has a tendency to accept, of course, that which is popular, for that which is popular in a society, of course, is considered normal. No one feels good being considered odd or strange, for in so feeling one does not associate well with what is called society at large. And indeed, it is a large society that you, as students of the Living Light, find yourself in.

And so this evening, let us discuss your solar system, the microcosm of the great macrocosm. It all works the same way. It is governed by the same law. That which governs the blade of grass is governing the solar system. The law doesn't change. Appearances are more than deceiving; they are an absence from reality. And what is reality? That which we are consciously aware of at any moment.

Ask yourself the question: Are you in this moment in reality? What proof, to your satisfaction, do you have that you are seated where you think that you are seated? Well, if you have someone to agree with you and there are enough people to agree with you, then you say, "Well, of course, it's a reality. I'm sitting in a room at a certain place with several other people." But is that fact or is that truth? If it was truth, it would not be dependent, students, would it? For truth, requiring no defense, requires no dependence. You see, for truth to require defense, then truth, by the Law of Defense, is dependent upon something.

Now facts require defense, for facts are dependent. It is a fact that you are seated physically where you are seated, but that fact cannot stand alone. That fact requires defense because its very being is subject to the Law of Dependence. Therefore, if someone says, "Where are you?" and you say, "Well, I'm in a certain building at a certain time." "Oh, where's your proof?" "Well, I have someone that was present, and they will state, yes, I was there at that time at that evening and etc. and etc." But then that's only one person you are now dependent upon. Perhaps someone decides that, "One witness is not sufficient. We require at least two." And so you search around in your class here, this little school here, and you find someone else that is willing to agree with you and to be inconvenienced and prove, to whoever you are trying to prove your fact to, that, yes, indeed you were there. You now have two witnesses. You are now not dependent upon the truth within you. You are now dependent upon two separate individualized beings.

Then the question arises, "Are they dependent? They tell me they will be my witnesses, but how dependent are they? I must now consider how much I think I am going to inconvenience them. For if I inconvenience them too much, they just might decide, being individualized, free beings and free agents, they may decide, 'This inconvenience can only come at a price.'" Well, then you have to investigate and you have to decide what that price is going to be. Because, of course, you're the one that has to pay—what do you call it, the tab? You call it a tab? Yes. Yes, a tab. You're the one that has to pay the tab.

So then the question arises in your mind, "That's too expensive. I'll try to find another witness. Perhaps I will find—there's several people to choose from." Well, everyone's going to be inconvenienced. So you must offer them something, and in your world I think you would consider that a bribe. So now you're the victim, by your own choice, of whoever you've decided that you can bribe and that will fulfill what it is that you want. That, you see, my children, is a mental world. It is filled with much diversity. It is filled with dependence. So let us carry on with this wonderful energy field of which we are all so interested in, and should be, as students of the Light.

Familiarity is an effect; it's not a cause. And so let us consider what familiarity truly is. Familiarity is an effect of our attachments to patterns of mind that, through error of ignorance, we believe that we are. And therefore, when someone asks us, "What are you?" we say, "Well, I am this. I am that. I am that. I am whatever I have attached myself to, through the error of ignorance of patterns of mind, that I believe that is what I am." And so when we move on in our thought and we say, "Well, this is what I am;" the question arises then, "Well, if this is what I am, I have a question: Who am I? I now know what I am, but I don't know who I am."

And which is the most important thing in life? To know who you are or only to know what you are? For, you see, what you are and what you believe you are is ever subject to whatever pattern of mind that you have attached yourself to. So what you are is in a process of constant change. So when you were 15 and when you were 17, patterns of mind, you believe, through error of ignorance, that that's what you are. And so at that time you had no problem saying to yourself, "This is what I am." The question rose at that time, "Well, this is what I am. Now who am I?" Well, "Who am I?" creates a confusion in mental substance because who you are is not what you are, for what you are constantly changes and is fluctuating, like the tides of the ocean that eternally wash the thirsty shore.

So as students of the Light, be not so concerned in what you are. Awaken the faculty. And in all your garnering and getting, get understanding that through that process and the receiving of understanding you qualify yourself to give wisdom unto yourself, for it's all taking place within yourself.

You see, a soul faculty has no dependence. It is not mental substance. Functions have dependence. We consider functions and say, "That's what I am." We consider faculties and ask, "Well, who am I?" We know what we are through effort of mental substance, our human mind. To understand who we are, that is not in the domain of knowledge; it is in the realm of wisdom. And how often, on Tuesday [we say], "This is what I am. I don't feel well. It's been a terrible weekend. A lot of things I didn't get to do that I wanted to do." Therefore, that Tuesday and your belief that that's what you are is not a good day for you. However, you might meet someone. You might get a call. And what you are, in the process of believing in the mind, suddenly changes. And now, for a time, you're something else. But that's not who you are. That is only the suit that you temporarily wear. It is so temporal. It is so, so limited. It is such a microscopic moment, *moment* in the eternity that you truly are.

So let us, in this class, spend our time awakening that we may express the faculty of joy and not be concerned with what we are, for what we are belongs to a world that these classes are not about, have never been about, will not even be about. These classes are about who you are. We are not interested, in our world, [in] what you are. Your world, a mental world, is interested in what you are. And in that sense, you are bound to the karmic wheel of repetition that, in time, in eternity, you shall free yourselves [from].

This is not a shortcut, an accelerated program in which you can move from what you believe, and are bound by, what you think you are—that is always having variables; that to one person they like you, only the next moment they don't, because you have the bondage of what you believe and mental patterns. That's not who you are.

These classes have always been, and continue to be, guidelines of reason that you may consider not again what you are, but that you may each moment consider who you are: whole, complete, formless, free Intelligence. That's who you are.

All other things you have added in your evolution. And because you have added them, you shall in truth and in time—time, the great illusion—you shall discard them. For that which is added, by the Law of Addition, is subtracted. And the more we add and the more we depend on what we think we are—not on who we are, but what we think we are—then we move from addition to multiplication to complexity to division and finally subtraction. Why take so much energy? Even though the universes and this solar system is being flooded with it.

How does it affect all things upon the planet from the smallest blade of grass to the highest human being? We're all susceptible to it, whatever patterns of mind that we continue to direct energy to, to believe this is what we are, and not move into the faculties.

"Who am I?" That question awakens all beings, for that question is a sincere and honest mind that is a servant and knows that there is something greater, [and knows] that without that something greater, mind, the substance that asks questions, *is*, by the very law, subservant to. Without that intelligent Energy, there is no mental substance. Without that intelligent, eternal, infinite Energy, there is no physical substance. It all returns from whence it has come.

And that's why you're here at these seminars. This is why you have come to this particular school, to this particular church, to this particular philosophy that you may learn for yourselves who you are. No one can tell you who you are. You alone know. In the stillness and honesty of your being, you alone know who you are. You are greater than what you believe; you are lesser than what you demand. You are greater than what you believe. Do not forget that great truth. However, you are lesser than what you demand. Be kind to yourself. Be not so demanding, for the law is clear: one first demands of themselves in order to place their being in a level of consciousness to demand from another. Be not so unhappy and so unkind to who you are by trying to please people, first yourselves, in what you are.

For when you leave your earthly clay, you have several vehicles that will transport who you are. [When] you leave this physical body, you have a mental body, a vehicle to transport your eternal being, who you truly are. You have an astral body. You have what is known as a spiritual body. You have a terrestrial body. You have a celestial body. And all of those things are like automobiles. That's all that they are. They are designed that way. You can repair them so many times before it's no longer practical or reasonable to repair them anymore. You can rebuild an automobile. Ah, but it takes God, the eternal Light, to rejuvenate a flesh-and-bone body. There are no mechanics on your planet that have such wisdom with flesh and bone. Only with steel and plastic. Yes, that is the domain, and rightly so, of a mental world.

Time for questions. Kindly raise your hand, should you have one. Yes.

Thank you, sir. Is the energy that is flooding the planet now and has been for these thirty years—

Thirty plus years, yes.

Is that going to continue into the future for a very long period of time?

Oh, indeed. Indeed, solar systems are like people: they're born and they, what you call, die. They're born; they're little children; they grow up; they become teenagers, adults. And then they become what you might call senior citizens. Senior citizens, that's a senior solar system. That's a junior solar system. That's a teenage solar system. And all intelligences that have composed it. Does that help with your question?

Thank you.

Certainly. Certainly. You see, you will not, for your expansion of time, limited by mental substance—you must see your own solar system from a different perspective for it is in the process of all of these changes. All universes, physically, have worked that way. That is a—the phenomenon is only a lack of understanding natural law. That's all it is, you see?

And so as the energy floods, ever-increasingly throughout the light years, so-called, ahead and eons of time, your solar system is already being affected. And so some time ago, I mentioned to you, your planet Earth, so-called, moves closer and closer and closer, microscopically perhaps in your limited views, to the source from whence it was born. It's known as your Sun in your solar system. Well, as this phenomenon, so-called, takes place throughout the universes, as the energy floods in varying directions by Infinite Intelligence, by laws that are, not to be, not has been, but laws that are. Which came first, the chicken or the egg? Neither one. Law *is*! Not mental substance. Law is. When did it start? Well, it didn't start because to start it has to have an end. Law is. Divine law is, has always been, will always be.

And so this flooding of energy directing to your solar system, affecting everything in its path, you understand that. It is not a partial, selfish energy; it works by natural law. Then your little planet, that little pinhead in the universe, called Earth, moving, moving, moving, slowly, surely to your Sun. Because that's the process. They all return to that which gave them birth.

They're big bangs if you want to consider that process a big bang. Well, then call it a big bang. It's just a very natural process. Does that help you with your question?

Yes. Thank you.

Certainly. Yes, please.

About this energy that's returning or that's, this energy field that's affecting the planet . . .

Yes.

Is it, is it—did it come from this planet and is it returning?

Well, you see, now there's the next class, isn't it? All things return unto themselves, but we don't want to take six hours for this class. But you have a question that is very important based on divine natural law. Hmm? You see, that's like, you know, I would love, really, to spend the hours with you this evening to give you those classes, but as we are, what you might consider rejuvenating our temple of God here on Earth, as we are in that process of the full restoration of our channel, who has been well prepared to do his 100 percent work for the Light of Spirit and under the banner of Spiritualism, you understand, we must not take six hours for that class when it's a preparatory class and there are several intermediate ones. You do understand that, don't you?

Yes.

Fine. And so based upon the divine law that all things return unto themselves, of course, I can tell you this: you are accurate—you understand?—with that question. However, there are many phases in between.

It's like the question: Well, where did man, intelligent man, come from? Well, is he evolved, as the Darwinian theory, of an ape? Well, let us consider the descent of man. Let us do the studies of the classes we already have, and then we'll have a greater understanding of what some in your society, still bound by "What am I?", would consider mixed marriages. Would you understand that? Whatever beings were here on the planet—and intelligences are always moving. I think you might consider that, well, whatever you call it, an intermarriage or galactic marriage? It doesn't matter what you call it. It's a matter, it's a matter of the descent of intelligence into the grossness of what is known [as] flesh and bone and form. You understand that? And so whatever was available at that phase of your evolution, whether you want to call them monkeys, apes, crocodiles—What do they call that, Crocodile Dundee? *["Crocodile Dundee" was the name of a popular movie that was shown to the students at the temple.]* Or is it Dundo? *[Many students laugh.]* Whatever you want to call it, it doesn't matter because, you see, the intelligence was infused in the evolutionary process.

Of which now we have all of these generations and no one wants to think practical, you see, and say, well, it used to be this way or that way. And so we look at someone on the planet, your planet, in the society of "What am I?" instead of "Who am I?" and we take a look and we see, "Those eyes don't look right. Why are those eyes slanted like that? Why is the color of the skin not the same color as mine?" And we ask our self the question, don't we? And we answer that question. We say, "Well, they're from this part of the planet. And they're from that part of the planet, and someone else is from that part of the planet." And we don't seem to understand the adaptability and the divine wisdom expressed through nature, what you call Mother Nature. So if you have beings on a planet and where they are constantly exposed to the bright sunlight of snow-capped mountains, sooner or later nature adapts and you call those people various names over periods of time. Is that not correct? Pardon?

Yes.

And so then we have other people on your planet, and we find them—well, their skin is a little different color. Might be reddish. It might be brownish. Well, some people like to say purple. Well, that depends. We don't have any—my channel likes to play that music. I've heard it several times called little "Purple People Eaters" or something: it's some silly, little ditty that came out in your world years ago. *[The teacher refers to a popular novelty song released in 1958.]*

So why and what happened? The pigmentation of the skin adapts. It is adapting, but it takes eons of time. And so here we find people, basically, as you study your own planet and its civilizations, some people are short. Some people are tall. Some people have blue eyes. Some have brown eyes. Some have black eyes. Well, it depends upon the evolution of the being and the climatic conditions and the environmental impact over a period of eons of time. Does that help with the question?

Thank you.

It doesn't seem to, but we are going to get—all things do return unto their source. But first we [have] got to take care of our understanding of the little people that are still in the earthly form so that their minds don't blow any—what do you call it?—any circuit breakers back here as we try to evolve these classes into a much broader horizon. Hmm? Yes. Thank you. Now [another student] has a question. Yes.

If, if energy is energy, then the infusion that the planet has been experiencing . . .

Yes?

. . . will work to our detriment or our benefit depending upon the patterns of mind that we establish?

Depending on the patterns of mind and on how much you believe that you are what you are instead of your awakening to who you are. Why, certainly. For example, if you believe that you are what you are, and what you are is demonstrable [as] an error of ignorance, accepting patterns of mind that you have attached your being to, and if, in those patterns of mind, you believe that life is such a struggle and you don't have any money and you don't have any time and you don't have any joy and you don't have any goodness, well, of course, that will all increase because there is a flooding of the universe of your planet of your solar system. Certainly, it will increase. But you aren't the victim of it. You have free choice. You can make the effort yourself at any moment to make that daily, constant effort. Flood your consciousness by your conscious choice. Let it not be flooded by what you believe, through error of ignorance, of what you are, which is only an attachment to patterns of mind that you alone have created by environmental impact and all other factors. Does that help with your question?

Yes, sir.

Any other question? Yes?

Then—

Oh, indeed, thank you. *[The teacher addresses the technician recording this class.]* You will just have to get another tape. You wait a moment. *[The teacher speaks to the student about to ask a question.]* Do you have another one?

Just flip it over? [The technician suggests turning the cassette tape over to record on the unrecorded side.]

Well, pause a moment and let him flip-flop over here these things.

[While the other classes in this series were recorded on video tape, this particular class, Seminar 33, was recorded on an audio cassette tape. After the tape is flipped, the class continues.]

Very good. Now your second question, please.

Then because the energy that is passing through our solar system is assisting the Earth—

Did I say passing through or coming your way and having affect upon your planet?

Coming our way—

And solar—well, you know, you see, you have to understand solar systems. Some are like sponges: they absorb everything they can get. Some, they have decided, "I have enough," and they let it pass by. So we have to understand the laws that govern your particular solar system. Your solar system isn't exactly identical to any other solar system. However, it is controlled, born, and dies by the same identical laws in principle. Do we understand that? But your solar system has a personality, you see? I don't see much getting past your solar system. It seems to be such a—what do you call that?—never enough type of sponge. Not personally, of course, you know, I'm talking about the planet. Yes, go ahead with your question.

Then our solar system, because the energy, because the Earth is moving closer and closer to its source—

Well, I didn't—well, the source in its particular solar system. You see, the planet Earth is moving—and [it] is measurable—closer and closer to its source. It is a child of what you call the Sun. Do you understand that?

Yes.

Now that's just one of the planets. Is that not correct?

That's correct.

Well, there you are. Now that's just one solar system. Is that not correct?

That's correct.

Well, now that solar system is another, in the entire solar—is a child. You understand that? Well, say that all of the little children of the particular solar system are once again reabsorbed and return into the planet into the sun. You now have one child, don't you?

Yes.

Pretty big one. A lot of energy. Would you not agree?

Yes.

Well? The little children have all died, the little planets, in that solar system.

Yes.

Now they've returned to its source in that solar system.

Yes.

Now, we've got the great lion and its roar. It isn't going to stay sleeping forever. And it's going to spit out again, if you want to put it that way. And a solar system, once again, is going to be created. You know, when you father a child usually you don't stop with the process of reproduction after just once, do you?

No.

Do you? *[The teacher addresses another student.]*

No, sir.

Well, there you are. I mean, you know, if you judge something is something, well, you know, there never seems to be enough of whatever one judges. Well, we're dealing with laws. These laws are infallible laws. Now how they are expressed by a planet, a solar system, and etc.—expression places one or anything into limit and personality. A planet has a personality. Would you understand that?

Yes.

A planet has a personality. It is different from another planet. It is composed of similar, but not identical, elements. Would you understand that?

Yes.

So in that respect it has its own personality chemically. Would you understand that?

Yes.

So here's a planet and it's composed—it's similar to other planets, but it has its own personality, chemically. Correct?

Correct.

Now you have the Earth planet—right?—in your solar system. It has its personality, because you go over to the Moon and it has a little different personality, but there are similarities of chemicals. Would you understand that?

Yes.

Now we'll move from there. Let's go to what we're going to be discussing soon: wars and rumors of wars are ever amongst all children of Earth. And so we now have Mars, don't we? Well, give us time—your world I'm speaking of—and all of their nice little, statistics and all their facts will be in, and you will see, "Well, there's different chemicals here. But, ah, there's some similar ones." Correct?

Correct.

Well, you haven't got to Mars yet, into your mental substance, but don't worry, that's on the way. So they all have a similarity, but they're all different. So one planet, physically, is composed of certain creatures, you understand, people, humans, animals, trees, plants, grass. And another planet is composed of something else. But it's only at a different stage of growth. You can't compare a five-year-old child to a fifty-five-year-old seasoned man. Can you?

No, sir.

There. Does that answer your question?

Yes, sir.

Well.

Thank you.

You're welcome. Anyone else have a question? Yes, please.

Are all solar systems born out of a sun?

Everything comes from the Light and returns to the Light. Now if you wish to understand that as a sun, then we'll call them all suns. Does that help you with your question?

Yes. Thank you.

They all come from the source. You see, without Light, there is no systems, there is no solar, there is nothing, there is no thing.

So what's the black hole? Aren't you—yes, you're usually interested in black holes, aren't you? This strange thing that happens in the universe. *[The teacher and many students laugh.]* That everyone has a theory about, and you make movies about them and all these silly little things to entertain yourselves with all of these little, purple—no—green people eaters and all that other superstitious foolishness. But anyway, it entertains your little minds for a time, doesn't it? Well, let's skip to what you call facts. I've always been in my life a person, practical, hopefully for you, down to earth. But I don't stay down here. *[Many students laugh.]* I have some of my own things to take care of. Yes, is there something—you need to be excused?

No, no.

Very well. Then please be patient with me.

Excuse me.

Yes. Certainly. Unless you need to stretch. Do you need to stretch?

No.

Very good.

Thank you. Excuse me.

Oh, I'll get to your question. I was on little green people eaters, wasn't I?

Yes.

And wasn't I discussing with you—you know, I'm not senior to the point of senility. Don't forget now, children, senility is ever relative to a decrease in productivity. That's totally based upon what someone wants out of you, you know. So let's not forget about seniority, senior citizens, senility, and all of those choice, little foolish—such childish foolishness. Not childlike, just plain childish. Don't forget they're what you call facts. Senility is relative to a decrease in productivity of what somebody wants out of you. *[The teacher laughs joyfully.]* All right. Now where are we? We're on black holes, aren't we?

Yes. Yes. [Many students respond.]

I'd prefer to call it something besides a hole. I don't mind calling it black. Let's call it a black vacuum, you know. Just something—all of these great minds can't seem to figure it out. Well, they look at the universes. Energy is released and there's a death of a solar system. Now another solar system is being born. So you get this transference taking place, and you people like to call it black holes. They never, never once called it a white hole. They're always calling it a black hole.

Well, why don't you be patient with yourselves, and don't be so dependent on the fickleness of scientific advancement? It's advancing very rapidly because there's always wars and rumors of wars. That will ever be amongst you people of Earth. Don't ever forget that. If you don't have a war, you have a rumor of a war. And if you have a rumor of a war, you're ever worried and concerned, "When will it take place?" Well, while you're in that process, you have all this technological advancement. Everything gets justified for the money because you are now in a process of defending your own personal self-interest. No government, no country, in any universe, in any world, at any time, ever got scientific advancement—that is for your stage of evolution, your planet and solar system—without wars and rumors of wars, for only through fear does man rise up to sacrifice so that he may defend, by the Law of Instinct, known as survival.

And so in that respect, that function—which is nothing more than directing your beautiful, intelligent, infinite, intelligent Energy into mental substance, and that you call fear. And then you do whatever your fears dictate based upon your beliefs of what you are, for your survival of what you demand, first of yourself, to survive in—what do they say in your world? What do they call that? Just a moment. These strange phases—phrases and things—"Living in the way that I am accustomed to." I think you call that luxury or something. Something you dream about and hope for—well, yes, living in the way to which you believe you are accustomed. Well, many of us are accustomed to dreams, before the dreams start dreaming us. So dreamer, dream a life of beauty before your dream starts dreaming you, and then you call that a nightmare, would you not agree, children?

Yes.

A real nightmare. And so then we ask our self the question, "What am I? Is this reality or is this a black hole? If it is, what's happening? Am I being sucked off into another universe because another universe is in the process of being born and is drawing all of this energy throughout the solar systems and it's affecting those things that have an affinity and proximity to it?" You understand that, children? Well, certainly! See, what is this great phenomenon and what is all this special stuff [in] your current affairs? And how does this, in any way, affect us? It affects us in all ways.

So now we'll speak about our school, its continuity, its purpose, once again, and our channel, who, by our own assistants and doctors, is fully restored and prepared to 100 percent, *100 percent*, spiritual, physical, and mental activity for the good of the Light that he has served for forty-eight years of his life. So we'll talk about those things, and free you from all concern, and free you from all fear, and free you from all demands of what it means to you as students. Students that have always been welcome, that are welcome this moment, that are welcome to remain and to be a part of the spiritual endeavor of the publication and the completion of the Living Light Philosophy, including this very class this evening. And so we'll talk about all of those things for a time. But I think, perhaps, you're even running out of tape. But that doesn't matter, I'll just speak with you as students of the eternal, intelligent, infinite Light of Reason, of which this school is but a small, little cornerstone in your world.

When I speak to you that to God, to Reason, to the eternal Light that you are, all things are possible, be not concerned with the appearances of *things*. For if we were ever concerned with the appearances of things, we would not be seated here this moment speaking with you, our students. To some of you, we are aware, there is much concern. Concern for who? Is it concern for my channel, when I am not concerned at all? Is it concern for the work he has to do, when we have not, nor are we, nor have we ever been, concerned? For we are the ones who brought to you the law that governs concern. It certainly is not good business. Is that not correct?

Yes, sir.

It's not practical. It brings no goodness into the life of an individual or to a group of people, to a church, or any of the work of God and goodness. It never has. It is contrary to the Law of Goodness. Concern is a function activated by fear. That's all that it is. Animals have concern. Animals fear. What are they basically concerned about, an animal? And what do they fear? They're concerned about their bare necessities of survival. Therefore, they fear and protect themselves. That's an animal, as a wild animal.

Now let's take the same wild animal and let's do what is done in your society to the animal. You say that you domesticate them. And so you take a cat or a dog or some other little creature and you bring them into your home. And you feed them and you care for them and you watch, slowly but surely, them become emotionally, with their feelings, attached. Would you not agree as students? Some of you, do you not agree as students? Pardon?

Yes. [Many students respond.]

Because most of you either have animals, have had animals, and many of your animals I see over here in our world. Fine. And so animals become attached. They move, animals do, when they're domesticated, they move from who they are to what they are. So, you see, what you are is an educating process through environmental impact. Now the animal moves from who it is and its survival in a jungle, free, etc., etc., based upon the society that the animal is born in with its own kind. Does anyone not understand that? And so if the animal is injured, the pack is always the first consideration. The injured animal must be left for the predators of the animal. Does anyone not understand that? And so what do I say to you, my students? A wise tiger never reveals his wounds in the jungle of creation. Ever, ever, ever!

For your benefit, as my students, my channel, you might say, was the sacrificial lamb. His wounds were revealed. I am here for his dedication and loyalty and honesty to the Light he has served since he entered your Earth planet has restored and rejuvenated him, and I am still here. Now I'm not going to take up a great deal of your time on this school and its continuity, because I am assuring you, as students of mine, that in your physical world, this school, its continuity, its true purpose of its foundation of being, the Living Light Philosophy, shall and is being taken care of by all our business assistants in our world, by all of our doctors that we have for our assistance.

In fact, because facts are so important to society, in fact, it is only within this last day that our good Dr. Collins, and now you might as well know his true dentist, counseled with a physical dentist and came to a harmonious agreement: no, [for] my channel, it was not necessary nor was it even beneficial to realign his partial. The physical Dr. Smith is very pleased. My channel is pleased. The receptionist has to mark an "NC" on the cost. All of you are pleased: you don't have to pay the bill; it's nonexistent. *[Some students laugh.]* And our assistant, our dentist, our doctor that's been with our channel for so many years—long before most all of you were in this association and in this school. There is perhaps one, one or two that were even in our school physically when that good doctor arrived, that dentist. Now why doesn't he have pearly white, perfect teeth? Well, he's in your world. He wasn't born with pearly white, perfect teeth, but he has no problem chewing, considering his age. So that takes care of the dentist, doesn't it?

Now we have the finest assistants in business. We have the finest lawyers. We have the finest that we have earned. They're not in your physical world, but our channel is directly responsible to our Council and is constantly monitored twenty-four hours, day and night, and has always been. We do not so freely give to your world the teachings that have taken us eons, eons to earn.

Are there any other questions, my children? Are you concerned that he will be sent to a Sunday morning church hall to work? Let me free you from those fears: it shall not be as a regular Sunday morning service to the public. Are you concerned that he will not be working here on Sunday? Why, of course, he will be working here on Sunday. Are you concerned that he will not be at a regular Thursday night seminar on the third Sunday of the month? *[The teacher misspeaks, but corrects himself in the next sentence. Seminars were on the third Thursday of the month.]* Why, of course he will be here on a third Thursday of the month. Are you concerned that it may be four times a week (your classes)? Be not concerned. We know you have other interests and should have other interests. Because without other interests, you cannot demonstrate to yourselves how the laws work for you.

This is not a monastery. We're not going to move him to an area like Tibet, though we have seriously considered it when other changes took place a year or so ago. Are you concerned, my children, that all of this will collapse? Be not concerned, for it is solid. It is a solid boulder. When it moves, you'll have your earthquakes; but in the meantime, don't hold your breath. Are you concerned that it looks dirty? We're having it painted. Are you concerned that the mortgage won't be paid? You're paying your just, fair share. I have a board of directors in your world to see that that is constantly monitored. Are you concerned there may be an increase in your just share of [$]936 per month as members of this Association? Be not concerned. We are not increasing your fees. Are you concerned that he physically or emotionally or mentally will not be able to continue to serve our Council? Be not concerned. It shall not happen. Are you concerned about reality? Then be concerned, my students, about what you are, and how valuable it is to make some daily effort to who you are. For who you are will take you through. That is the Light that will see you through. That who you are is your own honesty inside yourself. It's not the what you are that's dependent upon people. It is the who you are that will take you through eternity.

And before I go, because my channel has work to do with you—I will be leaving shortly, you understand? My channel has work to do with you for only a short time. For we have made a change, and we're going to see all of you over a cup of tea or coffee or whatever is available in our little temple. And we're going to see you, my channel will, and his guides—not me, his teacher. I have other schools to attend. I have responsibilities. I can't be spending all of my time in one and shirking my responsibilities in all of the others. So he is instructed. He knows what he will have to tell you. We've taken care of that. We are accepting volunteers for Friday, only volunteers, first with our board of directors. We understand everyone's commitments, and we will not interfere with them. We are accepting volunteer workers for Friday. We are accepting volunteer workers for Saturday. And *all* workers come to church on Sunday, for Sunday we have, and did last Sunday, what is known as a real church service for Spiritualism: God's love (work) made manifest.

We are in full accord with your world's national board. We are in full accord of the work we have to do. Be not concerned about money. Be concerned who you are, and then you will do your fair share and no one will be concerned about anything. And you will all be successful, be it your homes, be it your refinancing, be it your condominiums, or be it your apartments or so be whatever it be, by the application of law, which is demonstrable.

You know, I want to share with you this, because my channel certainly will not. In order to lighten his spirits through this so-called midnight of my students' souls (plural) and because everyone is sensitive and I, as your teacher and his teacher, consider him the most sensitive. Perhaps I'm partial, but I consider a person who clearly sees people's judgments and thoughts and concern very sensitive. And I haven't found the rest of my students with that—what shall we call it?—talent or ability that advanced or, let us say, that well practiced or performed, whatever we wish to call it. And so to lighten his spirits, for I'm the one that taught him, you know, humor is the salvation of the soul. So, child, let's begin with yours.

Now what is all this BSL that you're so emotionally hurt about? We named it, our little guide Crystal, if any of you recall—she's never been away. She's had no vacation. She's a worker. So what is this? She named it BSL. He was concerned about a look, studying him like a bug. And he was so concerned about it that we named it the BSL: the bug study look. Is he there? Is that him? Is that someone else? Well, we find no difference between the humor of this, which we named the BSL, the bug study look. He wanted to practice so that he would be able to do those kind of things with his directors, you understand, and some of his students, you see. And we said, "No, there's more important things to take care of. Why don't you stay with the dusting tai chi that you were so interested [in]—you know, the movement, you see. Some of our people have perfected such graciousness in cleaning the temple that it is most impressive to his mind that, you know: it takes a great deal of concentration to be able to move in, what he understands, is super slow-motion to get anywhere. *[The teacher refers to some of his students in physical forms who volunteer at the temple who move very, very slowly while dusting. A few students laugh.]* Now that really takes concentration.

So we are more interested, my youngest student, we are more interested in accomplishing something worthwhile without— There'll always be inconvenience to the mind, children. Why don't you prepare yourselves? You see, if we have a set schedule, [like, for example], you're here from 7 [p.m.] to 8 [p.m.] and that's all that you're here, then all that you have received this evening you would have missed. Or do you not understand what God or Light or Reason at our convenience has to offer to us as students? Does anyone not understand that? My channel's been through many students. They used to stay until a quarter to four and then we had to see fit that they were moved out the door so he could get to his morning meditation. *[Mr. Goodwin meditated every day at 4 a.m.]*

Have we absorbed, all of us as students, so much awakening and so much light and so much intelligence that what is offered to us is an inconvenience because we have so many things to accomplish?

Seek not money. It will destroy you. Seek the law. Seek not things. Seek not pleasure. It will destroy you. Seek the law that governs all of it. For when you seek the law that governs it, then you can choose it by conscious, conscious thought, by conscious choice, and it shall appear. Of what benefit will it bring unto you, spiritually, eternally, if all things are added unto you and you fail in your responsibility to the things, by the law, you have added unto you? Of what benefit, my children, can that possibly be? Of what benefit? What good can come from it? Only the weight, the heavy weight of responsibility.

We look forward, for you, our Sunday service here. We look forward, for you, our monthly seminars. Be not concerned. Is it Christmas? Is it Thanksgiving? We will see it will not be on that day that you may fulfill your commitments in a world in which most of your time must be spent for you are a part of society. But remember, that part of you that is part of society is what you believe you are. It's never, nor can it *ever* be, who you are.

And so I say to you good night. And also, I will see you again at a regular seminar on a scheduled time for those students who wish to remain on board with us. For our classes continue on. And I would also like to say, this is a public seminar. [Two students] are not members of this Association. Is that not correct?

Yes.

Well, we're not that type of an association. If anyone ever tries to shove a card down your throat, your responsibility is to let me know. You understand that? That's your responsibility, because, you see, you are members to our Light that we serve. You don't need to carry a card. All right?

OK.

And I don't want cards carried until people [say], "Well, let's see, I want to take on all this weight of responsibility called personality." No, no, no, I don't recommend it. And I'm not trying to decrease the membership, my child. I do hope you both understand that, as public attendees to our seminars. Someday you'll know all about that and our requirements. So if we bring anyone new, outside of [these two students], let us not forget, you will not have seminars like this. We will have ABCs and we'll begin at that point. And you'll wonder, real soon, what has happened. *[Many students laugh.]*

Thank you very much. My channel will see you at refreshments. Well, coffee's better than nothing—and tea or water.

Good night.

OCTOBER 20, 1988

A/V Seminar 34

Acceptance, the power; rejection, the force. Let us understand that the soul can and does all things create in a world of the soul. The mind can and does all things create in a world of the mind. The mind is designed to gather and to garner and to finally awaken to the burden or load that it is carrying. Now creation is the effect of a mental spin. As the mind spins, it gathers unto itself. That is mental creation. The soul is a retrospin. That is creation in a world of the soul. One gives in a retrospin and it is made manifest. The other gathers unto itself and one knows of experience.

Now we create many things with our mind. And when we use our mind to create things, we first create images in a mental world. We create them for we experience need, which is the effect of denial. These images that we create from our need or denial are shells; they are hollow. They have no life force nor vitality. Ofttimes these forms are used by decarnate, earthbound spirits in order that they may once again experience sensation, for without a physical body, there is not the experience of sensation. There is the need thereof, but not the fulfillment. Therefore, one should practice their exercises, especially when they lose conscious awareness.

Now the soul faculties are expressed by the soul through a conscious mind. The sense functions are experienced and expressed by a sub—so-called—conscious mind. When we harbor a thought, that is, when we entertain a thought for any length of time, we are creating the form, the image, or the shell of its fulfillment. If we do not, with our conscious mind, maintain and sustain that form of fulfillment that we have created, that shell or form is a house waiting for occupancy. Unfortunately, we are rarely, if ever, consciously aware of that happening, until so-called disaster strikes in our life. It is our responsibility to be aware of the forms that we feed. For example, a person may have a suppressed desire for a very long period of time. Not having the desire fulfilled, the form or shell of the desire remains empty and is filled in time by an earth-bound spirit, for they have yet to awaken to the freedom from the error of denial, known as need.

Now we have spoken on how resistance, the effect of resistance in a mental world is experience. What we accept in our consciousness, we free our self from. Whatever we deny in our consciousness, we are destined to experience. For example, we make a judgment denying personal responsibility for its fulfillment and in so doing, in creating that type of a form, like kind or earth-bound spirits enter that form, animate it, use it, and we sometimes wonder why we cannot free our self from a thought that we have created. That is the first step in awakening to what is known as possession. That which we have created and denied responsibility for, as a shell, is being used by another entity. That's known as the Law of Abuse.

Whatever you create, you create to serve the purpose of its design. When it no longer serves the purpose of its design, for you are no longer consciously using it, then you have denied its purpose of design and are abusing it. In so doing there are many who are waiting to use the shell, the form that you have created.

So each time you permit yourself to think and to feel rejected, you establish the law that guarantees, in a mental world, the experience.

It is indeed difficult for the mind to accept that it has what it desires, but by not accepting that you have what you desire, in keeping with the Law of Personal Responsibility, the alternative is that you reject it and, in so doing, experience the effects of that rejection.

A thought in our mind, a desire suppressed into our subconscious mind does not disappear. It continues to grow. And when it reaches maturity, it is animated and used by whoever and whatever is on the same level of consciousness in the universe.

We all like to think that we are in complete charge. We have no problem. We are the captain of our ship and the masters of our destiny. And indeed, we are. The sadness is we are not consciously aware that there is quite a crew that has climbed on board our little ship of destiny, and in so doing, like any ship, it can only hold so much of a crew before it sinks.

Be aware of your suppressed desires. Your expressed desires create no problem for you, for the payment of their fulfillment (or the lack thereof) is obvious to the conscious mind where the soul faculties express. It is the suppressed ones that are used by other entities after you have created them and simply put them on the shelf for one reason or another.

Now repetition is the law through which change is made possible. So when you have an experience that you find to be distasteful and uncomfortable, it is through conscious repetition that the energy which is sustaining that experience is dissipated. Exposure frees the soul for it permits the conscious awareness to express through the soul faculties rather than be suppressed by the sense functions of the mental world. Remember that force is the domain of the world of creation. It is the payment and attainment. It is not the world of the soul.

Now we'll take a few moments for your questions. Yes, please.

Thank you. You mentioned that we should continue to practice our exercises, especially during times when we're not in conscious awareness.

Correct.

For example, when we're asleep.

Because when you are asleep, that is when suppressed desires express themselves and, in so doing, be the open door for whatever entities of like kind on that level of consciousness, yes.

How, how is it possible to practice our, our spiritual exercises when we're not in conscious awareness?

Through repetition of flooding the consciousness prior to losing conscious awareness. It is extremely important prior to losing conscious awareness that one flood their consciousness. By practice and repetition, change will come about when the conscious awareness is set aside and the so-called subconscious, which is filled with suppressed desires, is expressing itself.

Thank you.

Yes. You're welcome. [Yes], please.

Sir, in keeping with this thought, would the playing of a continuous spiritual tape during our sleeping state accomplish the same thing?

It will have an effect, if the student floods their consciousness prior to losing conscious awareness. Definitely. Absolutely. You see, the thing is that in the course of one single day there are at least a hundred desires suppressed by the human mind, at least a hundred. For many people, they add into the thousands.

Now those suppressed desires express themselves during sleep. They create forms of their own fulfillment. Those forms are animated and activated during their sleeping time. The sadness is they don't stop there, you understand? Because, as I have said, a spirit that has left the flesh is no longer in a realm of consciousness where they experience sensation, which is in the physical body. And the only way they can receive sensation is through using the forms that people have created that they have suppressed. Suppression is one of the most dangerous of all of the functions. Yes.

Thank you, sir.

You're welcome. Yes, please.

Thank you. When we start to wake up to our suppressed desires, how—I've heard it said that, obviously, you can't fulfill all of your desires—so how do you go about, you know, educating the desires so they don't become further suppressed?

Yes. By, first of all, being aware of the suppressed desires and placing them in a priority, for they are unguided, undisciplined children. They are born in ignorance, and they have no guidance of the conscious mind. So they must be brought to the conscious mind, where reason prevails, and be educated to take their turn. Yes. Yes.

So—Thank you. How, how then do you educate them? Say you have a desire to, I don't know, purchase something materially.

Yes.

And it's just not possible at the time or it's not appropriate at that time.

Exactly.

How, how do you go about it?

You talk to the desire like you would talk to a small child. You make it very clear to them that, "Not at this time and don't ask me when, but someday." That's how you'd talk to a child.

Yes.

You must remember desires are children until they gain maturity and are activated and animated by earth-bound, decarnate spirits. That's what happens to desires. Desires that are not brought to the realm of reason become forms of fulfillment or maturity and are animated, activated by decarnate entities. That's when they become very, very dangerous. That's when you have a thought in your mind that you cannot free yourself from. Remembering that you have created the thought; it rises up and will not go away. That is when you know it is a suppressed desire that is being used by something that you are not in control of. Would you understand that?

I understand.

So what that means is that is the first stage of possession. It moved from possession to obsession, yes. Try to understand that when you create a desire and you do not educate the desire, the desire does not disappear. You have created it. It will return to you. It knows its parent. So it will return to you for fulfillment or education for so long a period of time, and then it will be activated, animated by other entities that you do not and cannot have control of. The only control that you can have is the control of the form or the desire that you have created. And it's difficult to get a tenant to move out when they've got a free rent. Do you understand that?

Yes, I do.

Yes, it becomes quite difficult indeed.

OK.

Yes.

Thank you very much.

You're welcome. Yes, please.

Yes. Thank you. The Law of Abuse that you spoke about, does that happen when . . .

Yes?

The Law of Abuse, when you, when they have moved in because you are not educating these particular forms, because they're using you, obviously, these decarnate spirits are coming in and using you. So is that the Law of Abuse?

The Law of Abuse is when you no longer take personal responsibility for the desire that you alone have created. When you no longer take personal responsibility for it, by either educating or fulfilling it, you abuse the Law of Use, and it becomes open game for any entity who has a desire of similar kind.

I see.

Yes.

Thank you very much.

You're welcome. [Yes], please.

When it's become possession and it's taken over the form, you said it's hard to get it out. Or hard to get the tenant to move out.

Indeed, it is. First of all, they are selfish by trying to use someone else's form to get a sensation. And they have a free ride, and they're not about to get off the train.

So the cleansing breath is, and, and redirecting your attention, and all the tools that we have...

It will take more than that once they gain possession. They're not so easily moved. Pardon?

Yes.

They're not so easily moved. Have you never had a thought that keeps repeating itself and will not leave you in peace when you want to do something else?

Yes.

Pardon?

Yes.

Well, now that is a thought you have created, is that not correct?

Yes.

Is it obeying you?

Not at all.

Then the Law of Use has been transgressed. It has now entered the Law of Abuse. And then it abuses you by taking up your peace of mind and [interferes with] what you want to do, is that not correct?

Yes, sir.

So what we find is, when we create a desire, if we do not make that effort—now there's only two things to do with a created desire: fulfill it or educate it. One of the two. If you don't do that, someone else is going to move into that desire from the so-called invisible world and demand that you give it energy, because that's how it gets its sensation and its feelings of the fulfillment of the desire that you have suppressed. Do you understand that?

Yes.

That's why it comes in to get its feelings and sensations when you don't even call it because you have transgressed the law by paying no attention to it after you have created it. Pardon?

Possessed with it—resisted rather...

Why, certainly. First you create something, and then you ignore it. When you create something and then you ignore it, you reject or resist it, don't you? Pardon?

Yes! So when it—

So when you create something, that's the Law of Personal Responsibility. It doesn't fulfill itself when you decide that it should, is that not correct?

It doesn't fulfill itself when I . . .

Well, you have a desire. And time passes and it's not fulfilled.

Right.

And you haven't made the effort to guide or educate it, correct?

Correct. Correct.

It doesn't disappear. It continues to grow up.

Right.

And when it is mature, those of like kind in the invisible world move in, and then you become aware of that desire that you had some time ago. And it starts to plague you. Do you understand that?

Yes, I do.

Because you have established the Law of Abuse. In other words, you created a child and then you decided, for some reason or other, that it wasn't doing what you wanted it to do when you wanted it to do it. And then you ignore or reject it. You see, if you ignore something or someone, you reject them. Is that not correct?

That's right.

You don't accept them. You reject them.

Right.

And so then you are robbed of your peace of mind when you don't want to be robbed of your peace of mind. And so the path through that is, first of all, to recognize that it is a desire that you have had. Pardon?

Yes.

Now you may have changed desires by changing priorities, but that does not free the creator, one's own mind, from their responsibilities of having created it. So first you must recognize it is your desire; second, you must accept it by the Law of Personal Responsibility; third, you begin to guide it to the light of reason. And when you do that, those freeloading tenants move out of that desire form and they stop plaguing you.

Thank you.

You're welcome.

Thank you very much.

Yes. Yes, please.

What is the process of maturity that a suppressed desire goes through?

For example, depending on the desire, it requires so much vital energy. It's not a matter of days, weeks, months, or years. It is a matter of energy. Now if you direct, through attention, a great deal of energy to a desire, it matures that much more quickly in the illusion of time. Do you understand that?

Yes, sir.

If you direct a little attention, perhaps once or twice a week, then it takes longer for that desire form to mature. Yes.

Thank you.

You see, a created form reaches a point of maturity; now it either fulfills its purpose of fulfilling that for which you have created it, you understand that?

Yes, sir.

Or educated it. You educate it (the desire); you bring it to the light. The light of reason cast upon desire dissipates the energy that went to create it. You understand?

Yes, sir.

Before it reaches maturity. You might call it an aborted desire. *[Many students laugh.]* I think you would understand that. However, if the desire is not brought, through exposure, to the light of reason during the time of its growth process of maturity, then you have something else to work with. You must use it to fulfill the purpose for which you have created it or invisible entities are going to use it for you. And use your vital life energy because that's where they get the sensation is from your vital life energy, yes. Does that help you—

Yes, sir.

—with your question there? Certainly. Of course, there is no escape from what you create, but there is growth, evolution, and awakening. So in that sense, though one could not call it escape, one certainly could call it growing up. Yes.

Remember, when you find yourself stuck in the functions, use the corresponding soul faculty. It's like when you find something, you wonder, "Well, how long is this going to take?" Stop worrying about how long it's going to take and it will manifest itself. It's when you worry about how long it's going to take that's the problem. Because, see, when you worry about how long something is going to take, you establish the Law of Resistance. You are resisting the process for it to fulfill itself. Your mind does not know how long it will take. Do you understand that?

Yes, sir.

So by resisting the process for its own fulfillment, you only make it that much longer. Do you understand?

Yes, sir.

See?

Thank you.

Certainly. Did you have your question there on rejection? *[The teacher addresses a different student.]*

I probably do, but I did have another question about this decarnated spirit that, that's entered this shell. Is it possible for this decarnated spirit that entered this shell to enter a human body?

If they have entered a sufficient percentage of the children or desires created by the mind of the individual, yes. Certainly. And [it is] well documented in your world.

And it can—can it cause, can it cause an effect on the person that it has entered for a feeling, for a feeding, if you're not feeding it? Say if you're not feeding—

Well, once an entity by—for example, if the entity has already occupied over 51 percent of the children created by the individual, then, of course, it can enter the—you're speaking of the physical mind and the physical form and the mind itself?

Right.

Certainly. Absolutely. Definitely.

So, I mean, when you're at this stage whereas, whereas in, well—OK, it's in control of 51 percent of the children that's been created.

It has to be in control of 51 percent of the person's desires before it can enter the form, that's correct.

Fifty-one percent of a certain desire, of a person's certain desire?

No, no, no, no, no. Fifty-one percent of their desires or 51 percent of the vital life energy that it took to create the desires in the first place. It has to be 51 or more percent, yes.

Oh, and it, and it—

It could be 2 desires or 2,000, you understand.

OK.

It's 51 percent of the energy or vital life force that it took to create them, yes.

And, and the only way that it's going to stay in this person's body is that it continues to receive 51 percent or more of their vital life energy.

No. No, it first has to have 51 percent of the vital life energy that it took to create the desire or desires. It remains in the body, in the mind, until such time as 51 percent of vital life energy is directed to the soul faculty known as reason.

Thank you.

You're welcome. Yes, please.

Thank you. I'm not sure that I am aware of what all the forty functions and faculties are. Can those be found in our class notes or are they—

They will be found in your class notes and in *The Living Light* book. Most of them. Not all of them have yet been given.

OK. Thank you.

Yes. Most of them are on the class tapes and the seminars. Yes, they are. You're welcome.

The most important thing to awaken to, as we have spoken before in our classes, is do not, through the errors of ignorance, do not suppress desire. Cast the light of reason upon desire. That doesn't mean to do without desire, but it means to keep it in the conscious awareness until you have full monitoring, control of that which you have created. A wise parent does not let their child go out into the world when he's only a child without some effort to monitor the child. Yes, please.

Is desire created in the conscious mind? Or does—

Desire is created in the conscious mind. Energy is directed into the subconscious where it is fulfilled. Yes.

When you create from the soul . . .

Then you're not creating in the mental world. The creation of the soul in a world of the soul is not a spin; it's a retrospin. It gives forth from itself for it is still aware of its Source. It doesn't gather unto itself. It gives forth from itself. That's the difference between the soul and the mind. That's one of the differences between the soul and the mind. Yes, please.

And do we go into a retrospin by a cleansing breath?

Oh, no. Many people do the cleansing breath and are totally in the spin, gathering unto themselves, instead of sending out from themselves, you see. The cleansing breath in and of itself does not free one from a mental world. That takes other spiritual effort, yes. What the cleansing breath does do: it does not permit any new thought to enter the mind. It is not possible, when doing the cleansing breath properly, for any new thought to enter the mind. So what it does offer to the student is control of their mind, if only for a moment. Yes. And so if it's practiced daily, then the moments increase. Yes.

Then the retrospin, we go into a retrospin if we can—

Retrospin is positive, and spin is negative. One attracts and gathers unto itself, and one sends forth from itself. One is a channel and the other is a dam. *[Many students laugh.]* Yes.

So the cleansing breath doesn't cleanse the forms that you have created?

The cleansing breath permits the person doing the cleansing breath to gain control of their mind, if only for a moment. Now when one gains control of their mind, if only for a moment, then they are not hounded by suppressed desires that are now mature that are activated by other entities. Pardon?

Thank you.

Yes. Yes.

Thank you. And do our affirmations, are they—[do] the affirmations begin the retrospin? Is that what . . .

Your breathing exercises and your affirmations are designed to permit one to rise to a soul-consciousness level, which would place one in a retrospin. Now the difference, as I said, between the spin of the mind is that it pulls unto itself by its own spin or resistance. The soul can and does create all things by retrospin. In other words, it becomes a channel for the Source itself. There's the difference between the two worlds, yes. So with one's cleansing breath, their power breath, their affirmations, and the various exercises that have been given, through that effort it will place a person, in time, into a retrospin.

You see, it is the denial, which is the destiny of the mental world from its own denial of the Source. The reason that the mind spins is because it believes it is without. It has denied its Source. The soul gives forth of itself for it is still relating to its Source. The mind does not relate to its Source and, therefore, is a vacuum that must constantly gather unto itself. Does that help with your question?

It does.

Yes. So because the mind does spin and gather unto itself, it is bound by its own belief. That is the bondage of mental substance, yes.

Thank you.

You're welcome. Yes, please.

Yes, thank you. Because the mind doesn't recognize the Source, is that the reason behind it garnering and gathering and garnering and gathering all this need and denial, because it denies its Source?

Well, you—yes, you must understand, even if you go to the allegories of the Garden of Eden, you must understand that the human race, called humanity or man, is whole and complete. It became aware of itself. When it became aware of its wholeness, its completeness, and its perfection, in that moment it entered the functions. Now in that moment, by entering the functions, it gained pride at the denial of the Source of which it is an inseparable part. Do you understand that?

Yes.

So, you see, you will find a prideful person is one who has much denial and great rejection. Do you understand?

Yes.

Because they have entered the bondage of believing that they are the source of all of their experiences. And they're quite correct, but not completely. Without the Source, the experiences could never happen. But they are quite correct: the experiences that they encounter are effects of their denial and their rejection of the Source itself. That is true.

So, you see, you have in your teachings, you have pride and you have the soul faculty of humility. So as more energy is directed to humility, there is less pride; as there is less pride, there is more humility. And a balance is brought about. Now reason is the very foundation of the soul faculties. Reason is the power that transfigures the mind. When the faculties are brought into balance with the functions, the light of reason dawns in the conscious mind, and in so doing you have a peaceful world within. Otherwise, you have the war of the world. You have the battle of the mind against the light of the soul constantly, with a few moments of peace, yes.

Thank you.

You're welcome. Yes.

Thank you. So I have a question about humil—humiliation. Is—

Yes.

Is humiliation piercing the pride that we possess, the experience—

Humiliation is an attack upon the judgments and the defenses of the sense function of pride. It is a direct attack upon it. For example, a person has pride based upon the judgments they have made that they are special, unique, different, or etc. But you must remember that a person's pride is dependent upon being unique and different.

Yes.

Now a person does not have pride until they first judge they're different. Now based upon their judgments of how different they are, they start to move in the growth of pride. And so pride itself, that function, is defended by the judgments they have made that put themselves on that throne in the first place. You see? You see, it's like, for example, a person, as time passes and the illusion known as time begins to take [its toll], Nature takes her toll, and man—by that I mean humanity's form—begins to change. Now those changes are not readily acceptable to the human mind. That is dependent on how much pride they experience in looking or being a certain way. Now the more pride, the more energy that was directed to the throne of pride, the more difficult it is for the person to make the adjustment or changes, which are inevitable. Pardon?

OK.

And so ofttimes the defense of pride will judge that it is a humiliation rather seeing humility for what it truly is. You see, a person cannot feel prideful when they are aware that they are an inseparable part of one Source; that difference is an effect of what they alone have created, but it does not last, you see? It never lasts. It is not enduring. There is no continuity. Absolutely not.

Whatever the human mind creates is born and dies. That is the law. It has birth and death, which is only birth. So birth and death are one and the same thing. Because man has not made the effort to awaken to see birth and death as one and the same thing, that does not change what it is. It is. Death is birth, and birth is death. And everyone goes through that constant cycle of evolutionary incarnation, yes. Now the ones who are very prideful are the ones who are earth-bound spirits because they will not give up that which they think they have gathered for something they're not sure, exactly, what it is. Well, they cannot be sure because in being sure, they just remain in the mental world. Yes.

Thank you.

Yes, you're welcome.

May I ask one more?

Certainly.

Thank you. I wanted to ask about the power breath. I don't know if I received that.

Ah, no. You are one of the students who have not received that. I will have the secretary this evening give you the power breath.

OK.

Yes, I will see that my channel monitors it because it is very, very important. And through practice—much practice, would you not agree? *[The teacher addresses a different student.]*

Yes, sir.

You will gain control. Try to understand that your breathing changes with the tides of the plan—of the oceans of the planet upon which you are. And that's how your breathing usually goes in rhythm with nature. Not always, but you must be able to consciously change your breath from spin to retrospin or from retrospin to spin. Because as you change your breath, you change whatever mental level of consciousness you are on.

OK.

For the time that you are doing it. Yes.

Sir, would you please elaborate a bit on the breathing and the spin and the retrospin in relation to the power breath?

Yes. Well, the left nostril is the negative or magnetic. That is a spin. You see, it attracts or pulls unto itself from without. The right nostril is a retrospin, and it gives forth from itself. It is able to give forth from itself because it is only a channel of the Infinite Source. Yes. And so one uses the power breath accordingly. Yes.

Should we be aware of the tide tables?

No, because you'll naturally be aware of them. Once you gain conscious control of the breath of life, once you've gained conscious control, you'll move into harmony with the tides, and you will see that your breathing moves from the positive to the negative, from the negative to the positive because that is the water center of the planet Earth. Yes.

What if one thinks they may be able to do the power breath competently and they still don't understand quite what you're talking about?

Well, you'll become very aware of it if you permit yourself to become emotionally upset or anything dealing with the emotions: you can be rest assured, you will be breathing through the left nostril only. You see, man does not breathe through both nostrils at the same time. We're all aware of that, are we?

Yes, sir.

Pardon? Well, if we're not, we should do some practice. Because you breathe either through your left nostril or your right nostril. Most all people breathe most of the time through their left nostril. That is an imbalance. That is because they spend so much time in the water center. Yes. Yes, please.

Would you explain the usage of the power breath as, I mean, the purpose, as a cleansing breath is to a person?

Well, a cleansing breath should precede all power breaths. Absolutely. As [that student] well knows.

Yes, sir.

OK.

You see, if the power breath is used to gather and to garner, then it is not serving its true purpose. Because you are continuing to deny the Source.

Whoever looks without for fulfillment is destined to grief and sadness. Because you must realize that like attracts like. If you look without for happiness, you will attract someone who is looking without for happiness. So they will look at you with a microscope and sooner or later they will find a defect. And it's over. Until the next time. So try to understand if you're looking without, whether it be for emotional stability, a relationship, material substance, then you are only going to attract that type of person. The law fulfills itself.

Now you may say, "Well, now this person's a very nice person," and find, surely, they are. But you must ask yourself the question, "Was I looking without for happiness and fulfillment when I met this person?" Well, if you were, the law fulfilled itself. You found a person now that is looking outside, denying inside, and looking outside for fulfillment. Well, the only thing they're going to find, after they blink their eyes a few times and put you under the microscope, is a defect. And then they'll go and look someplace else, you see. Because as long as you look without for what you think you need, you are still under the control of the destiny of denial.

Don't look outside for what you want to experience inside. Look inside for what you want and you will find it. Stop looking outside for what you think you want. Look inside, and you will have that fulfillment as quickly as you honestly look inside because it's all there. It was never anyplace else. For outward manifestations are only revelations of inner attitudes of mind. Look inside for everything you desire, for everything you desire has always been inside of you. You will not find it outside. You will only find like kind that's doing the same thing in the error of ignorance.

Thank you, friends, and good night.

JANUARY 19, 1989

A/V Seminar 35

Good evening, class.

Before we begin our class, I want you to know that soon you will be having a rest time from these seminars and classes so that you may absorb and apply and reap the benefits that you have been studying.

Now attention directed to the first faculty of being increases and multiplies the goodness that you place your mind upon. Now what is the first faculty of being? I ask some of my older students.

Duty, gratitude, and tolerance.

Duty, gratitude, and tolerance. Ofttimes in directing attention to that faculty of being, we don't seem to have a problem, so much, with the duty or even the gratitude. It's the tolerance that is our problem. And so, as all of you know, especially in this time of reaping, tolerance requires a great deal of understanding, which comes from acceptance. Tolerance is not difficult to the mind that truly accepts personal responsibility. Tolerance is difficult for the mind that denies personal responsibility through the error of ignorance known as dependence on something outside.

It is indeed a struggle in life when we permit so much of our energy and our time, in a world of time, to be so dependent on something beyond our control. The Law of Personal Responsibility clearly reveals: be dependent upon the laws that you alone create. If they do not reap for you that which you enjoy, then let us not forget that we are indeed a law unto our self; and in so being, what are we doing with the law that we are? Not what someone else is doing, for that error of ignorance robs us of reaping the harvest of goodness that we have earned.

Now I want to see some hands and questions here before you soon have your rest from these classes, a time to absorb and to apply what you've already received. So let me see the hands of interest, for the hand represents action. And it is by what we demonstrate, not by what we say, that we move ahead and enjoy life. We can say many things, but they only guarantee failure without the demonstration thereof. Now let me see these hands. Yes, please.

Tolerance, then, stems from—or tolerance stems from an acceptance of personal responsibility?

Yes. Tolerance is an effect of understanding. Now you cannot have understanding without a communication inside your own being. When you accept the demonstrable law for your own life of personal responsibility, you expand your tolerance, the first soul faculty—duty, gratitude, and tolerance—you expand your tolerance and you experience success, yes, in your endeavors. Does that help you with your question? Yes.

Thank you, sir. When we find ourselves moving into intolerance, what can we do to redirect?

Become aware that you are dependent upon that which you are intolerant to, and being dependent upon it, you are controlled by it. Do you understand that?

Yes, sir.

You see, a person is not disturbed by anything that they are not first, by denial of personal responsibility, what they are not first dependent upon. You must first depend upon something for that something to disturb you. As it disturbs you, it controls you. It is the denial of personal responsibility that creates the problem. The solution is very clear: personal responsibility. Take charge of your destiny, yes.

Thank you.

You're welcome. [Yes], please.

You said that tolerance comes from understanding, which comes from acceptance?

That's true. That which we accept, we place our self in a position in consciousness to communicate [with] and understand. Yes. Ofttimes in life we are intolerant to people because we have not communicated with them, and we make a judgment based upon our own experiences with our reference in our own mind. Therefore, communication is indispensable to understanding. And without understanding, there is no tolerance. Yes.

So the acceptance, then, is not of the other person, but of our self?

The acceptance is quite simple. The acceptance is of our own personal responsibility that the intolerance that we are experiencing is what we alone have created through an error of ignorance in our own experiences. For example, if you pluck an apple from a tree and by the law you have established the apple that you have plucked is rotten, that does not, to a reasonable person, dictate that all apples on that tree are rotten—only to the person who denies personal responsibility of effort to thoroughly investigate. So it is a very foolish person that would judge one apple from a tree when there are so many to be tested. Does that help with your question?

Yes. Thank you.

Now [another student] was waiting, yes.

Thank you. So if one, if one finds oneself in the experience of being intolerant . . .

When one finds oneself in the experience of being intolerant, then one, in that moment, must accept they are romancing the love affair with their own judgments. Yes. They are in a romance stage at that time. Of course. Go ahead.

OK. So what would be the first step to take, because already, if you're in a, if—because isn't it so that you're already experiencing not having, not taking personal responsibility; so you're upset. At that point what would be the first step to take?

To accept that you have created the experience by your own mind. And because you have created it by your own mind, you alone are responsible for your mind. And you can change your mind at any moment that you consciously choose to do so. Yes. Yes.

Is it—if, if the experience you're having is including someone else, which it usually does include somebody else, because I, at least, start blaming the outside—

Well, I would like to say it is a rare person that is intolerant with their own judgments. *[Many students laugh.]* I mean, the reason they express them so freely is because they love them so dearly. Yes.

OK. So would it—is it wise—so in this communication, then is it best not to communicate with someone else? But just communicate with yourself.

That's where it started, isn't it?

Yes.

That's the only place it exists, doesn't it?

Yes.

That's the Law of Personal Responsibility, isn't it?

Yes.

So that which starts somewhere should end somewhere within one's own self. You see, because, otherwise, you are now involving, through the Law of Denial, your dependence on a person that you have become intolerant of. Do you understand? So you're right back where you started. And then you say, "Well, I can tolerate this part. We've had communication. I have better understanding. But there's all those other little things that I can't tolerate." And so you're back on the old treadmill, you see.

Yes.

Because you've denied your own individuality. You have denied it, and you have become dependent on what someone else thinks, feels, or does. Yes. Yes, indeed. Yes.

So it would be best—my tendency is to want to include somebody else in the communication.

That reveals one's need of dependence. Yes. Pardon?

So it's best not to—it's best to just communicate with oneself first and then the need to communicate with someone else wouldn't be necessary.

Well, of course not. Once you communicate with yourself and you direct your attention to where it should be (to the first faculty of being), then you move on in consciousness.

Now the other individual has a divine right to notice the change or not notice the change. And in noticing the change, work with themselves. Perhaps they get an opportunity to grow. But if they are dependent upon you for their growth, then they will come to you with whatever they come to you with, which reveals their dependency upon you! Not upon God. Not upon freedom. Not upon personal responsibility. You see, without this personal responsibility, there's no freedom. There is not. It is an absolute denial of the individualization of the being. The denial of personal responsibility is the denial that you are captain of your ship and you are master of your destiny, yes. Does that help with your question?

Yes. Thank you.

Very good. [Yes], please. [Another student has] been waiting.

Then when or would it ever serve any purpose to communicate with another on any particular subject?

In respect to tolerance and intolerance, then, of course, it's dependent on whether or not your life you've made dependent upon them. Because, you see, that which is in our universe is there by the Law of Attraction and Adversity, for adversity and attraction are one and the same thing, you see.

Yes.

You see, you have this attachment from the attraction, and you have this repulsion from the adversity, as everyone has. So if you look at those laws and personal responsibility, a person will see a change within you based upon their perspective. They may or may not ask you what has happened. Do you understand?

Yes.

But that's really not important, is it? When you are personally responsible for your own life and you are not personally responsible for their life.

Right.

Pardon?

Right.

You see? So if a person wants to think that another person is a certain kind of a person that they don't want around them, that's fine. Even though they may witness a change within the individual. But that's *their* growth, you understand.

Yes.

Yes. Does that help with your question?

Yes. Thank you.

Very good. [Another student] has a question, please.

I'm trying to formulate—

Well, I'm expecting some hands and questions out of this class. Or while you're thinking about it, I'll speak to [another student]. Thank you.

Sir, would it be in the student's best interest to, during the course of their meditation, attempt to determine what level of consciousness and plane of expression that they're on based upon what was given to us in the Living Light?

Yes.

About the dimensions of the different planes.

Definitely. Because, you see, you'll have the personal experiences as you're ready. For example, if a person wants to feel good, and we all want to feel good—feeling good is a necessity, you know; it's not a luxury. It's a necessity. It's the law. That's God within, the sustenance. [If] a person wants to feel real good in their meditation, they visualize a person they cannot tolerate. Pardon? *[A different student coughs loudly and the teacher addresses him.]* Are you all right there?

Yes.

Yes. You need a glass of water or something?

No. Thank you.

Very good. All right. Now you visualize a person. You know, pick someone that's really choice in your consciousness. *[Many students laugh.]* Usually there are several, but try to pick the most choice one. Because in so doing, in so doing you will experience all the references that you alone have created and all the defenses of all your judgments with that person in your mind. You will prove to yourself that, "All of these experiences, I've created. I created all of this. No one else created it for me. It's my mind. It's my thought. So it's my error of ignorance. Now here I look at this place, person, or thing, I just can't tolerate the visualization of it." Do you understand? And you will start to grow inside and see how that came all about. It will be revealed to you, you see. You will find that it is based on fear, a function, the animal instinct function. It is based on fear.

You see, whatever one person has, all people have in potential. Now they don't like to look at that, but that is the facts of life. The potential exists because you are part of a human race. So what you cannot tolerate in another is what you, in truth, fear within oneself. So, of course, it is advisable for an advanced student, such as yourself, to make that effort to visualize that which they absolutely cannot tolerate because that very vibration is held together by fear. Now once you face fear head-on, it disappears. It disintegrates, and you move on. So when an advanced student is making that effort and that practice, as in the Living Light and in the higher studies, then one looks at that and becomes aware of themselves and what they have created. And because they have created it, well, they can uncreate it, you see? But they must first have the incentive. They must first see clearly that something they have created is controlling their mind, and by controlling their mind, it's controlling their entire life and creating all of the experiences that disturb them, so that it may grow larger and larger and larger, you see?

Yes, sir.

You see, you see, when you took control of your mind, the problem situation started to disintegrate. It started to weaken because, you see, the truth of the matter is like attracts like from the universe. You change it within and you'll experience the manifestation of the change without. Does that help you with your question?

Yes, sir. Thank you.

You're welcome.

Sir, I have one more.

Certainly.

In relation to—

Yes.

—identifying the level of consciousness. Should we make an effort to put that label on—self, service, student, preacher, teacher, etc.?

Yes.

Or—and if we do that and something comes to us, how do we know that it's not a desire from within, if, particularly if it's above the upper—

Exactly. Well, usually you will find, when it is not a desire, you understand, it's not usually so attractive. Now, you know, it's like communication. If you tell a person what they want to hear, then you're getting the straight dope, right? But if you don't tell them what they want to hear, they'll argue with you of your source. *[The teacher laughs joyfully.]* Is that not true?

Yes, sir.

And so, you see, it's the same way that takes place within oneself. And so one in making that effort, you know, "I don't like what I'm hearing *for me.*" Pay attention to what you hear that you don't like for yourself.

Thank you.

That'll help tremendously, like it will with any student, you see. But you must remember, as without, so within; and as within, so without. When we hear something in our universe, in our mental world, whatever, and we judge it isn't what we like, we instantly question the source. Don't we?

Yes, sir.

Now if it's something that we like and we agree with, why, we don't have any problem at all accepting it. So, you see, ofttimes in life the stone the builder rejects becomes the cornerstone; that is so applicable in that respect. It comes to you in keeping with the law. You don't like it? Well, don't like it. But accept it and you will see the message that comes with it. You see, don't throw out the message-bearer that comes with that and lose the message because you don't like the bearer of it. You understand?

Yes, sir.

You see? You see, God works through man, not to man. And anyone who deceives themselves that they're directly in communication with God—we're an indispensable part of God. But, you know, you ask one level, "You believe in God?" "I don't believe in God!" "Do you believe in God's spirits?" "I don't believe in God's spirits!" But then if you go to another level of consciousness, "Why, of course, I do!" So each level is convinced, depending upon its own survival and its own selfish desires.

So here you find the pancake consciousness; it's a flip-flop, you know. It's like a morning hotcake, you see. *[The teacher and many students laugh.]* And [it's] usually known as a, as a fickle mind, you see, because you're dealing with so many levels of consciousness and you're dealing with so many desires bombarding the consciousness for position. So you would talk to a person at one moment [and they say], "Yes, that's exactly what I want to do. Yes, that is what I'm definitely going to do." And you blink your eyes, you go get a glass of water, you return, and it's totally changed, you see? You see, it isn't that they have twenty or multiple personalities, no, no, no, no. It is because man doesn't yet understand the eighty-one levels of consciousness. Now when he understands the eighty-one levels of consciousness, he will understand himself and he'll say, "Well, they're just off on that level this time. And I hope they don't stay too long." Does that help you with your question?

Yes. Thank you, sir.

You're more than welcome. Now have you prepared yourself? *[The teacher returns to the student who was earlier formulating a question.]*

Yes, I did.

Fine. See, we mustn't move until we prepare. *Siempre preparados.* I think that's the motto you should try to remember.

Yes.

Prepare yourself and raise your hand. Go ahead, please.

Thank you. The question was the difference in making a decision when one is making changes or resolving, versus a judgment, and a judgment may be from lack of tolerance versus a reasonable decision.

Well, lack of tolerance is lack of communication and lack of understanding of *oneself*.

Right.

Of oneself. So one works to understand, through communication—you see, people don't communicate with themselves. You see, they have this defense mechanism [that says], "Well, that's not the thing to do. You know, nuts walk around talking to themselves." Well, you don't have to give it a verbal sound to communicate with yourself. And ofttimes a person is much better off communicating with themselves than communicating with someone else because they're not prepared yet. They're not ready for the barrage they're about to get. Isn't that true?

It's true.

You see?

Yes.

Yes. Does that help with your question?

Yes.

Communicate with yourself and what—and understand yourself.

Yes.

Understand that there are eighty-one levels of consciousness; there are forty functions, and there are forty faculties—all triune.

Right.

And there's one divine, sustaining Power that sustains all of them.

Yes.

Indiscriminately sustains all of them. Yes.

Thank you.

You're welcome. And [another student] has a question, please.

Is fear the function of tolerance?

Fear is man's faith in his own mind. We've discussed that many times. Absolutely. Fear is our faith directed to mental substance and its limits.

Thank you.

Yes. Now [another student] had another question.

How, how does one begin to understand the eighty-one levels of consciousness?

By making the effort, through personal responsibility, to understand oneself. To understand why you feel one way at one moment and why you feel another way at another moment. How many times in the course of one, single day does a person say to themselves, "Why, I don't feel right." You see? No, what they usually say [is], "That so-and-so." Just out of the blue it comes into the mind. All right? Seemingly out of the blue. Now what they don't pursue is—and they're not aware of: they have descended into a level of consciousness within themselves, and on that level a dependence was created with another person. Now that person may be very upset at that time, do you understand?

Yes.

And then this person says, "That so-and-so!" You understand he gets all emotional. But a person's not making the effort to know themselves. You see?

And first of all, there's personal responsibility. We establish all these links in our life. Dependence on this one, dependence on that one, dependence on that one. And so depending on the rapport that we have established and how solid the bridge is that we have created, years could pass and if that person is upset, because of the bridge we have established, we feel all upset and we don't know why. But if we make the effort, we'll soon learn why, you understand, and we'll go inside our self and say, "OK, this is the price that I'm having to pay to disassemble the bridge that I have created. I wish I hadn't made it so strong. It'll take me a long time to disassemble it." *[The teacher laughs joyfully.]* Because you either disassemble it or you find yourself controlled by what you have depended on in the past. You see, what you have depended on in the past you are still controlled by in principle until you free yourself through honesty within your own consciousness. Pardon? Yes.

Thank you.

You know, that's like being angry at a person and having created a chain to that person and you don't want to talk to them and you won't look them in the eye or anything else; it reveals, you see, your dependence. You haven't got through your own dependence yet. But you should look them square in the eye, communicate with them very clearly, and tear a few more bricks down on the bridge that you're trying to get destructed. Yes.

Thank you.

You're welcome. And [yes], please.

Thank you.

Yes.

My question is about interaction with other people.

Uh-huh.

And how do we remain in tolerance when we are being tested in sort of an abusive manner by—

Yes. By accepting that we are testing our self. Because that's what we're doing. You see, first of all, through the Law of

Personal Responsibility we have clearly demonstrated that we have placed our self in a position to test our self. You see, we do test ourselves, you know. Pardon?

OK.

And so a person speaks to a person in an abusive manner; it is the responsibility of the individual to clear it up, unless they like being abused.

OK.

Pardon?

I understand.

You see? But remember, whenever you stand for the soul faculty of respect, self-respect, you understand, you must be willing to pay the price.

OK.

There's a price to pay for all the faculties. There's a price to pay. If you're willing to pay that price, you understand—you see, remember, disrespect comes from familiarity. Familiarity offers to the mind, well, it knows a person, you see. And the temptation is to control what you're familiar with or that you know. Because there's no way possible to control what one doesn't know.

Yes.

You see?

Yes.

And so there is that tendency, through familiarity, you understand, through an involvement or an interchange of communications that a person loses perspective. They lose it temporarily. And then it's the responsibility of the individual, of the individual to once again declare their right of perspective, you see?

Yes.

And self-respect. That's up to the individual. Definitely.

OK.

And pay whatever price is necessary depending on how valuable self-respect is to one.

Yes.

Pardon?

And then tolerance comes in paying that price.

Absolutely tolerance comes in paying that price because there's been communication, there has been understanding, you see, and the effort has been made and tolerance is expanded. Pardon? And success is absolutely guaranteed.

OK.

Yes.

Thank you very much.

You're welcome. Yes, please.

I'd like to ask a question about communication and tolerance with respect to what you gave us in the last class. For example, a person creates a desire, but then puts it on the shelf, doesn't sustain it or fulfill it, and then it's open. It's a hollow form, open—

That's correct.

—for an earth-bound entity to come in and animate.

That is correct.

OK. So the person then finds himself, now, he's bombarded with that. And he's in that situation. Where does he begin? And how does he communicate in order to get his understanding in tolerance in that situation?

Well, first of all, he accepts the responsibility, of course, that he created the shell, the hollow shell and that [he did that] through errors of ignorance. So he's tolerant with himself in his days of ignorance. And he talks to himself and he makes the effort to create no more of them because he doesn't want to experience any more of them, you understand? Because, you see, whatever you create in your mind you're responsible for. Now when you give up your responsibility for it, it's like an automobile. You buy an automobile and you pay the price and you park it out on the street and leave the keys in it and the door open. Well, [if] you leave it there for weeks or months, not taking care of your personal responsibilities, you can't cry when one day you go out and it's gone. Somebody decided it was a nice car and now they're driving it. So it's the same way in creating your desires and not educating them or fulfilling them. You put them on the shelf. You've already created them, like an automobile, and some passenger says, "Say, this is a real nice vehicle here." Steps in and has a joyride. Does that help you with your question? It's your responsibility to make that effort.

Thank you.

You see? Not to sit down and feel sorry for yourself [and think], "Oh my, how many of those things have I created? And how many of them now possess me?" No, no, no, no. Your responsibility is to wake up. Say, "All right. I have created them. Now I'm booting you people out of here. You astral, earth-bound entities have had enough." And that's it. And you can't do it just once. You see, you flood your consciousness.

A person doesn't even know what their consciousness is being flooded with. The consciousness is flooded constantly. It is the responsibility of the individual to consciously know and consciously choose what they're flooding their consciousness with. That's the individual's responsibility. So if you don't know what thoughts and feelings are in your mind, then you be rest assured there are some there and you didn't consciously put them there because you don't consciously know anything about them. The effort hasn't been made, you see? You see, that's like going to say hello to a person and say, "Well, hi, Mary Jane," when her name is Betty. You see, it's the same thing. You know, you so deny personal responsibility [that] you can't even call them by the name that you know that they are, you see. Does that help you with your question?

Yes. Thank you.

You're welcome. Yes.

So what higher purposes are we sometimes advised by the spirit to wait rather than to stand up for self-respect . . .

Oh, definitely.

And to communicate?

Oh, yes. Definitely, definitely, there are times when, asking for guidance, the angels will look into the laws that have been established. And there may be a period of time for a person to have to wait until they're able to completely accept the Law of Personal Responsibility. Because if that Law of Personal Responsibility is not completely accepted, they will repeat the experience. Oh, definitely, absolutely. You see, whenever you run from an experience you have created, you establish the law of its return. Now it doesn't necessarily mean the same person.

OK.

But it certainly is the same experience. Do you understand that?

Thank you.

So there are times when that is looked into and [they] see, "This is the time span (approximate) that it will take this individual to face the fullness of personal responsibility. Otherwise, face the alternative and just repeat the experience again and again and again and again." So, you see, that constant repetition does bring about change in time, but it is not the wisest path to take when all of those repeated experiences could be overridden with a higher law of the full acceptance of personal responsibility. You see? So the higher purpose is served that way.

Thank you.

Does that help with your question?

It did.

Yes, certainly. [Another student] has a question, please.

Yes. I recall that you have to use the triune faculty to make it work. So without duty and gratitude, tolerance isn't sufficient either, is it?

Why, certainly not.

And when you are intolerant of—and let's say you're having the mean reds at that moment. Would a cleansing breath help you come down to earth and to accept responsibility?

As long as the effort is made within the consciousness of flooding the consciousness. Remember, intolerance is an adversity created by an attachment to one's own judgment. See, it's just the other end of the pole. The more attached we are to the judgment here, *[The teacher gestures to his left side on the table at which he is seated.]* it goes out into the universe and we find the intolerance there of the adversity. *[He now gestures to his right side.]* So, you see, it's one and the same in that respect. Yes.

Thank you.

But communication grants understanding. Duty, gratitude, and tolerance will free you from it. Because you must remember, everyone will agree what they are attached to, they are emotionally controlled by. Is there anyone who will not agree with that? Everyone who's had a meaningful relationship or marriage or any of those things, you see, will agree, I know, will agree that whatever you are attached to, you are, to the degree of your attachment, controlled by. All right? But then try to understand, an adversity is only an undeveloped attachment. It is growing. It is an attachment. A person says, "Well, I'm adverse to this," or "I'm intolerant of that." That's what it is. You are creating and solidifying a judgment.

Oh.

And in so doing you're guaranteed to service it someday in your life. So the more adverse you are to anything, the more intolerant you are, the more you are controlled by it, until you serve it as a complete attachment. That is the law of that function of attachment and adversity. So take a good look. I mean, everyone is familiar and knows their attachments. Few, very few people are even aware of their adversities. They push them aside. They don't even want to think about them. Yet those adversities are growing into very strong attachments, and they will be servicing them in keeping with how great that attachment is. For an adversity is a growing attachment because you direct energy to it. That which you direct energy to and that you have created begins to grow up and grow very strong. Yes. And then a person wonders, "Why did I have this experience? I wasn't attached to this." No, you were adverse to it and did not accept the demonstration that an adversity is a growing attachment. Yes, you had another question.

Well, I would like to know—I'd like permission to learn the power breath. I've never been shown it.

Very well. I will see that it is given to you by the students that I had selected here the last time.

Thank you.

Very well. Privately.

Thank you.

Yes. *[The teacher addresses another student.]*

May I also be included in that?

Did you think of it before or just now?

Actually, I thought of it last week.

Always speak—Knock and the door shall open. Speak and you shall receive. Yes. All right, yes.

Could one be flooding—so one could be flooding one's consciousness knowing what, with an affirmation, let's say, but then if you're not communicating with yourself, then there's still— you still will have the experience . . .

Because the level that is accepting the flooding of the consciousness of the vibration is not the level that needs to be worked on. That level's closed down. The door's closed; [there's] no communication with it. If you take a look inside, you'd see the windows are all shut and the shutters are up and the doors are locked. It doesn't want to hear anything like that. You know, some people are so controlled by those various levels that it becomes blatant. They'll close their eyes. They'll look up at the ceiling or down at the floor. Because they don't—their level that is controlling them at the moment doesn't want to hear what it is hearing, you understand. So it closes down. And in very advanced cases it shows physically. The level shows itself physically. Or they'll sit, you know, and they'll go to sleep or this or that because the level that's controlling them at the moment is not one bit interested in what the ears are hearing—you understand?—and it wants nothing to do with it. And the level has that much control over their body. Do you understand that?

Yes.

Yes. Those are extreme cases. Extreme cases, yes. Yes.

I also asked last seminar about the power breath. So I would like—

Very well, you will receive it.

Thank you.

[You students] make sure of that. Yes, please.

Thank you. The, the awareness of, of the need to communicate and educate a level arises at a different level, not in the level that needs the communication.

That is correct, until one makes the effort to be aware of their levels. The level shuts down and will not receive it.

Right.

Pardon?

Yes.

Yes.

Then how, how does one open the door to that level from another level at which you recognize or become aware of the need to, to educate that other level?

Through reference. See, all levels are interconnected through reference. So use reference because reference it cannot deny. The door must open for reference. Do you understand? You see, there's an interconnection of all of those levels of consciousness. So what affects one level in an experience has its repercussions throughout all of the levels. Do you understand that?

I do.

Now those experiences are recorded in all of those levels. Do you understand?

Yes.

Now when you go to educate the level that is holding tenaciously to it, so you will not make changes, which are indispensable to the Law of Evolution— you understand?

Yes.

Then what happens, they close down. But you can use reference through your memory par excellence to reopen them. Because you have experiences in that level. Do you understand that?

Yes.

And by reference—you see, you can be on a conscious level of reason—you hear me?

Yes.

Which is a soul faculty. And you can take that little lamp of honesty and descend with that down into the realm where survival is running wild with its judgment and its defense mechanisms. Do you hear? And you can cast that light of honesty and reason will prevail; and you can see what particular judgment is demanding your survival. You see, to the human mind you call it survival. You understand that?

Yes.

To the level that is sending the message to your mind, it's the survival of one particular experience. Do you understand that?

Yes.

You see? So what is survival to the mind of one's whole life, you hear, to the conscious mind, ofttimes is one little, bitty experience many, many years ago. Do you hear? But the message is sent up to the mind to use all defense mechanisms to protect itself. Isn't that interesting? But that's the way it really is, you see.

Does, does that level, does that first experience in that level attract other or create other experiences to re—

Reinforce it? Oh, [it] absolutely does. Definitely. And so when you experience survival, it is working with all of its troops to make sure it is protected and it maintains its authority. But remember, a level does not consider any other level of consciousness. You do understand that? Unless, through reference, it can get some troops to do its work; that's the only way it considers it. Pardon?

Is that what you referred to before as, as the bridge in the, in the example of building, tearing down—

Yes. Because that bridge takes place inside before it can take place with a person outside. You see, what happens so often, time passes and a person becomes aware that they are dependent on another person. Do you hear me? Now, they say, "Well, why did they take so long to become aware of that? It never was a problem before?" Isn't that true? Well, what it is, is a certain level of consciousness has been awakened that wasn't awakened before. *[The teacher laughs joyfully.]* And so usually—you know how people are when they awaken. They don't awaken very graciously, usually rather irritable, *usually*. And so that level has woke up and says, "Say, what's been going on around here? And how long has this been taking place? And . . ." *[The teacher again laughs joyfully.]* Do you understand that?

Yes, I do.

Yes, that's what happens. You know, people get their meaningful relationships and their divorces and involvements and all of those, well, what it is: they didn't check with *all* their levels of consciousness when they got started. You hear me? And some of those levels, they say, "How long has this been going on?!" And it's furious. Do you understand? Well, that's what happens. Yes, all the time. It happens all the time because people, through the lack of honesty and understanding, they don't consider all of their levels of consciousness. [And ask], "Now is this the best for me?" And then maybe some of the levels say, "No, I don't want to do this. Absolutely not! Do you remember the experience that we had before?" You see, it'll speak to you in your mind, you know, if you're honest with yourself. Then you have to make the decision to put them in their place and keep them there—you understand?—or there cannot be any relationship, you see. It will deteriorate because they're always trying to get back up again to take control, based upon their own fear, you see, of what they've experienced before.

So what good is there for a person who lives in their has-beens of what used to be? Pardon?

Yes.

You see, it's like the good old days. If they were so good, well, why did we ever leave them? "Why did I come to my world, if they were so good?" Don't you understand, you see? Does that help you with your question?

Very much. Thank you.

It's very, very important. It's very important to understand oneself because then people wouldn't have to run around being sorry for this and filled with regret and anger and battles and all of those things. To understand oneself and not be dependent upon others, you see? Hmm?

Yes. Thank you very much.

You're more than welcome. Now someone else over here had a question. *[After a short pause, the teacher continues.]* Well, you know I [have] not come here at this time to beg you for your questions. If you're not interested in the philosophy, I have many other schools to take care of. Yes.

May I be taught the power breath as well, sir?

Yes, you may. Yes.

May I also?

Yes. Yes.

I also? And, also, I have a question.

Yes. Go right ahead. Yes.

Why do we so often choose to be dependent on another person?

Because we deny our Source. You see, we would not experience the need if we didn't deny our Source. You see, we are never absent, that which we are. We're never alone. It is not possible. It does not exist. It is a delusion created by the mind to find more dependence. It is from a denial of our Source. When we deny our Source, we experience a need to be wanted, because we have denied what we are an inseparable part of. And by that denial, we're always seeking outside for what finally becomes hidden inside. You see? Yes.

Does every level have its own denial then?

Oh, absolutely! You ask [that other student]. One of the levels awakens years later and blatantly denies what—that's why the level says, "What's been going on here? How long has this been going on?" Isn't that true?

Yes.

You may not hear it clearly in the mind, but I can assure you that's the way the levels work, as [that student] well knows. They'll rise up and that's what they're really saying. "What's going on here?! How long has this been going on or that been going on?!" It denies the right, you see; denies it. Because, you see, it wants that sensation of supremacy, that sensation of uniqueness. Pardon? You know, it's like the roller-coaster of old creation. [It] has a ticket taker: you get a thrill, you get a ride, but you pay the ticket taker, right? Well, now the ticket taker, he gets paid. He's got his hands on the control, and if you don't pay him, you don't get another ride, isn't that true? So, you see, creation's a price tag. Choose it wisely, very wisely.

You know, it's more than a phenomenal expense to permit oneself to deny their Source and become dependent on what others do, for there is no way that anyone can control what others do. It can only appear that way during the time of temptation. During the time of temptation, you draw the shades. You can only see one thing: the desire that is tempting you. You can't see the whole picture. There's no way possible to control another person. Pardon?

You see? And you have an experience: you find that you're dependent on a person, and you find that they are dependent on you. And you take a look and say, "Well, they've denied their Source. I've denied my Source and here we are." It's only a matter of time, then there you are not. And on to the next roller-coaster ride of experience. That's the way it is.

And then some people say, "Oh well, you know, some people, they're together their whole life." Well, physically they may be; they separated long ago and that's how come they managed to survive and be physically together in their 90s or whatever. *[Many students laugh.]* Because they separated up here long, long ago. *[The teacher points with both hands, using a finger from each, to his head.]* Would you not agree?

Yes.

Well, there you are, you see. So we can all separate in consciousness and physically be under the same roof. There's no problem. You know, people do that all the time, you see. They space themselves out someplace else. And they say, "Say, come back for a while so you don't have to ask me this question twice. I've already answered it, you see." You see? They call it spacing out or bombing out, you see. Their physical body's there, but they're off someplace else, you see. But that only guarantees failure in anything, you know. It takes all the bodies together to have some degree of success, yes. Does that help you?

Yes.

Yes, and [that student], please.

Thank you.

You're welcome.

It seems like it boils down to having greater faith in God or a great faith in God.

Without that, man must pay the price of the roller-coaster and keep paying the ticket taker, yes.

Right. So what are the steps that one can take or I can take to have greater faith in God?

There are many steps. There really are. One of those many steps is the declaration of truth: "That which is mine knows my face [and] is already on its way to my heart. And I'm not going to tell you, God, what that is." You understand? You remember that?

No.

"That which is mine knows my face and is already on its way to my heart." Now it'll be on our tape, so you remember that, won't you?

Yes.

Declare that. Flood your consciousness with that declaration and don't dictate to the Divine that sustains you.

Yes.

You see?

Yes.

Because the letter of the law kills us. You know, so many people they want to know exactly what's this. You tell a person, "You know, I really feel good." [And they ask], "Well how— why do you feel good? What happened?" "What happened?! I accepted the Source of which I am an inseparable part." You know, that's what happened, you see? So tell yourself that you feel good, because when you do that, your mind will tell you, "Well, so-and-so's not doing such and such." Right?

Yes.

That's what the mind will tell you.

Yes.

Then you have an alternative. You say, "I'm feeling really good today." And in the instant that you finish that, that statement, your mind will tell you, "Well, he hasn't changed at all. In fact, he's even worse," or whatever the problem may be. So then you can say, "Let's see, now while I said I was feeling good today, I felt it for a split-second. Then this thing in my mind came over and tells me this. And I feel terrible all day long. I'm going to start working on this side over here: that's the declaration of my divine right." Do you understand that? Now you make that effort. And you know that that is around us, you understand?—

Yes.

—can only survive by being in rapport with us. You do understand that, don't you?

Yes, I do.

So if a person makes an effort to grow within themselves, that that's around them grows or goes. And what does it matter, if the person themselves is growing and feeling better. Isn't that true?

Yes.

So, you see, it is not easy to wrench oneself free from dependence, the dependence taking place within one's own mind.

Yes.

You see, it isn't a person out there. There is no such thing as a half a soul. God did not, by the divine law, impulse into being half-souls.

Yes.

No, no, no, no, no, no. It is a delusion created by titanic, uneducated egos. There is no such thing as a half-soul. Now there is such a thing, for the promulgation, the promotion, and the continuity of physical substance, there is such a thing as a half-body. And when the two halves get together, you got another one. Do you understand? Because of the descent of man, you hear me? Because man, in his evolution, was self-reproductive—you understand that, don't you?—like the ear of corn, you know.

Yes.

And—but it's man's evolution. As man became more gloried in his uniqueness, the separation began. Do you understand? As he started to become greater than anything else, unique and special, he separated himself from the Source.

Yes.

And has become dependent upon others, feeling like a half a soul ever since.

Yes.

Thank you very much. And good night.

Thank you. [Many students respond.]

FEBRUARY 16, 1989

[This was the last recorded class of the Living Light Philosophy given through the mediumship of the founder of the Serenity Association, Mr. Richard P. Goodwin. On February 24, 1989, Mr. Goodwin passed from this world to his true home.]

APPENDIX

The Divine Healing Prayer

I accept that the Divine Healing Power
Is removing all obstructions
From my mind and body
And is restoring me
To perfect health, wealth, and happiness.
My heart is filled with gratitude
For the Divine Law of Acceptance
That is healing both present and absent ones
Who are in need of help.
Peace, the power that healeth,
Is guiding my thoughts, acts, and deeds
As God and I go hand in hand
Living a life of joyful abundance.

The Total Consideration Affirmation

I am the manifestation of Divine Intelligence. Formless and free. Whole and complete. Peace, Poise, and Power are my birthright.

The Law of Harmony is my thought and guarantees Unity in all my acts and activities, expressing perfect Rhythm and limitless flow throughout my entire being.

Without beginning or ending, eternity is my true awareness and sees the tides of creation, as a captain sees his ship.

As the Light of Truth is sustained by the faculty of Reason, I pause to think and claim my Divine right.

> Right Thought. Right Action. Total Consideration.
> Amen. Amen. Amen.

Divine Abundance

Thank
(Gratitude)

You
(Principle)

God
(Divine Intelligence)

I'm
(Individualizing)

Moving
(Rhythm)

In
(Unity)

Your
(Realization)

Divine
(Total)

Flow
(Consideration)

The Controlled Spiritual Environment Affirmation

You are in a controlled spiritual environment of truth
and freedom
Where peace and harmony reign supreme.
Be awake, be aware, be alert.
Your purpose of being is freedom from what has been.
Thoughts of self are foreign to this environment.
Take control of your mind and experience the joy of living.

[In Seminar 33, the teacher refers to a pamphlet that was published by Serenity many years earlier. The name published on the cover of the pamphlet is "The Descent of Man," but the title page has two titles, "The Celestial Marriage" and "The Descent of Man." Here is the text of that pamphlet as it was published. An asterisk indicates a page break.]

THE CELESTIAL MARRIAGE
or
THE DESCENT OF MAN

A FABLE
FROM
THE BOOK OF LIFE

*

GIVEN IN HUMILITY
TO ALL
HUMANITY

*

One day in great **ASPIRATION GOD** sent forth from itself **WILL**, and the sons of **WILL** became. Now the sons of **WILL** were of **GOD**, yea, they were **GODS** sent into form, but knew not because of form. The sons of **WILL** roamed the universes for eons and eons of time ever seeking other forms. After much searching they met to consider what they must do. For seven days and seven nights they discussed, and at the seventh hour **ILLUMINATION** fell upon them and said, "Behold, sons of **WILL**, within thyself is **COMPASSION**, know it, and unto thee shall be given." Alas, the sons of **WILL** knew **COMPASSION** and that night the daughters of **DESTINY** became.

In the morning when the daughters of **DESTINY** awoke to the sons of **WILL**, the **GODS** and **GODESSES** of nature danced in jubilee.

Now the sons of **WILL** married the daughters of **DESTINY** and all nature wept with joy.

One day in **TRUTH** a son was born, his name was **INEVITABLE**, and the sons of **WILL** were greatly pleased. Now the daughters of **DESTINY** were quite unhappy for they **HOPED** for a daughter, and so that night in **DESIRE** a girl was born, her name was **LUST**.

Now **INEVITABLE** grew in the warmth and sunshine of the day. Oh how he loved the sun, for to him all **LIFE** was **LIGHT**.

LUST grew up to be a beautiful and lovely woman with a great fondness for the moon and darkness, for had she not been born in the night of **DESIRE**.

Time passed on, and one day **INEVITABLE** felt he would go into the night to find **LUST**, for he had heard so much about her, and had sent her many messages asking her to come into the **LIGHT** so that they may know more of each other. **INEVITABLE** went down, down into the darkness of night, and as he descended a great **FEAR** overcame him, but he found **LUST**, her face glowing so beautiful by the reflection of the sun. From the shadows where the **LIGHT** of the moon shone not, a voice spoke unto **INEVITABLE** and said, "Behold the beauty and the glory thou hast found, is it not worth the descent into our realms?" But from within, a voice spoke to **INEVITABLE** and said, "Take her to the realms of **LIGHT** that you may see more clearly in a day of **REASON**."

The senses won, and that night in **DESPAIR** a child was born, her name was **GRIEF**. The years passed and **GRIEF** could not be comforted, for she had been born of **LUST**, in the night of **DESIRE**, by the promptings of **PASSION**, and knew not of **TRUTH**.

INEVITABLE wandered on and on with the daughter **GRIEF**, hoping to return to the realms of **LIGHT**, but no, the centuries passed and only **SORROW** did they know.

Then one day a bird from the realms of **LIGHT** landed on his shoulder and sang this song, "In **SORROW** doth thou stay for self-pity knows no way."

INEVITABLE thought and thought of the meaning of those words, then he thought of his homeland **TRUTH** where he had been so very, very happy; and in **CONCENTRATION**, he found himself leaving the realms of darkness, passing through the lands of **IGNORANCE** and **EXPERIENCE** to return to his blessed land.

LOVE ALL LIFE
AND KNOW
THE LIGHT

*

OH MAN THINK HUMBLE
YET WELL OF THYSELF
FOR IN THY THINKING
IS CREATED
THE VEHICLE OF
THE SOUL

www.ingramcontent.com/pod-product-compliance
Lightning Source LLC
Chambersburg PA
CBHW030144100526
44592CB00009B/114